A SYNTHESIS OF
HUMAN
BEHAVIOR

A SYNTHESIS OF

HUMAN
BEHAVIOR

**an integration of
thought processes
and ego growth**

by

JOSEPH C. SOLOMON

Assistant Clinical Professor
of Psychiatry, University of
California; Consultant,
Mount Zion Hospital, San
Francisco, California

Grune & Stratton

New York   1954

Library of Congress Catalog number: 54-7258

Copyright 1954

Grune & Stratton, Inc.

381 Fourth Avenue

New York 16

Printed in the U.S.A. for Grune & Stratton

FOREWORD

In this book the author has attempted to categorize human behavior according to the growth of ego development. His codification pertains to physical maturation, and psychosexual and ego development. These stages are traced through infancy, early childhood, adolescence, maturity, and later aging.

It is interesting that Doctor Solomon, in his discussion of the latency period of development, states that no experimental evidence or observation upon animals demonstrates a latency period. It is also noted that Freud himself called the latency period a purely human phenomenon, although many cultural groups that have been observed by anthropologists do not appear to undergo a latency stage. The absence of any hormonal changes at this period is shown by endocrinological study. All evidence therefore seems to point strongly "to the fact that there is no true physiological latency period." This conclusion I would agree with, from my own observations and knowledge. The latency stage would then be an arbitrary period, so marked off for what social or cultural influences can be detected.

Almost exactly three-fourths of the book is devoted to synthesizing growth and development from infancy through adolescence, and this is as it should be, since by the early twenties, the average young man or woman has attained a rather full maturation and personality development. If we accept data from the Kinsey studies of human sexual behavior, the average young woman by this time will not have reached her full sexual capacity, although the average young man will have already begun the downgrade of capacity and even performance. Whether these facts may affect the success of early marriages has not been established. Doctor Solomon's discussion of falling in love and of marriage is clear and interestingly presented.

The analysis of the concept of parenthood in both men and women is especially well handled. Here the psychoanalytic formulations have been carefully synthesized, and interesting conclusions are reached. For ex-

v

ample, the strength of home-making interests in the young woman, the devotion of the young man to his professional or occupational fulfillment, and the wishes of both for children are clearly described, as are the adjustments that can be made by well-integrated young people to various problems, the wife's career, for example.

There is the usual attempt to arrive at a concept of values whereby to measure the mature adult. I question whether these estimates are helpful. Full maturity, with the attainment of a good set of values and of happiness, usually comes as a kind of bonus to experience and to the performance of one's various duties in his career and home. Just as no one should set out to be happy, so no one should strive to become, per se, a mature adult. Doctor Solomon has much to offer in his analyses of basic values and in his tracing of the way in which an individual successfully develops the various autonomous ego traits.

An especially good discussion follows of the so-called middle years. The serious conflicts both in professional and in marital life that may arise in women around the menopause and in men at a comparable age are discussed. The author applies the term "sophomorism" to the perpetual quest of both women and men, though by somewhat different means, for youthfulness. Here Doctor Solomon has been particularly successful in tracing the continuous change of personality, whether for growth or for regression. Some time ago I was asked to prepare a paper on the development of personality in the aging individual. I find that actually very little is known about this area which is so important because many people now live to be old. The various problems of old age are discussed. Some attention is paid to the fact that high intelligence and a proper mental attitude toward old age may favorably affect longevity and productiveness.

Considerable evidence also points to the fact that persons who age successfully continue until very late years to have as active a sex life as possible. They continue to keep up their intellectual and occupational interests, to cultivate interesting avocations, and to keep up their personal appearance. They continue to have sexual relations with their spouses, and if the spouse dies they seek to remarry. Some evidence suggests that the organic deterioration of senility may result from the breakdown of psychic defenses and ego traits formerly of value to the individual. These facts Doctor Solomon has noted. He also admits that psychoanalytic avoidance of therapy in older and even in very old people has not been wholly justified. By now, therapists report that psychoanalytically oriented therapy achieves good results in old persons, and that behavior can be modified in the elderly. Serenity is seen by the author as the special achievement of old age.

Doctor Solomon's tracing of the ego's cyclic development and of the thought processes characteristic for each stage of growth ought to be very useful. This synthesis of what is known about the masteries and accomplishments of maturity and about the types of disorganization liable to occur allows one to see how the well integrated person progresses from infancy to old age.

KARL M. BOWMAN, M.D.

Professor of Psychiatry, University of California;
Director, Langley Porter Clinic, San Francisco, California

PREFACE

Many books have been written on the subject of human behavior. Almost all of them have been concerned with the "analysis" or breakdown of human activity and thought. This involves the retrograde action of retracing the origins of these processes to childhood events and cultural patterns. This book has an entirely different approach. An attempt is made to effect a "synthesis" of human thinking. Instead of going backward, the orientation in this book is the movement forward. The newborn babe is followed progressively to maturity and ultimately to old age. I have tried to establish a correlation and understanding of the developmental sequence of human character from the facts that are thus far available from all the disciplines devoted to the study of human thought.

Out of the accumulation of observations by many students of the subject, including those of my own, a *Table of Ego Organization* has been prepared, and appears in the Introduction. In order fully to follow the text, the reader is advised to refer frequently to this table. It is almost necessary to do this at the end of every chapter.

The clinical data, from which the points discussed have been drawn, are not always presented, nor are all the ideas which have been gleaned from readings and from the teachings of others always given full credit in the bibliography. This is unavoidable, both because it would make the text too ponderous and because one cannot always trace the source of a particular idea that has become common knowledge. The references are largely psychoanalytic, but the descriptive material is mainly an outgrowth of my own twenty-seven years of training and experience, not only in psychoanalysis but also in pediatrics, child guidance, and hospital psychiatry.

No book is worthy of publication unless it makes at least a small contribution to the general body of knowledge. In addition to the *Table of Ego Organization*, a few other items may be noted. Infantile anxiety is described in this book in purely perceptual terms. This is a continuation of the ideas of other investigators. The idea that an infant can frighten himself by his crying is one which does not appear elsewhere in the literature, as far as I have been able to discover. This concept is in marked contrast to the ideas of Melanie Klein and her followers, who attribute the anxiety of infants to an elaborate system of fantasies that exist almost from birth. The basic idea presented in this book is that when such fantasies exist, they are regressions from the Oedipal age, at which time there is already a high measure of conceptual thinking. I have introduced the term "secondary perceptual thinking", which consists of the merging of the memories of infantile primary perceptions with ideas and "meanings of things" that have been learned at later age levels. The secondary perceptual thinking and new learnings or concepts which arise from life experiences and maturation are followed through the various age periods until senescence. This theme of perception dominates at least the first half of the book, and then takes on background status as the discussion begins to deal with more familiar things.

I should like personally to acknowledge my debt to former teachers and colleagues. I owe much, in particular, to Drs. Seigfried Bernfeld and Lionel Blitzsten. Also I am indebted to the influence of Mr. Erik H. Erikson and Dr. Bernhard Berliner, whose ideas permeate the text. For suggestions on the preparation of the book I should like to acknowledge the help I received from Drs. Stanislaus Szurek, Leo Bartemeier, and Malcolm H. Finley. Finally, I should like to cite the aid of my son, George Freeman Solomon, Stanford University medical student, who is responsible for many corrections in rhetoric and who rendered invaluable assistance in clarifying points which otherwise might have been too abstruse.

San Francisco, California   JOSEPH C. SOLOMON, M.D.
January, 1954

CONTENTS

A SYNTHESIS OF
HUMAN
BEHAVIOR

INTRODUCTION

The study of the nature and operation of human thinking is a continuous operation, inasmuch as all human behavior and symptomatology is connected with the thought processes. The muscles, organs, and glands which bring about the actions and reactions of the organism are agents of the thinking apparatus. As far back as we can go in recorded history, man has attempted to discover the relationship between thought and behavior. Thought is often considered something quite apart from another mental phenomenon, that of perception, thought being looked upon as occurring in the highest level of the brain, where it acts as a relay station or clearing house between sensation and motility. If perception and thought are two separate phenomena, then thought would be the function of the utilization and storage of ideas; whereas perception does not involve ideation. This dichotomy may be essentially true, but it must be remembered that all memory does not consist merely of the storage of *ideas*. There must also be a reservoir for the storage of experienced *sensations*.

For purposes of description, the type of psychic process involving the storage of sensations will be referred to as perceptual thinking and the process involving the storage of ideas as conceptual thinking. The purpose of this presentation is to allocate the relative roles of these two modes of thinking in ego and superego development. There is a great deal that should be said about perception and concept formation before embarking on our central theme, but this would involve considerable speculation into the realm of metapsychology. It will suit our needs to be satisfied with the arbitrary formulations that perception or perceptual thinking is essentially the same as nonverbal thinking and that concept formation or conceptual thinking is essentially verbal thinking.

In this connection it will be remembered that Freud [1] considered all of consciousness as part of the sensory system. If we examine consciousness more closely, we can see that it ranges from pure sensation to the highest orders of abstract thinking. Learning, or cognition, has been described as perception plus "thinking". Let us consider perception first. At the risk of over-simplification, the suggestion is offered that *perception represents sensation plus the memory of sensation.** This definition implies sensations that arise from outside stimuli as well as those arising from stimuli within the organism. Both sources of stimulation are part of the receptor system.

The sensations that bombard the organism from the external world are invested with varying degrees of effectiveness depending upon the strength of the outside stimuli and the ability of the receptor systems to register these stimuli. From the inner world of the organism, sensations arise out of the very nature of the structure and function of the organs themselves. Freud refers to this energy investment as "trieb". It has been variously termed as "instinct", "drive", "motivation" [2], "drive signals" [3], or "inborn memory patterns" [4]. It is generally agreed that these motivations, which can be referred to as instinct, are exclusively directed to the preservation either of the self or of the race. These inner perceptions follow fundamental laws of sequence of development coinciding with the orderly maturation of the individual. Both the internal and external perceptions are related to the release or the increase of energy tension by the organism, resulting in an appreciation of either pleasure or pain. When the inner organ pressures, such as those of an empty stomach or a full bladder, are associated with the memory traces of pleasure, the drive motivations or signals appear as appetites. When the perceptions are associated with the memory traces of pain (or hunger), they are appreciated by the organism as alarm signals. The subjective aspects of pain or pleasure lead to effector reactions. The total

* Some investigators of human behavior, notably Wundt, have felt that perception includes some involvement of the effector or motor system. It seems that when motor or secretory effects are produced by a sensation we are dealing with the emotions. The motor display of emotion is perceived but this is essentially a new stimulus. There is also a subjective aspect of emotion which is the affect. Pure perception, however, only involves the sensorium. Freud, in his "Totem and Taboo", makes a statement which could be construed as being close to the one which is being offered. An excerpt from his statement is as follows: "The thing we project in outer reality can hardly be anything else but the recognition of a state in which a given thing is presented to the senses and to consciousness, next to which another state exists in which the thing is latent."

response is appreciated as "feelings" or "emotions". As a further complication of the phenomenon of perception, it must be pointed out that the memories of sensation need not be of the same character as the actual stimulus, so that the perception may represent an actual distortion of the reality factor. These points will be elaborated upon later.

Many investigators, including Vigotsky [5], Kasanin [6], Piaget [7], Cameron [8], and Goldstein [9], have shown that the development of conceptual thinking coincides with the acquisition of language. Ideas or concepts seem to have a direct transitional sequence of transposing percepts into words or word forms as symbolic representations. In so doing, the process is routed through higher cortical centers. This involves increasing complexities of thinking which range from states of awareness to the highest levels of abstract reasoning. As will be pointed out later, the application of language gives the perception a different internal significance. Thus it can be said that percepts are converted into concepts. This change, embodying a conversion from perceptual to conceptual thinking, is of vital concern to psychoanalysis, as it is directly related to ego development. Proof of the importance of this clinical point lies in the well accepted fact that there is a parallelism between disturbances in conceptual thinking and lack of ego organization.

There is more than academic interest in the question of this differentiation between perceptual and conceptual thinking. Freud in his early papers stated that therapeutic assistance could be afforded only when emotional traumata had occurred after the onset of verbal thinking. Freud later suggested that preverbal or, preferably, perceptual thinking can be therapeutically influenced. Evidence has subsequently accumulated to substantiate this view. The modus operandi of successful psychoanalytic treatment seems to be, at least in part, the gradual conversion of perceptual into conceptual thinking. Conversely, in therapy, before we can deal with the perceptual or "id level" of thinking, we must work through a maze of conceptualized defenses. There seems to be general agreement that therapies that are directed to purely philosophical or intellectual approaches are usually ineffective. By the same token, we have learned that therapy cannot proceed with sole emphasis on the physiological functions. Hence, from the therapeutic point of view, our attention in recent years has been directed to the ego. This will be the major concern of this presentation. It is the ego which routes the stimuli from the outside world, or from the inside world of the organism, through the higher levels of cortical organization and allows the organism to obtain gratification in terms of reality. By "allowing" the organism to obtain gratification or by dealing with reality, there is implied a definite active role for the ego. It would be very simple to say that the ego is a part of the motor system, but this is actually not true. However, we can say that it is closely bound to the motor or effector systems. According to our definition, we might say that perception is at one end of the ego and action is at the other. Thus we can say that the ego records, evaluates, observes, warns, wards off, modifies as well as executes, directs, organizes, and integrates. These actions are vastly more complex than the simple spinal reflex motor actions of pulling the hand away from a flame. The ego is more the outgrowth of individual experience. Thus the ego is a development of the "meaning of things", or in short, conceptual thinking.

In order to carry out the theme of the emergence of increasing levels of ego integration, it will be necessary to follow the maturational development of the individual from birth to old age. The information which will be used is part of the body of general psychoanalytic knowledge. The main emphasis in this presentation is on the development of a synthesis, the desired outcome of all fact gathering, rather than on an analysis. For real completeness the specific methods of child training and parental handling, and cultural influences both inside and outside the home should be included; however, this will not be attempted. Our attention will be directed to what goes on inside the mind of the individual as a result of the interaction of these forces with the innate energy drives of the organism. An attempt will be made to offer a sequential arrangement of both normal and faulty ego traits which develop in the growth of the person.

The contributions of Erikson [10] and Hartmann [11] have given the greatest impetus to the understanding of the nature of the ego. Erikson gave us the idea for listing ego traits in an arrangement which coordinates with stages of psychosexual development. Hartmann furnished the useful concept of autonomous versus conflictual or secondary autonomous traits. The concept of autonomous ego traits is a derivative of the work of many previous investigators. Federn's [12] term "ego boundaries" came close to what is being considered here as the area of operation in the ego of both instinctual and inhibiting motivations. Allport [13], on the other hand, used the term "functional autonomy" to refer to a set of motivations which may have been derived from the instincts but have quite different aims. He believes that the infantile drives are transformed in the course of growth into new contemporaneous systems of motives. Although he offers the ingenious suggestion that a tree has no resemblance to the seed from which it came, the analogy does not hold. Psychoanalysts in their daily work are able to see the instinct derivations in all ego manifestations confirming the fact that there are unconscious or conscious id elements as part of the trait motivations. Freud stated categorically that the structure of the id never changes. Hartmann concedes the possibility of some change in the instincts but never, as Allport believes, are they completely extinguished. As offered in this presentation, the ego traits consist of excitations from the zones of erogenicity in the characteristic modes of action of the physiological processes as described by Erikson—plus the memory traces of their gratification or lack of gratification and defense adaptations. Although there may be a set of growth motivations or "instincts to master" [14], we do not need to postulate a set of "ego instincts" as described by Silverberg [15] as being anything different from the basic impulses toward survival which are described in this presentation as stemming from the excitation of the organs seeking nutriment. This work will attempt to name the various traits as developments of perceptual and conceptual thinking and will offer suggestions as to the formation of symptoms when such traits are in conflict with each other or with other energy derivatives.

Let us be mindful that cultural patterns are basic determinants in the emergence of particular ego traits. There are also basic biological forces which are given meanings to the organism and to his outside world by the culture. These meanings may be different and thus may produce differing traits, but the fact remains that in all cultures there are some meanings which have a degree of universality.

Although we discuss stages of development as though they were different entities, it must be remembered that each stage is influenced by the stages which preceded. Thus a particular phenomenon described at one level does not exclude previous phenomena, but is either modified by that which pre-existed or exists with it side by side. The term "external object" is used frequently. This term generally refers to the mother in the early stages of the individual, but also includes father, siblings, playmates, business associates, children, etc., depending upon the stage of growth we are discussing. Autonomous ego traits represent the results of the mastery of the instinctual forces through knowledge of the ability to discharge energy with the external object. This discharge is accompanied by a feeling of pleasure, comfort, or relief. Actually, we can say that this configuration will represent the stored memories of gratified impulses. The term "sentiment" can be applied to the memory of instinct plus external object plus gratification; as such it constitutes a pleasant emotional association.

When there is frustration or pain in connection with an attempt by the organism to reduce instinctual energy (drive motivates or signals), there is recorded the memory of pain. Alarm signals or shock reactions [16] activate specific emotional responses such as fear and rage when pain is precipitated on a primitive level. Painful affects during later stages of development, it will be shown, are colored by less violent phenomena such as disgust, shame, remorse, disgrace, etc. The memories of these affects become the internal imperatives or commands which constitute the superego portion of the ego. When the organism strikes a compromise between the impulses and the memories of frustrations, traits may develop which differ from those which develop as a result of the memories of pleasure. These traits are what can be termed, through Hartmann's influence, secondary autonomous traits. They result from the operation of the defense mechanisms. It will be shown how these conflictual traits generally drive the organism toward widely divergent poles of motivation. Often this polarity is actually a duality because both extremes are detectable in the same person.

With this introduction to the subject, let us turn our attention to each of the maturational levels of the organism and follow the ego in its growth from the newborn babe to the aged. As the ego is a manifestation of the thinking of the organism, we must endeavor to study all of the thinking processes of the individual. To assist us in following these stages, I have prepared a *Table of Ego Organization.*

table of ego organization

Although there may be some objection to the codification or categorization of human behavior, there are enough points of interest in the growth of the ego to warrant such an attempt, and many such attempts have been made. The chart presented here may contain many flaws, but it is an attempt to stratify ego development in both its normal and abnormal growth. It does not attempt to include all of the symptoms or manifestations of disorganization that the human organism may suffer. The emphasis is largely upon the ego and the manner in which emotional disturbances are handled at various levels of maturation.

The first column of the table lists the maturation phase. The age period for each of these maturational phases varies to some extent in different individuals. There are to be considered the factors of physical and organ maturation as well as differences in intellectual maturation. This not only applies to the tempos of development in different people but to the marked differences in total functioning that various individuals are capable of attaining. Highly endowed individuals in the intellectual sphere may show differences in maturational processes from the poorly endowed. Hence some flexibility in the application of the chart to all individuals must be maintained.

The second column is the psychosexual stage development. Here are listed all the innate drives of the individual. The various terms which apply to the excitations or needs of the organism, which have been termed as instinctual or libidinal in nature and referred to as the id, are arranged in a sequential order of their usual appearance. In the text these forces will be referred to as "primary motivation". They have the property of directing the organism toward survival, toward reproduction, and toward various aspects of satiation and protection of self and others. Just as a leaf turns toward the sun for its survival these inner forces are directed in a positive way toward external objects, hence they are referred to as constituting a "positive tropism". This refers to an orientation toward a source of stimulation or toward the object which will discharge tension.

The third column is concerned with the principle external objects. There is little need to comment at this time concerning this aspect of the table. It is quite self-explanatory. It will be noticed that the term "isosexual" is used. This is done in order to avoid the pathological connotations of the word "homosexual".

The next column is the one labeled the Mature Ego. This represents the autonomous portion of the ego. It consists of the learnings which the individual has acquired from the successful mastery of his instinctual drives. As such it contains a stockpile or reservoir of memories of the pleasant emotional experiences which are stored within that individual.

Table of Ego Organization

Maturation Phase	Psychosexual Stage Id—libido Drive Instinct Need Primary motivation Positive tropism	Principal External Objects Persons concerned with gratification or frustration of instincts	Mature Ego Pleasure—comfort—relief Direct mastery Nonconflictual sentiments Primary integration Primary autonomy Character traits	Superego Reactions Frustration Pain-shock Reproaches Internal commands Controls—restraints Slogans—mottos Axioms—maxims Negative tropism Secondary motivation	Neurotic Ego Traits Conflictual Defensive—adaptive Reparative mastery Secondary integration Secondary autonomy Foibles—idiosyncracies
Infancy Nursing situation Teething	Early-perceptual Vegetative Oral-sucking Self-preservative Anaclytic Passive movement Fascination Late-perceptual Oral biting (sadistic) Upper segment motility Acquisition—incorporation Mimicry	Mother Grandmother	Trust Reliance Security Faith Primary identification	Rage Anxiety	Basic vulnerability Sensitivity Listlessness Apathy Awayness Dependency Insatiability Greed
Toddler Training and indoctrination	Early-perceptual Anal sphincter (libidinal-sadistic) Locomotion Lower segment motility Time sense (two dimensional) Late-conceptual Language Urethral (phallic) Exhibitionistic Scoptophilic	Mother-Father (Grandparents) Mother-Father Siblings (Grandparents)	Patience Generosity Autonomy Self-esteem Creativity Pride Ambition Competition	Suspicion Doubt Disgust Shame Remorse	Procrastination Appeasement Compliance Ingratiation Impetuosity Opposition Defiance Obstinacy Stinginess Perfectionism Bashfulness Hypoactivity Taciturnity Inferiority Envy Wastefulness Disorderliness Ostentation Hyperactivity Loquaciousness Boastfulness Spite

Stage						
Oedipal Age	Genital Procreative Time sense—3 di- Menopausal	Mother-Father Siblings	Assertion Courage Love		Belligerence Bravado Dominance	Jealousy Inadequacy Submissiveness
Latency Prepubertal	Social instincts Group relations	Isosexual contemporaries (peers) Extrafamilial prototypes defining religion, culture, mores	Group loyalty Leadership Initiative Body image acceptance Adventure Sportsmanship Secondary identification	Social anxiety Disgrace Dishonor	Bossiness Over-gregariousness Impertinence	Shyness Isolation Meekness
Pubertal	Sexual (mating) impulses	Heterosexual contemporaries	Identity Charm Romance	No new forms of reaction	Brazenness Arrogance Rebelliousness Dramatization Dare-devilness	Prissiness Unobtrusiveness Subservience Eidetic imagery Cowardice
Young Adult	Matrimony Goal realization	Mate	Reciprocal affinity Confidence Industriousness Reliability Parenthood		Sophistication Conceit Over-extension	Stagnation Naivete Inefficaciousness
Mature Adult	Home life Work life Social life	Mate Children Business associates Social contacts	Fidelity Poise Sense of values Perseverance Altruism Sincerity Enterprise		Infidelity Doggedness Pretentiousness Ruthlessness	Abstemiousness Disillusionment Cynicism Irresolution
Middle Years Climacteric	Involutional Menopausal Loss of reproductive functions	Mate Children Grandchildren Society at large	Dignity Self-acceptance Tolerance Charity Caution		Sophomorism Rigidity Intolerance Pomposity	Progerism Resignation Pliancy Unctuousness
Senescence	Survival Return to narcissism Physical debilitation	Mate, if living Children Grandchildren Great-grandchildren	Serenity		Irascibility Querulousness	Suspiciousness Despair

These include not only pleasure as such, but also the memories of the relief of pain and the affordance of comfort or relief from inner tensions or external threats. This is an area where there is no conflict. It contains the pleasant sentiments which allow the organism to leave one stage of development and move on into the next one. This does not mean that there have been no obstacles, but it means that there has been mastery. Because of the absence of conflict, this mastery will be referred to as *direct* mastery. It contains all the traits of character which are in keeping with the highest level of stability of the individual.

At this point I wish to stress an important and possibly controversial point. It is the fact that *all learnings are essentially inhibitory in nature.* The great neurophysiologists of the past, notably Hughlings-Jackson [17] and Sherrington [18], spoke of the inhibitory effect of the higher centers. Modern investigators such as Magoun [19] and Linn [20] are bringing added knowledge to the physiological aspect of the perception of emotion upon the cortical function and the effect of cortical function upon the emotions. Even a gratifying result from the pressures of an instinct has the effect of inhibiting the instinct. For example, if the child remembers that when he was hungry his mother appeared and he was fed, he will not react as strongly to his hunger as he would if he had some doubts about it. In this way the primary autonomy of the individual is a learned process of an inhibitory nature. As such it constitutes a direct mastery or primary integration of the ego.

In the next column are recorded the various reactions that the organism presents when there is an obstruction to the gratification of the primary motivations. The reservoir of memories of pain and frustration form the basis for the superego. In our presentation we are adhering to Freud's original formulation that the superego is the equivalent of the internalized prohibiting or punishing parent. The internalized loving or protective parent is represented in the previously discussed column as primary autonomy. The internalized punitive images are at the roots of emotional conflict. They are the instigators of painful emotional reactions, the nature of which differs at the various levels of maturation. In the text there is described a perceptual, nonverbal superego and a conceptual or verbal superego. Both of these comprise a volume of internal reproaches or commands. On the conceptual level the controls and restraints may take the form of slogans, mottos, axioms, and maxims. These superego reactions motivate the individual in a direction essentially opposite to that of the primary motivation. They are considered in the text as secondary motivations. As the orientation is away from the threatening stimulus, it is labelled a negative tropism.

The last column is subdivided into two columns. We have here the abnormal ego traits which have been formed as a result of compromises, defenses, and adaptations on the part of the organism when there is conflict between the primary motivations and the secondary motivations. The new level represents the establishment of a secondary autonomy. The adaptive ego traits may have a number of different manifestations at the different maturational levels. They seem to divide themselves into a polarity of extremes. Both extremes are neurotic. They make up the deviant personality traits whose manifestations are the idiosyncracies and foibles of the neurotic character.

Stern has introduced a term which appears to be very useful in the establishment of secondary autonomy of the ego; his term is "reparative mastery". By this he means the retroactive attempt on the part of the organism to correct traumatic experiences magically which it had been unable to avoid. This process involves the use of the various defensive qualities of the ego such as denial, displacement, and reaction formation.* The reparative mastery renders the memories of traumatic events or conflict situations less harmful to the self than they had seemed at the time of their occurrence.

The phenomenon of reparative mastery produces a *secondary integration* of the existing motivations. Secondary integration involves a learning by inhibition. In bringing about this integration the organism is obliged to inhibit or repress part of the energy arising from the emotions and motivations emerging from the conflict situation. It operates in the manner of a joining of forces for the purpose of establishing as nearly as possible a single channel or outlet for the complexity of motivations. The situation is comparable to the manner in which a series of rivulets can be joined together to form a single large stream by setting up barriers and dams which redirect the flow. Failure to establish a secondary integration leaves the organism with diffuse unbridled impulses and consequent symptom formation and weak ego structure.

It is hoped that the reader will understand that the various items

* Other defense mechanisms which appear in the text are repression, projection, introjection, identification, rationalization, somatization, condensation, dramatization, regression, libidinization, sublimation, generalization, and intellectualization.

which appear at any horizontal level only represent the major point at which a particular manifestation appears or at least is of sufficient strength to become a noticeable phenomenon. After the trait appears, it can remain part of that individual for a lifetime or can be modified by future maturation and experience. Thus each stage is superimposed upon each of the preceding stages and contains all the elements of what went before it. The memories of what went on before may be repressed but they will remain as islands to which the organism may retreat when overwhelming difficulties are encountered in the later stages of development.

orality and perception
· early ego autonomy
· early ego disturb-
ance · ego growth in
late infancy

THE INFANT

Much more understanding of human behavior would be available if we really knew a great deal about the thinking processes of the infant. Because there is no verbal communication between the infant and the external world, what information we possess has, of necessity, been accumulated from indirect sources. These sources are (a) dreams, fantasies, and memories of adult patients in psychoanalysis, (b) the verbal production and behavior of schizophrenic individuals, (c) direct observations of infants, and (d) the interpretation of spontaneous play and drawings of small children. It is little wonder that there have been so many divergent views of the internal psychic processes of the infant. A dynamic psychology, including all the known facts about infant thinking, would be very helpful in explaining many human characteristics. In this presentation, material will be borrowed freely from all the aforementioned approaches in order to obtain as complete a picture as possible for elucidation of the subject at hand.

Being mindful of the definition of perceptual thinking as consisting of sensation plus the memories of sensation, we can safely say that the newborn infant is a purely perceptual being. Because there is a direct connection between the stimulus, whether it is from the outer world or from within the infant's body, and the recording of the stimulus in the infant brain, the term primary perception or primary perceptual thinking is being used. This is in direct contrast to secondary perceptual thinking which will be described later. There can be little doubt that by the time the infant is placed in its first bassinet there have already been recorded many sensations from the intrauterine period and from all the events surrounding the process of being born and beginning an extrauterine existence. Many of these sensations, particularly the intrauterine ones, are pleasant, whereas the phenomena of being born and the experience immediately following that event are mostly unpleasant.* The pleasant sensations or "feelings" result in relaxation or comfort. The end point of comfort and relaxation is sleep. Unpleasant feelings produce other reactions in the infant, the most noteworthy of which is the phenomenon of crying. The "emotion" or feeling tone accompanying the motor discharge of crying is describable as anger or fear. Sleeplessness is characteristic of these feelings.

There seems to have been an insufficient degree of attention to the actual phenomenon of infantile crying. Whereas Bühler [21] and Gesell [22] have revealed that 90 per cent of the newborn's waking time is spent in crying, this may not apply to the Indian baby who is carried about by its mother almost constantly. How this relates itself to the perceptual system will be described.

To pursue the subject further, let us look at the infant directly and delineate the factors which give him comfort and pleasure in contrast to those which cause discomfort and pain. It will be noted that either the pleasure phenomena or the pain phenomena are directly related to the basic physiology connected with self-preservation. The infant needs to breathe, to be warm, and to take nutriment. The importance of these factors seems to be in the order named. Even a hungry baby cannot feed if he is cold, nor will he nurse if he cannot breathe freely. There seems to be no particular fluctuation in the respiratory or cutaneous-thermal demands because they are constant. These demands require constant gratification in order to insure relaxation. When there is interference, a diffuse alarm reaction takes place. The alarm reaction, manifested by sudden violent crying, occurs, of course, where there are any causes for pain or physical discomfort. Nutritional demand is cyclical because it is related to the filling and emptying of a hollow viscus. There is little doubt that hunger is the major perceptual stimulus which provokes an infant's premeal crying. Crying after meals may be due to the pain accompanying indigestion. In converting these phenomena into social terms, we can say that satisfying hunger (as well as sup-

---

* There are considerable variations in this respect depending on whether the baby is born after a prolonged hard labor, or by Cesarean section, or in a relaxed normal healthy fashion. It is difficult, however, for me to conceive of birth in any form as being a pleasurable experience for the infant.

plying air and warmth) can be subsumed under the term "get", whereas denying these needs results in what can be termed a "threat".

Although emphasis has been placed in the previous paragraphs upon the physiological aspect of hunger, it is very well known that the sucking and swallowing apparatus itself possesses inherent properties for attaining pleasure. The pleasurable emotion is of a primitive vegetative nature. Nevertheless, the demand for gratification of sucking impulses seems to be necessary over and beyond the mere demands for nutrition. Freud has shown us how the mouth is endowed with properties that can be termed "excitability", which can be relieved by sucking alone or by sucking and swallowing. It is this excitability of the oral areas which can be said to be closely bound to the impulses for self-preservation. Actually hunger is the more basic impulse, but sucking need is the accompanying internal perception which coordinates with food intake, and to the infant it seems as though sucking in itself has the property of preserving the organism. This idea is corroborated by the fact that most any sort of physical discomfort on the part of the infant, including overeating, can be temporarily relieved by furnishing a stimulus for gratifying the sucking impulse (e.g., the pacifier).

orality and perception

Sucking and swallowing, from the motor point of view, have a "taking-in" quality. However, we cannot be satisfied with observing them merely as motor phenomena. Let us concern ourselves mainly with the process from the sensory point of view. To adhere more closely to Freud's formulation, it is more than sensory; it is "sensual". The total picture of the sensation depends upon the excitability of the end organ (the mouth and perioral area) [23] plus the object which reduces or "discharges" the excitability. Failure to reduce the excitability seems to provoke further excitability and eventually to spread excitability to other excitable areas. Conversely, frustration or discomfort in other sensory areas may intensify excitability of the oral zone. Spitz [24] demonstrated that babies that were excited by genital stimulation resorted to intensified oral sucking. Before we go further, let us examine other aspects of the infant's perceptual system.

The other organs of sensation which are vitally concerned with the perceptual system are the organs of hearing, the visual, vestibular, gustatory, and musculo-cutaneous receptors, and to a lesser degree the olfactory organs. Of these, perhaps the hearing sense is the most fully developed at birth. In fact, there are distinct evidences that the fetus responds to auditory stimuli before birth. Sudden sounds, for example, cause motor responses of the fetus that are quite unmistakable. The infant seems to be particularly sensitive to high pitched sounds and responds with alarm to sudden or loud sounds. Vision, on the other hand, is probably only slightly developed at birth. Most observers conclude that vision for light and dark is about all that the newborn can discern. Clear delineation of objects is thought to develop at about two months. When it does develop, it has been shown that only near vision can be appreciated by the infant with clarity. As to the appreciation of pain and temperature, there is probably less in the newborn than in the older infant because sometimes babies have cold hands and feet and do not seem to object as strongly as one would expect. Nevertheless, cold seems to be a factor in perceptual threats; e.g., the reactions of the infant after kicking off the covers, etc. A case of unusual sensitivity to cold, seen by the author, seems to have had such a background. Visceral pain, particularly of intestinal origin, likewise is of great concern to the infant, as of course is hunger.

All of the sense organs are capable of recording stimuli which are appreciated by the organism as either pleasant or unpleasant. Sweet tastes, for example, provoke sucking movements and motor responses of a nature which approaches the oncoming object whereas bitter tastes provoke grimacing and avoidance movements. In this connection, the vestibular, proprioceptive, and cutaneous receptors concern themselves with the interesting phenomena of passive movement through space and of clinging. This latter has been given the term "the anaclytic impulses", the former is the precursor to the motives for locomotion. Although the infant is frightened by the sudden loss of support when it moves quickly through a short space (the Moro reflex), actually a slow or rhythmic motion affords an infant a great deal of pleasure and comfort. During gestation, the child is carried about a great deal as it moves whenever mother moves. After birth, however, in our culture at least, the infant is placed in a motionless crib or bassinet. In previous generations and in many other cultures, the cradle was an indispensable piece of furniture. It is amazing how much motion an infant can tolerate or even welcome. Older children would find it very disquieting and annoying to be subjected to such stimulation. When the infant has the chance to cling, there is less need for any motion. It seems that both of these perceptual systems are designed to attain some sort of contact between the infant and mother. An infant will often fall asleep if he can at least hold on to the fingers of the parent. Walking the floor or carrying the baby about, seems to be related to the gratifications of these basic demands of the infant. In the presence of illness or pain, the infant does not relinquish this demand, and the parents seem more inclined to yield to it.

The parallelism that exists between the sensory system and the oral end of the digestive system can be demonstrated by giving a common language to both processes. The common denominator is that of the function of "intake". Stimuli in the form of sounds, light, temperature, smell, and taste, as well as muscle sense from various areas as in sucking and being rocked or held, are all taken in and properly recorded in the brain in the form of awareness or consciousness. Indeed, Freud has said that all consciousness is essentially sensory in nature.

When the state of consciousness of the infant is in repose or is receiving pleasant stimuli, there is a relaxation and a tendency to release the motor discharge of smiling. Indeed, even at two months the baby smiles in his sleep, or what is more natural, responds to the pleasant social approach by any person, particularly the mother, by smiling. This social approach is auditory, visual, and tactile. On the other hand, at about four months, an infant can be made to cry by subjecting him to an angry look. This reaction is not easily explained. It is a very important one, playing a major role in subsequent human behavior.

The baby who cries when he is subjected to the angry look may, by simple conditioning, have associated this facial expression with loud or unfriendly sounds. This may be true but does not seem to be a sufficient explanation for the observed phenomenon. Psychoanalysis can supply additional understanding by the study of dream, fantasy, and "regressive" behavior of older persons. As pointed out previously, the infant clearly demonstrates his pleasure in attaining a feeling of unity with mother. This feeling of "one-ness", which extends from the intra-uterine period, is a very strong motivating force in the infant. It is only natural that he use all of his available equipment in order to attain this goal of one-ness. Achieving the goal helps maintain a homeo-static equilibrium. As pointed out, the main organs for attaining this equilibrium constitute the perceptual or more specifically the swallowing or taking-in process. The feeling of union with mother becomes equivalent to the desire to take in the mother or to be taken in by her. This is tantamount to swallowing or being swallowed or to incorporate or be incorporated (the latter representing the return to the uterus). Through this device, the infant acts in a manner which gives a quality of one-ness and it is as though the mother is part of the self or the self is part of the mother. As such, the baby "knows" or "feels" what the mother must be feeling when she is angry because he already knows what it feels like to be angry. Thus, when he perceives anger from the outside world, it is as though it is already something on the inside and as such becomes a threat to his bodily integrity. By the same token, the infant appreciates stimuli that arise inside of the self as though they were arising outside of the self.

Before we attempt to understand how either pleasant perceptual stimuli or unpleasant stimuli become "internalized" or "built-in", let us return to the subject of crying. As stated previously, crying represents a primitive form of communication. At all times it represents some disturbance in homeostatic equilibrium, even though there may be some questioned salutary effects such as exercise, etc. Although at first it may be saying, "I am hungry" when it reaches a point of intense expression it usually serves to say, "I am very angry". This vocal expression of anger produces a sound which in itself can serve as an auditory perceptual threat. Many mothers can confirm the observation that babies seem to frighten themselves by their own crying. This is a point of vital significance because if it is shown that tension can engender new tension in this manner, an important element in the perpetuation of anxiety in the adult can be delineated. To throw some light on the question as to whether babies scare themselves by their own crying, the author investigated a series of congenitally deaf babies. An attempt was made to determine whether such babies had a lesser degree of self-perpetuating or crescendo type of crying than normal babies. Questionnaires were submitted to fifty mothers of congenitally deaf babies. The results of the study showed to the author's satisfaction that, except for those cases where there was intercurrent illness, such as colic or otitis media, congenitally deaf babies are "good" babies in the early months of infancy. There was an almost uniform response that deaf infants do not spend as much time in crying as do normal babies. It seems hardly tenable that this condition can be due only to the absence of sounds from the outside. The absence of self-perpetuating crying must be due to the fact that the child, not hearing itself cry, has a lessened degree of self-imposed perceptual threats received by its auditory apparatus.

If it is true that tension has the faculty of perpetuating or prolonging itself, as in the infant who frightens himself by his own crying, then we can better understand the meaning of the phenomena of "incorporation", "introjection", and "projection" as devices of infantile thought. As stated previously, the experiences of the organism are recorded as memories. The memories of the sensations which have arisen in connection with the external object cast permanent shadows on the thinking processes of the child. By virtue of the taking-in impulses which had surrounded the motivations for nutrition and self-preservation, the perceptual imageries of the pleasant or unpleasant aspect of the parental figures can be appreciated as forces actually within the body of the organism.

As part of the taking-in and introjection mechanisms there are two other observable processes which lend weight to the subject at hand, namely fascination and mimicry. Bernfeld [25] called our attention to this interesting phenomenon in which the infant seems to find a particular object which grips his attention. His impulse is to take that object in his mouth. This motivation is directed toward the things that give him pleasure. It includes foods, bright objects, and the bottle, breast, or total person of the pleasure-giving mother. The sounds, motions, and facial expressions of the mother which arrest the infant's attention lead to the imitation or mimicry of the object. Fenichel [26] conceives of this mimicry as serving the purpose of mastering the intense stimuli which the organism perceives.

early ego autonomy

This shadow of the external object is sometimes referred to as an "introject". The primitive imitation of that which is perceived is referred to as primary identification. In the case of pleasant experiences with the external object, the introject corresponds to the feeling of possessing the "good mother" or, as Klein [27] believes, the "good breast". It is based upon the association in the mind of the infant that

when it "wants", it "gets". This leads to the early development of the
knowledge that needs can be satisfied in a cause and effect relationship.
As such, it forms the basis for the primary trait of reliance or trust.
In this respect it forms the groundwork for the establishment of magical
thinking. Hunger disappears, mother appears, pleasure prevails, sleep
supervenes. These are the phenomena which contribute to the magic.
It is good magic and as such has been described by Ferenczi [28] as
giving the infant the feeling of "omnipotence".

A point which cannot be overstressed is the fact that the emotional
state of the child bears a direct relationship to the emotional state of
the mother. If there is a high degree of stability in the mother and with
it a wholesome attitude to the infant, there is an almost intuitive understanding of the needs and interests of the infant. Thus, the pleasant
perceptions that the child receives are but a reflection of the pleasant
perceptions that are received by the mother. Where the mother is disturbed by her own neurosis and is not capable of affording the child
the necessary ingredients for his early gratifications, the infant uses
every means available to make his needs known. The feeling of omnipotence is but a reflection of the infant's use of his powers to attain
gratification. The memories of the feelings and emotions that come with
the interchange of reciprocal pleasant perceptions constitute the reservoir
for the magical notion that all is well.

This good magic is a necessary ingredient for infantile development;
perhaps it is even necessary for actual survival. The knowledge of this
fact has led to a change in emphasis in recent years in the care of
infants from studied neglect and rigid discipline to increased cuddling
and self-demand schedules. On the other hand, a persistence of continual prompt gratification of all impulses for an indefinite period of
time throughout childhood may interfere with a true testing of reality.
Carried to an extreme degree, reality may become synonymous with
good magic. Such a state produces the so-called "spoiled" child in
whom every demand is expected to result in prompt gratification. Such
a state interferes with wholesome ego development.

There is some gratification afforded to the infant when the sensations
or perceptions have a quality of being similar to sensations that have
already been experienced. There is established a feeling of continuity
when there is afforded a stimulation of that which is familiar. This
feeling particularly concerns itself with the mother but can apply as well

to the room and to various objects, but there is another element of gratification which is just the opposite; it is the pleasure that is obtained by change. This is more noteworthy with taking the child into another room, or presenting new playthings or changing in position. It offers new interests for experience and experimentation.

Thus there is present in the infant two sets of motivations: (a) the desire to be subjected to familiar perceptual patterns and (b) the desire to receive new perceptual patterns. These can both be looked upon as primary motivations or positive tropisms. They have far-reaching significance. On a superficial plane the former represents the security of "sameness" or the memories of past gratifications. Change, on the other hand, stimulates new excitations (as in adults going on vacation) and counteracts the ennui of prolonged stimulation by the same set of stimuli. The relative emphasis on the desire for sameness or the desire for change depends entirely upon which of these motivations has been gratified or frustrated. It follows then that either one or the other becomes a more dominant motivation. This basic principle becomes attached to other life experiences and to other learnings which occur later in the developmental phase.

It has become a dictum of psychoanalysis that ego growth develops out of the mastery of the frustrations of the instinctual processes [29]. This means that all growth is associated with some frustration. Indeed, even the phenomenon of birth itself is a frustration. As pointed out earlier, the infant is constantly subject to threats from the outside world and from within himself so that the forces of mastery are constantly called into play. When the learning processes are such that the threats are no longer the menace that they first appeared to be and when they are such that the demands which arise from the operation of the instinctual excitations can be relieved and gratified by the external world, then the infant has attained a feeling of faith, reliance, or "basic trust". It is with the perceptual knowledge that there is a prospect for relief from discomfort or excitation that the beginnings of ego strength are crystallized.

Most of the writings of psychoanalysis stress the concept that the ego starts to form when the infant begins to appreciate the difference between himself and the external object. He comes to understand where he ends and his mother begins. Certainly we have seen regressed schizophrenic individuals who show this lack of differentiation of the self from the mother or mother substitute. What I wish to stress is that this differentiation of the self as an entity does not necessarily come about by natural maturation. It develops out of the stored memories of gratification and pleasurable mastery of the instinctive forces. When the child learns that he can influence the outside world and that someone on the outside can and will relieve his discomforts, he begins to appreciate his own self in relation to the external objects. Conversely, when the gratifications are not forthcoming, there may be delay in the differentiation of the self. However, when favorable conditions for mastery have occurred, there is produced a happy baby. This normally is an accomplished fact by the age of ten months. It implies that the "good magic", "good mother", or "pleasurable perceptions" have been internalized or incorporated within the self. In this way the internal representatives of pleasure memories replaces to a large extent the continual dependence upon the outside world and with this comes the feeling of being in possession of one's own body.

The accumulation of memories of gratification of the primary self-preservative demands of the infant which results in the phenomenon of trust can be looked upon as a direct mastery of the instincts. When this trust is solidified or crystallized as a part of the self, it constitutes a base for ego development. This process will be referred to as primary integration. The ego trait of trust becomes a trait which is identifiable in the child and can exist as an autonomous psychic structure. Having stemmed from direct mastery it can be referred to as primary autonomy in contrast to secondary autonomy which will be described later.

We can then say that the gratification of individual demands resulting in pleasure, comfort, or relief enables the body to function as a balanced, organized machine. This balance or homeostasis is essentially life-giving or self-preservative. However, it is probably true, as Szasz [29] pointed out, that without the presence of some types of frustration there cannot be any biological differentiation of function or purpose. Therefore, complete perpetual gratification does not exist and would not be highly desirable if it could exist.

We may say, in theory at least, from what we have learned about tissue cultures, that were it not for the fact of birth, the fetus could grow in that manner indefinitely. However, birth does occur and as such probably represents the greatest frustration that the organism ever endures. Because of this, much care and protection, at least in the human mammal, is necessary to help prepare the organism for new frustrations and denials that will come later on. It is during the period of infancy that the groundwork should be laid for later training and indoctrination. New learnings and acculturation can occur smoothly when the ego trait of faith or basic trust is firmly established. This is the first example of the autonomous ego. When a matrix of faith has been established, the infant has learned to begin an existence apart from the mother. With this faith in the external object is the beginning of faith in the self. Notice must be taken of the fact, however, that this trust is on a purely perceptual level. It is still contingent on the availability of the external object in whom the infant invests a great deal of emotional energy. Freud used the term "object cathexis". It represents the beginnings of the sense of "belonging", a precursor to "object love".

At this level of development the infant is as yet the central figure of his still limited world. He accepts demonstrations of love and tenderness from the external object without giving anything in return. The pleasurable perceptions are accepted as gifts and in return he directs his first feelings to those persons who are willing to afford the gratifications. Abraham [30] particularly stresses the gratifications as being specifically directed toward the fact that the mother touches the child and evokes pleasurable sensations through the stimulation of erotic zones. There is some question as to whether the mother creates new sensations by stimulation; more probably she is capable of giving gratification to areas of excitation which innately appear as part of the maturation process. The fact that these gratifications are all centered within the self has led to the use of the term "Narcissism".

early ego disturbance

Just as the memories of gratification lead to the built-in feeling of faith, the memories of pain become internalized and continue to operate even when the perceptions of immediate threats are not present. This produces a state of constant alertness to distress. It is the picture of infantile anxiety or of the unhappy or sleepless baby. Let us try to consider what is happening or will happen to such a baby. On the basis of incorporation, Klein speaks of the baby reacting to the internalized "bad" mother or "bad" breast. Or more spectacularly, it reacts directly to the mother's internalized penis or penises of the father. This type of thinking implies an imagery which we are unable to prove exists in the infant. Such thinking is more likely a result of tensions that occur at a later period of life. This will be discussed later under secondary perceptual thinking, particularly the archaic type or that type of thinking that is primitive in nature and embodies the concept of a return to the nursing situation. Stern discusses infantile anxiety in purely physiological terms. He adapted Selye's [31] ideas concerning stress and the general adaptive reaction to the infant and small child.

Even though anxiety has physiological origins, there are psychological concomitants. The nature of the anxiety stems from the dangers that the infant experiences (1) from the outside world, (2) from the internalized threats of the memories of painful perceptions, and (3) from the effects of the instincts themselves. This categorization corresponds to Anna Freud's delineation of objective anxiety, superego anxiety, and instinctual anxiety. The last named would seem to be of the nature of the fear arising from the child's own instinctive demands or the reaction to their frustration, namely, rage. Later in life it could lead to an imagery which can be formulated in such terms as "If I don't get what I want, I will be angry. If I am angry, I am afraid I will burst". On a purely perceptual level, however, it is the body, or more specifically body regions or organs, which is appreciated by the infant as something dangerous. Thus the excitation of the organ can be considered as a "bad object" which produces a threatening situation and its consequent anxiety.

The infant who has not mastered his needs is the one who feels the impact of "bad magic" as a trigger device. As pointed out earlier, when the instinctual excitations are associated with lack of gratification and repeated frustrations, then the demands themselves serve as alarm signals for the organism. Thus the demand can become in itself a basic threat. By virtue of the failure of the organism to attain sufficient gratification, it is unable to predict the relief of discomfort or excitation and there results a continual state of disequilibrium or disturbed homeostasis. It may well be that this disturbed homeostasis represents nothing more than the perpetuation in memory of the stress of birth itself. At least it may be said that the reactions to the perception of danger repeat, in form, the prototypical reaction of birth. Whereas, as was pointed out, the feelings accompanying gratification or the predictability of gratification are essentially life-giving, the threat or danger signals are tantamount to expectancy of physiological death, and the disturbed homeostasis calls forth defensive processes which attempt to ward off such a calamity. Thus a traumatic situation or the anticipatory reaction of the perceptually recorded memories of traumatic experiences is capable of calling forth physiological responses to the approach of danger.

When the danger signals do not lead to discharge of energy as can be afforded by the establishment of primary perceptual communication with the external object or through relief of tension by stimulation of the excitable sensuous areas, then a state of shock is produced [16]. This state of shock is more than merely an instability; it can extend to a state of complete physiological disorganization.

Although the small infant in its waking state can be said to live in an almost perpetual position of anticipatory anxiety, this condition only persists when the perceptual system has been bombarded with a high degree of shock-like stimuli. Thus, instead of developing the ego trait of faith or trust, there is developed instead a state of basic vulnerability or mistrust. It may well be that the deeply seated fear of loss of love in later life has such an origin.

To return to the actual disorganization of the physiology of the infant, we see that much of the explanation of the varying degrees of ego disintegration in the psychopathological pictures of older children and adults lies in the presence of an overwhelming anxiety in the infant. Many students of infant behavior, notably Ribble [32] and Spitz [24], have supplied clinical data for much of the more theoretical formulation of early analytical observations. It has been clearly shown that when anxiety reaches a peak and gratification still does not supervene, the organism attempts to defend itself by surrendering the demands for gratification. Freud terms this the withdrawal of the cathexis from the perceptual system. Such an infant becomes listless, anorectic, and apathetic. An extreme degree of this phenomenon produces a state of "awayness" or a catatonic-like state where contact with the outside world becomes lessened or lost, a condition which may lead to marasmus. Spitz has shown that even death itself may be the result of such complete withdrawal from the fundamental processes of life. Partial deaths in the form of the production of basic personality traits that lead to the depressions and schizophrenias of later life probably have their roots in such physiological phenomena. On a lesser scale, the withdrawals, denials, negative hallucinations, and even the process of repression stem from this early form of perceptual defense.

We cannot fully appreciate what goes on in the mind of the infant when the physiological manifestations of basic vulnerability and repression take place. On the one hand, vulnerability suggests that the infant reacts to dangers which may not exist, and repression suggests that the infant reacts as though the impulses or the threats do not exist. This implies that there is already developed in the brain of the infant a function which can begin to interpret reality. Thus we can say that there is formed an ego which both "experiences" and "observes".

This observing function of the ego "anticipates a situation experienced in the past and projects it into the future under conditions of the present" [16]. The question arises as to what the internal imagery of the child is when these internal observations are in operation. The formulations of Klein have already been alluded to. There is reason to believe that the imagery is probably associated with organs of perception themselves as well as with the areas of excitation. Whenever an instinct is associated with the memory of pain or the lack of its gratification, then the instinct itself is endowed with the properties of a threat so that a basic impulse can become a basic threat. This type of thinking is one of the fundamental elements in the formation of anxieties. As Freud states, the ego behaves as if an outbreak of anxiety threatened it not from the direction of the instinct but from the direction of the perception. To go a step further, the organism can project or introject the organs of perception as threatening forces. This internalization forms the basis for the primordial superego. The matter is complicated further when we recall what we said earlier about the child frightening itself by its own crying. In terms of some kind of internal imagery of the memories of crying or anger, it appears that a portion of the mind is geared to receiving threats that may have originated from the child's own rage. From what we have learned about people who show what appears to be an archaic form of thinking or infantile reactions to anxiety, there appear in the imagery various ingredients of the perceptual system, particularly eyes, ears, and mouths, As a force which acts as a damper upon the expression of instincts, it can be labelled a *perceptual, preverbal superego*. This force must be considered as an entity in contrast to the verbal conceptual superego which will be described later. The perceptual superego can be endowed with the same properties as the external threats or can have the same mode of expression as the instincts themselves; e.g., a devouring superego.

Lewin [33] is of the opinion that the early superego is a representation of the breast. He speaks of the devouring or encircling breast, which is an outgrowth of the actual encircling or choking phenomenology of the nursing situation plus the mother's desire to swallow or be swallowed by the infant. Thus the encircling breast produces the danger situations that go to make up the infantile superego. I am trying to stress the primary perceptions of danger as the outgrowth of the child's own physiology, these perceptions being appreciated as threats from the outside world when frustrations of instincts ensue. Danger or alarm signals set in motion the self-preservative impulses which would be similar in nature to the desire to relieve homeostatic imbalance by the return to the pleasure (or ecstasy) of the nursing situation, but on such occurrences the alarm signals become threats in themselves. Our point here is that the encircling or devouring breast is not a primary perception, but is a secondary perception which is described later as secondary perceptual thinking.

A case illustrating this point is that of a young man who was consciously afraid of women's breasts. The imagery was indeed related to the idea of being devoured. But the facts of the case were that he had not been a breast-fed baby. In fact, he was a premature infant who had not been picked up or handled for the first six months of his life. He had been fed at first with a Breck feeder because he was too weak to nurse. Klein would say that the devouring breast idea was an "unconscious" fantasy existing as an inborn heritage. Most observers do not subscribe to this view. The reader is referred to the many writings of the two authors mentioned. The pertinent publications appear in the appended bibliography.

Although the true nature of infantile or archaic thinking cannot really be studied first hand, we may gather some conclusions by the study of the archaic form of secondary perceptual thinking which will be discussed later.

A young man, aged twenty-three, suffering from a schizophrenic process, is a case in point. He presented intense feelings of anxiety when he was looked at or when he was subjected to any situation of authority. His fears of authority were related to the sound of the voice as well as the gaze. He reported many dreams where eyes and eating were related, but one dream in particular illustrates the relationship of the mouth and early superego formation. He dreamed of a god which was all mouth. "I was afraid of the voice. I felt that I must feed it. I must have known how I felt when I was hungry. I obliged the voice. I had to appease it."

An even more convincing case proving the existence of a preverbal superego has come to my attention. An infant of thirteen months of age was left in the care of a neurotic aunt who screamed and admonished the baby for sucking its thumb. She pulled the thumb out of the child's mouth as she registered her vocal disapproval. After the third time she did this, the child placed his hand with the thumb extended under its back and cried violently. The child continued to do this for many weeks afterward, every night. The hand would be tucked under the body as if to prevent itself from getting the thumb while he wailed with rage, even when no other person was present to issue the prohibitive command. This baby grew up to be a shy, inhibited boy. He maintained a marked aversion to his aunt. There seems little doubt that here we were dealing not only with the precursors of superego, but perhaps also with an already developed preverbal superego at a very early age.

From the foregoing case it can be seen that the infant is able to exert some internal pressure at curbing his own instinctive demands. In order to renounce an impulse or to repress its presence, a strong counterforce is needed. Freud introduced the term "counter-cathexis" as a function of the mind which binds primitive reaction impulses in such a manner as to inhibit their immediate discharge. Simmel [34] suggested that the counterforce which effects the repression, springs from the original devouring impulse which he equates with the instinct for self-preservation. He pictures the phenomenon as a swallowing or an internalizing of the impulses which cannot be gratified. Although it has been said by some observers that an infant cannot appreciate a prohibitive command, there is reason to believe that this is not true. What may be true is that the infant cannot appreciate specific prohibitive commands, but that it can, as a result of the bombardment of painful sensory stimuli described in the previous pages, develop into a non-specifically sensitized organism. This process produces the picture of the sensitive child.

There is reason to believe that the perceptual superego is more clearly evidenced and is of greater intensity when the external object which had been the source of supply for good magic becomes the threat or symbol of bad magic. This point is being illustrated by experimental work with puppies.* When the loving figure becomes the threatening one, there is an exaggeration of the threat by virtue of the cathexis which had been invested in the original object since a formerly protective force now becomes a powerful force which can hurt or destroy. The experimental work seems to show that the internalized prohibitive threat or command becomes stronger when the agent which institutes the threat had been an important source of libidinal supply.

A sensitive child can be observed to be constantly attuned to distress. He cries easily, over-reacts to mildly nocuous stimuli, and is quite unhappy most of the time. Because of his sensitivity to perceptual stimuli, he is more vulnerable to new threats from the outer world than the child who has developed the ego trait of trust. He is apt to be vigilant to danger to such an extent that he sleeps very poorly. Thus sensitivity can be looked upon as an ego trait which has developed defensively in order to cope with threatening stimuli but which renders the organism increasingly vulnerable to new stimuli.

However, because of the increased perception of the sensitive child to the stimuli arising outside and inside the self, there is an increased demand for pleasant perceptual gratifications from the external world as well as from the body itself. Let us first engage our attention to the relations of such a child to the outer world. The anaclytic or clinging impulses drive the infant to make demands for their gratification in order to allay the exaggerated discomforts. These demands lead to the ego trait of dependency. There exists in the sensitive child a prolonged state of demanding assurances that instincts be gratified and discomforts be relieved, making it not only more susceptible to new hurts, but also causing it to resist being weaned from the source of its supplies.

As an accompaniment of the prolongation of dependency, there is maintained for a longer period of time than is necessary, the feeling

---

* I am indebted to Dr. Ernest Hilgard for calling attention to this work which is being done at Harvard University by Dr. Richard Solomon. By personal communication, Dr. Solomon states that his experiment is based upon an "elaboration of associationistic conditioning and learning theories."

of one-ness with mother. It must be remembered that there is a great difference in the origin of such dependence, when the demands have been constantly granted and frustrations have never occurred from the cases where the infant "hangs on to mother for dear life" in order to get what supplies are available or to attempt to neutralize by pleasure the memories of pain. Dependency itself can later on lead to new complications because it places the organism in a perpetual state of being at the mercy of the external object. Later in life the persistence of such a trait can result in the phenomenon of gullibility which can produce many new complications of personality. It is in this state that the orally incorporated suggestions from the external object become internal commands. Thus, a strong perceptual superego lays the ground-work for an intense superego on a conceptual level.

Let us take notice of other ego traits that take form in the face of the infantile superego forces. As a result of the unbalanced homeostasis resulting from the disturbing forces, the infant may attempt to strike a balance by resorting to repetitive activities such as playing with its feces, sucking activities, or rocking in bed. Such activities are essentially masturbatory in nature and represent rescue phenomena on the part of the infants from their desparate situations. As a more satisfactory mastery of the deprivations, the organism can attain an equilibrium by putting increased demands for gratification upon the external world. This reaction can produce, through the process of secondary autonomy, the ego trait of greed or insatiability. This trait of greed or selfishness manifests itself as a perceptual search for pleasure. It may be for food, but can include all forms of demands for attention. When babies have mastered their needs, they begin to exhibit varying degrees of self-sufficiency. This is not so when the phenomenon of greed has taken hold. It is this trait with its interminable search for pleasure or relief from minor discomforts which gave Freud the original ideas concerning narcissism or the love of one's self. It can hardly be called "love" in the sense which we will describe later, but represents a cathexis or emotionalization of the self as a defensive process operating against the frustrations of early perceptual needs. Instead of really loving the self, the organism displays perpetual cravings that seem never to be satisfied. These cravings, when not gratified, may lead to new frustrations or may seek discharge in substitute or perverse gratifications at later stages of life.

The knowledge of the effects of deprivations during the oral phase of development is becoming increasingly clear to psychoanalysts. It has reached the point where the nursing situation is regarded as the theme for the understanding of nearly all personality aberrations. Certainly in the extremes of personality disorganization the thinking processes are devoted to early infantile language expressions. But even in lesser states of pathology, the affects of oral traumata may be disclosed. A case in point is as follows: A thirty-six year old woman came to analysis because of feelings of inadequacy, irritability, and compulsive shopping. She reported feeling stupid and empty. Her problems were traced back to her infancy when she had gone through a prolonged period of hunger. She had cried a great deal before it was discovered she was nursing on comparatively empty breasts. Her later imagery consisted of being a bad person, the imagery proving to be an introjection of "bad mother" and an "empty" person which was an internalization of the "empty breast".

ego growth in late infancy

Although many of the anlages of human personality have been described thus far in terms of perception and in terms of sucking and swallowing, notice will now be given to the phenomenon of biting. Chronologically this phenomenon appears in the infant at the teething period. However, it may put in its appearance earlier, particularly when there is some evidence of early frustration, such as sucking on an empty breast. It will be recalled that the behavior of the infant in its early months was typified by the word "get". Even the muscular movements, which are mainly of the upper extremities, function in this same direction. The hand grasps objects and tends to bring them toward the mouth. Both the grasping and the attempt at ingestion involve getting. The late oral or biting phase shows accompanying muscular movements which can be considered to be akin to biting; e.g., picking (at objects or the self), clawing, tearing, or striking. The biting, chewing, or clawing vaguely resemble the eating habits of the carnivores. The main language of instinctual expression seems to be to "take" or "grab". Inasmuch as this motor aspect of this expression can lead to some discomfort to external objects, it can become part of the language of the infant to express anger. Erikson suggests that the association is brought about because the child has pain in teething and relieves the pain by biting. The expression of anger with biting need not be universal, because biting out of affection is the rule. After all, the child eats that which tastes good and can try to bite the object which it wishes to incorporate. A suggestion made by Bell [35] regarding the biting of soft and hard objects as having some meaning is very ingenious. He suggested that the child's biting of hard objects is the first appreciation of "hard reality". The author cannot confirm this suggestion from any clinical material, although it is of some interest. It is true, however, that biting itself may become a phenomenon of behavior as in bruxism or teeth grinding and later in nail biting. The latter condition seems to have both the element of the action of biting and the denial, as in biting off the claws that may have aggressive qualities, so that it actually represents a form of suppressed anger, released on one's own body.

The phenomenon of biting can be looked upon as the primordial expression of the destructive impulse of the organism. Out of it develops the ego trait of cruelty. Infantile cruelty, of course, may have no relation to the cruelty of later childhood or adulthood because it does not bear the conceptualized connotations which are acquired later. But cruelty it is, as judged by the performance. Such cruelty may be shown toward the object upon whom the infant is dependent, as in biting the hand that feeds him. This is the first or oral form of ambivalence, loving and hating the same object.

When the imagery in the perceptual superego contains elements of the infant's own oral sadistic or biting impulses, the organism experiences the fear of being bitten. This has its effects in later life when some sensitive persons are constantly alert to criticism or to the "sharp tongue" of others. In other words, one of the ingredients of the child's fear of others comes from his own wish to hurt.

Although the phenomenon of "taking" can later develop into the habit of stealing, it does not mean that the biting phase of development furnishes only the destructive aspects of the personality. Bartemeier [36] has shown that the muscular aspects of eating and biting are related to the phenomenology of work. He pointed out many parallel imageries. They will be discussed later.

Theoretically at least, the consequences of biting should be more marked in the case of breast-fed babies than in the case of bottle babies. When the baby bites the nipple, the mother reacts and undoubtedly makes some impression upon him. On the other hand, bottle babies bite the nipple freely and no consequences result. Whether this lack of reaction leads to a seduction into free expression of aggression can only be conjectured upon at this time.

Another aspect of infant physiology, which seems to have some bearing upon the development of the personality, is vomiting. This phenomenon may be transitory or can become quite a prominent feature of an infant's reactions. It is only in the latter instance where it seems to have any bearing. There are many people who have been vomiters since infancy and use vomiting as a body language to express many things. It has a "getting-rid-of" meaning, which can apply to the wish to ward off some unwanted impulses, to get rid of certain traumatic situations or to get rid of certain "introjects" or the incorporated images of pertinent people.

Pediatricians have become accustomed to using "spitting" and "vomiting" nearly synonymously, the former term being reserved for the type of regurgitation which flows out of the mouth and vomiting to that which is forcibly ejected by a reflex action of a particular set of abdominal, diaphragmatic, and chest muscles. True spitting, however, as adults know it, which consists of a voluntary contraction of the muscles of the mouth, tongue, and glottis, does not exist as such in the infant. However, as was pointed out earlier, the infant reacts to bad tastes and makes some attempts to rid itself of the contents of the mouth that appear unpleasant. It is these reactions which form the basis for the phenomenon of disgust which develops later in the toddler period. It is also used by the organism to get rid of unpleasant perceptions or impulses which are unwanted. These form somatic reactions in later life.

In summarizing the discussion of the infant, we can see that many of the basic structures both for the formation of the personality in its healthy state and for the formation of the precursors of future difficulties are developed in this period. In the healthy growth of the infant, the child learns to anticipate pleasure and that he will both "get" and has some of the equipment with which to "take". Out of the integration of these phenomena develops the sense of reliance. The child is not necessarily dependent upon his environment, but can rely upon the gratification of some of his most primitive self-preservative instincts.

This lack of dependence, as was pointed out previously, is an outgrowth of the development of "faith", but even further enables the child to begin to extrapolate into the future the feeling that things will lead to satisfaction, developing the phenomenon of "hope". In such a setting the child is prepared to meet the new frustrations that reality will have to offer later on, so that he can then be amenable to the processes of training and indocrination that will follow.

Conversely, when he has had a sufficient degree of friendly internalized memory patterns, he is the possessor of a groundwork upon which future happiness and enjoyment of life can be based.

Before we leave the period of infancy, we can already anticipate some of the developmental phases of later childhood. Although the infant is nonverbal, he already understands the meaning of many words. Furthermore, there are other nonverbal meanings that may in some measure be understood, as for example, which is the right end of the bottle. Some aspects of socialization have already begun. Survival on a purely physical basis seems to be the more primitive process and is involved essentially with perceptual thinking. Social survival or relating oneself to external objects in reality terms seems to be more involved with conceptual thinking. If one were to consider the strong or well-functioning ego as a "conceptual" ego and the weak, sensitive, or poorly organized ego as a "perceptual" ego, it would be in keeping with the theme of this presentation.

CHAPTER **THREE**

the role of sphincter
control · time and
space concepts · de-
velopment of speech ·
late toddler phase

THE TODDLER

Whereas the infancy or oral phase of development
has formed the groundwork for the personality of the organism, we
can say that the toddler phase forms the framework for the super-
structure. Once the basis for survival as an independent being has been
established, we reach the stage of the beginning of character development. One of the most noteworthy developmental phases which influences
the thinking processes, is that of active motion through space. Before
the child learns to walk, there is first the stage of creeping or crawling.
Let us engage ourselves with the new areas of experimentation and
temptation that enter into this phase of existence.

Silverberg [15] has called our attention to a very important aspect
of child development which he calls the "see-touch-swallow" sequence.
Although these phenomena have already been described in the previous
chapter as aspects of perceptual thinking, the new addition at the
toddler phase of growth is the concept "go". Thus, locomotion will help
the child see new things, reach them, and then try to incorporate or
ingest them, obviously bringing complications into the life of the child
because not everything that the child can see or reach is fit to be taken
in the mouth. Not only does the mother find it necessary to interdict
the handling of sharp objects, but sometimes is obliged to take things
out of the child's mouth or have him spit out some "unclean" or "bad"
substance.

Depending upon the manner in which the child is handled, this "see-
touch-swallow" sequence can lead to pleasurable experiences or painful
ones. The painful experiences can be appreciated by the child as pro-
hibitions of each of the three components. It can not only be wrong or

35

naughty to swallow; it can become naughty to look or to touch. This forbiddenness may have far-reaching significance. We might add that it may also become wrong to "go", but this will be discussed further on the matter of locomotion.

Because of the intervention of the parent in the "see-touch-swallow" sequence, the child "thinks twice" before giving way to the motivation. This "thinking twice" implies a recognition of both the pleasure motive and the alarm signal. When one of these forces is stronger than the other, the organism gives way to the dominant motivation. As pointed out previously, the deprived infant may have greater motivation for instinctual gratification than the one who has already the built-in sense of basic trust. Thus the deprived infant not only is drawn more intensely toward searching for some sort of pleasure-giving stimulus, but also thereby invites more and more prohibitive commands. Add to this the basic vulnerability that some disturbed infants already demonstrate, and we can see how the early toddler (or creeper) can be thrown into a quandary. Thus both forces can become very strong. The "thinking twice" may be repetitive, like the swing of a pendulum or the oscillations of an alternating current. This type of thinking forms the basis for what has been termed "ruminative thinking". It corresponds to actual physical rumination; viz., regurgitation and reswallowing. Rumination or treadmill thinking as a process, is an intimate part of the obsessive-compulsive neurosis which will be discussed later.

Although this ruminative thinking is connected closely with an understanding of the meaning of things, it is my contention that in its most primitive form it is essentially nonverbal and closely connected with primary, perceptual thinking. What is more important at this point is the process itself rather than the content. In some respects the thinking process is an end in itself and has survival qualities of its own. As such it serves the ego as a defense mechanism against overwhelming anxiety and serves to establish homeostasis. Later this can become a merry-go-round detour leading to ritualistic, useless activity, but at its inception it serves a purpose.

Rumination is not the only means of defense that the early toddler will begin to show. There is also the matter of fantasy formation or speculative thinking, the beginning of secondary perceptual thinking. Here the content begins to take on measures of importance. What the child does is to remember when "things were good". This is clearly, as

Silverberg [15] and Lewin [33] as well as others show, the recall of
the nursing situation. As such it may represent a true nostalgia with
attempts actually to re-establish in action some of the elements of the
nursing experience. The most successful of these, and one which sometimes remains a persistent driving force, is the "bid for attention".
This desire for attention is a projection outward onto the parent of the
"see-touch-swallow" sequence. It represents "look at me", "touch me",
and "swallow me". The "swallowing" may take the form of being picked
up and cuddled, but also by a process of reaction formation can produce
a return to fundamentals in the idea, "feed me". When the little toddler
has not fully attained the feeling that he can exist as an entity away
from his mother, he may do everything in his power to prevent being
separated from her. The sensitive child cries over small hurts to get the
mother to his side. He hates to go to bed alone, but finally accepts a
compromise by taking a favorite toy or stuffed animal to bed with
him. These are remnants of the feeling of one-ness or the wish to be
still a part of the physical body of the mother.

Although Klein and others have attributed elaborate fantasies concerning breasts and penises to the infant, as stated before we have no
proof that this mode of thinking exists in the very little child. However,
these fantasies exist somewhat later in the toddler period when the
child begins to speculate in terms of the meaning of things and of
possible solutions for his stresses. Questions no doubt arise on "Why
can't I have mother's breast?", "Who has it now?", "Maybe daddy has
something equally good", etc. These modes of thinking arise from the
elaboration of imageries stemming from the primary perceptions of the
infant and constitute the most archaic forms of fantasy formation. The
child can have vague remembrances of the time when things were good;
but conversely it can also remember if things were bad. Therefore, on
new lines of maturation, new pleasures can become threats, just as basic
needs (instincts) were shown to become basic threats. Perhaps this
process can be a basis for the feeling that any kind of pleasure may be
bad.

Let us now return to the little fellow who is happily exploring the
world and who is only mildly menaced by what results from his putting
things in his mouth. He may still get great pleasure out of seeing and
touching, but to swallow requires some differentiation. It is part of the
first true example of ability to take his place on an autonomous basis

when he learns that some things are edible and some are not. In addition, he may obtain great pleasure out of "getting into things" at times to the discomfort of the parent, although here too there must be new "learnings" as to what the limits may be. Mention should be made here of the necessity for consistency on the part of the parent, because inconsistency will only tend to encourage the ruminative type of response rather than to permit the child to work toward a goal.

the role of sphincter control

On the matter of training and indoctrination, nothing offers a more fertile field for combat between mother and child than the question of bowel and bladder control. Although all the textbooks still state that in our culture there is a strong tendency to rigid and early bowel training, in actual practice there seems to be a slackening of pressure in this direction, just as there has been a general lessening of rigidity in feeding schedules. This relaxation may be due to the emphasis that psychoanalytic investigators have made upon the importance of not creating too many issues on this matter because of the significant personality changes that can result. In spite of this teaching, the battle of the sphincters is still a most vital element in the development of the child.

Although evidence has been brought forward that reactions of the children stem from "giving up their feces" or by pleasing their parents through "offering feces as a gift", there is some question that these are primary reactions. The movies of severely deprived babies shown by Spitz seem very convincing on the latter point, i.e., the gift quality, but nevertheless this too may be secondary to previously imposed disciplinary attempts. It is becoming increasingly agreed that the complications that arise from the processes of defecation and urination are direct outgrowths of the prohibitive and primitive commands of the parent or person in charge of the training. By these prohibitive commands the pleasure or libidinal discharge associated with the act of defecation is converted to other gratifications or compromises.

From the point of view of pure sensation or inner perception, the full bladder or rectum leads to some degree of discomfort, which when evacuated, leads to a feeling of relief. This feeling of relief is pleasurable, but is probably not as intense in the young toddler as other pleasures because urine or feces are not retained but are promptly expelled. There is probably some pleasure for awhile when the urine or feces is still warm. Perhaps the most pleasure or relief comes when the expulsion of the excrement is delayed and there is already some discomfort.

In essentially the same manner that the creeper "gets the idea" that some things should not be put in the mouth, bowel and bladder training are effected. That is, he can learn only after he "gets the idea". We may see some variation, of course, with intelligence differences. It seems that with the onset of locomotion, the major interest of the organism shifts from the oral area and upper extremities to the pelvic area and the lower extremities. From the disciplinary point of view, the child need not take full responsibility for placing things in the mouth or touching things he is not supposed to. The parent is there to help remind him of what he can or cannot do, and the issue may well be settled. With bowels on the other hand, there is no retrieving the action when it is done. The act must be inhibited before it happens. The full responsibility for control rests upon the child himself.

Now, what is it that the child must learn about his bowels? It certainly is not *how* to have an evacuation. Reflex physiology takes care of that. It is only *where* to have the movement or *when* to have it. This control brings into play two very important concepts; namely "place" and "time". Spatial relations and temporal awareness are thus two maturational forces which emerge during the toddler period. Let us lay these aside for a moment and turn to the consideration of the bowel activity itself.

Even though the toddler may get some pleasure out of wetting or soiling himself, the mother's attitude toward the acts stands in sharp contrast. In fact, the child may himself find some discomfort out of being wet or cold. The pleasures of eating are quite different since here the mother can make a big fuss over the very thing the child may naturally enjoy. This does not mean that the child enjoys all foods equally well. Actually, here too there may be distinct differences of opinion by mother and child as to what is palatable and what is not. "Eat your spinach, it's good for you!" "Don't put that in your mouth, it's filthy!" "Pew! let's open a window!" With bowels or bladder, the preponderance of feeling from the outside world is heavily on the side of the naughty or nasty. This attitude becomes equated in the mind of the child with the "dirty" or dangerous things that he might put in his mouth. These evaluations are bound up with unpleasant emotional experiences.

However, long before the child actually comes to the acceptance of this point in his indoctrination, his young mind has been very active. Certainly his thoughts are reflections of the manner in which he has been handled. For example, the mother cannot possibly react to bowel function in any manner other than that which is a result of her own acculturation. Furthermore, mothers can accept a baby's bowel movements with equanimity, but become alarmed, disgusted, or threatened when the runabout is still soiling his pants. This changed attitude also prevails in other ways with many mothers. They can be perfectly fine mothers to their infants, but when the infancy period is passed and the toddler begins to get into mischief, the romance is over. Conflicts regarding the desire to maintain the state of helplessness and the need to turn out a "perfect product" serve to act as devices which interfere with the ego growth of the child.

Bowel activity specifically is the particular function which pits the will of the child against the will of the mother. However, this is not the only area in which the child expresses himself in a manner antagonistic to the parent. Exactly what goes on in the mind of the child when he is motivated to say "no" is hard to say, but no doubt the negating attitude springs from physiological sources, as Freud pointed out. When the child perceives the pressure to curtail a pleasure or to accept an unpleasantness of any sort, the body rebels with a reaction of avoidance. This avoidance can range from failure to heed the command, to open defiance. Actually, when there is a measure of self-sufficiency, the defiance can be looked upon as a wholesome ego reaction. The defiant attitude represents the refusal of the child to yield to the demands of the external object and the maintenance of the motivation of satisfying his own demands. In such a situation the child may obtain gratification out of the defiance itself. Thus the power that the child feels in having mastered the obstacle of the parental command, can become a source of pleasure and can be incorporated into the ego as a personality trait. This defiance can be an end in itself and is quite apart from the hedonistic aspect of merely gratifying the impulses without concern for parental authority. Indeed, such traits also occur, but these have been described in the previous section under oral greed.

The predominating emotional tone in defiance is anger. This anger can range from the violent rage, which is more characteristic of the infant, to subtle feelings of opposition, which do occur in the toddler phase. Thus the child may act in the manner of the sit-down striker (negativism) or he may do the exact reverse of what the parent asks him to do. These are merely degrees of disobedience which the child is capable of showing at this age. In terms of bowel activity, the child can show his defiance by having his bowel movement where and when *he* wants to or he can retain his feces to such a degree as to not have any spontaneous bowel movements. In this manner, bowel activity begins to take on a form of language for the child. He can symbolically say "I am angry" or "I won't" by means of his lower intestinal tract. This form of anal expression, where the child can attack by expulsion, or retention, is termed "anal sadism". This defiant attitude can be manifested by actual smearing of the feces. These phenomena can later be made socially acceptable (sublimated) in the form of playing with dirt or mud and still later in life with messiness or gossip.

These manifestations of defiance are closely connected with anal libido. But they may show themselves in other ways, as general stubbornness or obstinacy, for example, or as a refusal to eat or to be coerced into other activities. Also, it may be mentioned that sometimes defiant attitudes about bowel activities may be the result of the clash of wills with mother on issues other than bowel training, but the child uses soiling or constipation as his means of asserting himself.

Let us now consider the sensitive child, both the one who is anxiety-ridden from the infancy period and the toddler who becomes intimidated by stern disciplinary measures at this age. Such a child does not dare to maintain an attitude of defiance. The best adaptation he can make is to be compliant to the demands of the parent. Here the predominant emotional tone is one of fear. This compliant attitude, if extreme, can show almost automatic obedience and relinquishment of all individual demands. As to bowel function, expulsion can be performed to appease the mother and retention can be effected in order to be clean.

It must be remembered that both defiance and compliance exist in the minds of all children at this age. In fact, the polarity of defiance vs. compliance or opposing vs. appeasing, represents basic forces in the thinking processes of all people. In some, both extremes are very marked; in others, one or the other of these poles will predominate. It is the oscillation of one to the other which adds content and meaning to the ruminative thinking which was described at the beginning of this chapter.

A most unfortunate circumstance exists when the organism reacts with both motivations at the same time. This produces a picture of emotional tension because the motor discharge cannot gain access in either direction. When persons exhibit this type of behavior they resemble a car in gear with the motor racing and the brakes on.

On elaborations of the defiance-compliance theme, we find the defense mechanism known as reaction formation. In this situation, the opposite motivation from the basic one reaches the surface as an ego trait. Thus the polarity at the conscious level may be the reverse of the one which had been the original motivation. Such phenomena as clean vs. dirty, kosher vs. trafe, messiness vs. orderliness, moral vs. immoral, have their origins in the early reactions and secondary defenses to the disciplinary situations of the toddler period. They all operate essentially on the all-or-none principle.

When the results of the basic training period are such as to avoid the extremes of defiance or compliance on the part of the child, he is afforded the opportunity of mastering his own impulses in terms of the demands of his parents. The term "will power", which has more popular usage than scientific, can refer to the exercise of energy by the ego to withstand the demands of the external objects, but it also refers to the motivation for exercising energy to curb the instincts. However, here too "will power" itself, which can reach in either direction, is a defense mechanism of the ego, a mechanism capable of giving the organism the pleasure of mastery. As a child once reported, "I am the boss of me." Obviously this is the culmination of the development of the ego trait of autonomy. When a child says "No, I won't!" this presupposes a concept of "I am I", the realization of self as a separate being. Out of this characteristic emerges the very important trait of self-esteem or self-reliance. The child can get great satisfaction out of feeding himself or doing things on his own.

Mention was made in the previous chapter concerning the early establishment of precursors to the superego. During the training and indoctrination period this development proceeds further. At first the parent, particularly the mother, represents a force which establishes "external controls". As these controls become internalized or incorporated, a set of "inner controls" develops. These inner controls have the capacity to give the toddler a sense of gratification in themselves because in carrying them out the child can establish communication with the parent on a new level.

In addition to the feeling of acceptance by his parents that the child feels for having established the inner controls, he is to some extent freed from the parent because it helps the child establish a sense of independence. It is as though he has his mother within himself all the time. This becomes supportive and protective if the parent had been actually such a person in the prior period. If, for reasons of poor handling on the part of the parent, there is disturbance of the establishment of the internal controls, the child is delayed in the establishment of the dominion over himself and remains perpetually sensitized to external controls and parental attitudes. This is particularly true when the parent has not been sufficiently supportive in other respects for the child to accept readily the notion of inner controls. However, it is when the inner controls become established that autonomy and self-esteem are present. It is this feeling within the toddler that motivates him to express the concept, "I am a big boy!"

Let us discuss a bit further the ego trait of self-esteem from the point of view of primary perceptual thinking. Self-esteem arises from the incorporation of the esteeming external object. When the child feels that he is being highly regarded by the mother, and at this stage by the father too, then the imprint of their personalities leaves indelible impressions upon his psychic processes. The esteem that the child perceives from the parent involves the fact that the training elements have been sufficiently mastered by the child while his own basic impulses are either gratified or relinquished in favor of the pleasures arising from the mastery of the total situation. By virtue of the introjection of the esteeming parent, the child begins to become a parent to himself and this starts the march to an independent existence.

Let us return now to our original theme of perceptual and conceptual thinking. It is true that by this time in the development of the child there is already considerable progress in the understanding and expression of language. Nevertheless, the meaning of things is largely tied up with pure perception. The prohibitive commands are not instilled on the basis of pure reasoning. The mother either yells at the child in loud, angry tones or administers physical pain in the form of a slap or spanking. These commands, as they become internalized, are essentially auditory, not so much in the interpretation of the verbal commands as communicable concepts, but rather as loud or angry tones. At this age, as in all ages, the auditory apparatus can also respond to pleasant stimuli. Pleasant tones, cooing, lullabies, and the friendly glance can still make the child relax and their opposite can bring forth the specific manifestations of the anger-fear reactions.

In relation to the feces, the phenomena of remorse and disgust are elaborated. Remorse represents a reaction of the organism to an act committed, which it wants to undo. As a precursor to appeasement, remorse is involved with some aspects of fear. Disgust is a reaction which is more physiological in nature. It is closely related to nausea and is the psychological equivalent to the reaction of the refusal by the organism to ingest unpalatable substances. Both remorse and disgust are phenomena which enter into making up the superego. It is to ward off these phenomena that the defiance-compliance theme is brought into operation.

Another aspect of the compliance-defiance polarity which has been particularly stressed by Bergler [37] is the element of mockery. Even the toddler is able to comply in a manner as if to burlesque the parental demand, so that there can be elaborated such combinations as compliant-defiance or defiant-compliance. Here is a case in point: A patient in analysis suffered from the ruminative thinking so typical of the obsessive-compulsive neurosis. As far back as she remembered, she had tried to be very compliant with her mother's demands. All acts became tasks. Even a bowel movement was known as a "jobby". She reported a memory that consisted of going to a barber shop as a very little girl. She said she was very relaxed, as if she were at home. Her mother laughed about it and made her feel as though she were being criticized. "I was embarrassed. I thought 'I'm not supposed to be relaxed. O.K. I never will be again. From now on I'll never relax in such a situation again' ".

This memory not only illustrates the point of burlesquing the compliance, but brings out two other points which will be discussed later; namely, the "from now on" theme and the phenomena of being teased and ridiculed. Before discussing these, we must go back to the "where" and "when" themes which we left some pages back. Also, there are two other concepts that emerge from the anal instinctual energy; namely "do" or "make" and "give".

The language of the bowel not only arises from the inherent nature of bowel function itself, but from the implications of the activity in terms of the language of the mother. The child can feel that he is capable of producing something in having a bowel movement. This "something" is not merely the material which he has created, but also it has odor and can produce a reaction in the mother. Furthermore, many mothers speak of "making a-a" or "wee-wee" or "doing duty". This idea of making something not only forms the basis for the ego trait of creativity, but fortifies some of the beliefs of the child in the phenomenon of magical thinking.

The ego trait of generosity stems from the concept of "give", which arises from the communication of child to mother by means of the bowel activity. When there are new conflicts added to the generosity trait, which disturb the homeostatic balance, secondary autonomy may be established at a later date by the person's becoming either very extravagant or its opposite, very stingy or penurious. In these instances, money becomes equated with feces.

time and space concepts

In returning to the spatial theme, we are confronted with the "where" concept. In the previous chapter we spoke of passive movement through space. This movement is pleasurable. The next developmental phase veers more and more to active movements and also to the active search for the location of objects. Locomotion is the culmination of the child's mastery of active movement through space. Here we are dealing with the concept "go". Inasmuch as the same term is applied to the bladder and bowels, we are dealing with not only the fact of "going" or expulsion, but in the location of "where" to "go" and the actual movement through space to get there.

Walking or running becomes a distinct pleasure in itself to the runabout. In addition to the new worlds of exploration that it offers, it also serves the organism as a means of getting away from painful situations. Thus mastery of locomotion is a distinct boon to the ego growth of the child. As a "getting away" or physical escape phenomenon, locomotion serves as a defense mechanism in the service of fear or anger. But locomotion can also serve as a means of releasing direct aggression in which the going may be toward an object for purposes of doing harm or for retrieving objects that have been taken away or are desired by the child. These purposes for which the child uses locomotion can get him into direct trouble with parental authority.

Locomotion is subject to the same modification processes by the organism as bowel function in order to satisfy the ego traits of defiance or compliance. Thus, as compromises with conflictual forces around the locomotion experience, secondary autonomy can be established around the pattern of hyperactivity or its opposite, hypoactivity. Clearly these are defense adaptations, which operate in the direction of personal survival. This matter of locomotor hyperactivity is of more than passing interest. In a recent study by Wilcox and me on arthritis, it was shown that hyperactivity as a defense is a characteristic feature of these cases. When conflicts regarding motility occur at a later phase of life, the stage is set for the development of the arthritic symptoms.[38].

As stated previously, one of the learnings of the toddler is the concept of "when". These ideas revolve around the meanings of "now" or "later". It is during the toddler period that the organism develops an appreciation of the concept of time. In the order of development, an understanding of tenses probably follows the sequence of (a) the knowledge of the meaning of the present, (b) the acceptance of the existence of the future, and (c) an appreciation of the past. This fact may be of vital significance in the understanding of the neuroses because in such states the organism finds it difficult to realize that some things are already in the past and are not in the present, nor will they be in the future. Bonaparte [39] goes so far as to state that the appreciation of the meaning of time is equivalent to the sense of reality. Indeed, where the reality sense is disturbed, as in stages of ego disorganization, there is a complete temporal disorientation. This confusion in appreciation of past, present, and future may be the basis for the kind of thinking seen in obsessive-compulsive individuals, who react to current situations in the manner of "from now on, it will be ever thus". The confusion in time appreciation may be at the root of the organism's dealing with memories as current realities.

The manner in which the child learns to handle time depends, of course, upon the realities of his life situation. He may treat time as a commodity which can be spared or expended. By frustrations at either level of psychosexual development discussed thus far, the child may develop the idea that "I must have it now" or "I must get away immediately". These responses are not formulated conceptually, but are automatic learned responses and lead to the ego trait of impulsiveness or impetuosity. Such children are said to have low "frustration tolerance".

The opposite pole in the handling of time is represented by the defense adaptation known as procrastination. Here the child uses time, either to prolong the pleasure he is engaged in or to postpone facing an unpleasant situation. In the former situation, the child may hold his urine or feces until the last minute because of reluctance to give up a particularly pleasant play situation in which he may be engaging, e.g., "I'll hold it back now and go later". In the latter instance, namely that of postponement of unpleasantness, there may be an actual delaying action which can sometimes be successful but after which procrastination often becomes a weapon to defeat the mother. As such it becomes a tool in the service of defiance. Witness the exasperation of the mother when the child persistently dawdles.

Mastery of the sense of time is manifested by the autonomous ego trait of patience. The term suggests a quiet waiting for what the child desires, but it also refers to the ability to complete tasks that require some time to accomplish. There is another quality in the mastery of time which is not exactly covered by the term patience, but for which the author has no other terms to offer, and that is the quality of taking action at the propitious moment. As a suggestion, this may be termed "action-timing". When there is confusion in the mind of the individual in regard to the question of timing, there is missing the ego trait of "hope", and as a result there are activated the alarm signals characteristic of the infancy period. When the organism has not mastered the use of time, it does not have available one of the most useful elements for the avoidance of pain. "Time is a healer" cannot become a useful concept when time itself is not a mastered function. Mastery of time as an ego function then applies both to the proper postponement of response and to the proper and adequately timed responsible action.

The foregoing paragraphs on the understanding of the meaning of time are general statements and are meant to indicate merely that the toddler shows the beginnings of these understandings and not that they are fully developed at this age. As a matter of fact the toddler does not have a real understanding of three dimensional time, namely a clear knowledge of what is the past, what is the present, or what will be in the future. It is more nearly two dimensional or like a flat surface. Everything that happened in the past seems to be part of the present. It is akin to some modernistic paintings where the background and the foreground are on one plane. A current stimulus makes the present resemble the past and the future resemble the present. This is the reason that the thinking processes of the toddler period contain this "from now on" phenomenon. There is no real understanding of the meaning of the word "tomorrow" and only a beginning of the true significance of "yesterday".

development of speech

By the time the toddler has reached the age of two, he not only is able to understand nearly everything that is said to him and a good deal of adult conversation that he may not be expected to comprehend, but he has a good sized speaking vocabulary of his own. This accomplishment places verbalization on a reciprocal level. Much can be said about the phenomenon of speech development which would be very interesting and enlightening. It is a complicated subject and is especially important for our purposes here. It bears a vital relationship to ego development. As we stated previously, conceptual thinking is essentially the same as verbal thinking because concepts or meanings are generally recorded in verbal form. This subject needs further elaboration at this time.

Speech can be dealt with by the child as a distinct function such as eating, defecation, or urination. These physiological functions presumably possess a "body language" that may express meaningful elements of communication, but the development of speech is a unique development which characterizes the human being as a thinking animal.

The infant or preverbal child expresses needs or registers objections, both real or imaginary, by the use of some aspect of bodily physiology. By the acquisition of language, the child is better enabled to handle instinctual drives or to express dislikes enabling ego mastery to proceed in an accelerated fashion. Fenichel refers to the use of speech by the organism as a device for helping to tame the id. Words are more suited for precise communication, both for the acquisition of pleasure demands and for the anticipation of displeasure. As such, speech becomes involved with the thinking processes. Indeed, it becomes so much a part of thought that speech and thought become almost interchangeable.

We can study speech from the standpoint of pure intellectual growth on one hand and from the emotional standpoint on the other. Let us first consider it as a function of intellectual development. There seems to be a sequence of speech growth, which can be arbitrarily divided as follows:

a. *Utterances:* These are vocalizations having no relationship to particular forms or structures which have been learned from the outside world. They are expressions which may communicate something to external objects or may merely express the state of being of the self, without concern as to whether there is any element of communication.

b. *Naming:* The first real word forms are nouns. Objects and pertinent persons are given names. This naming may have little or no relation to function or meaning, hence, this process cannot be thoroughly considered a part of conceptualized thinking.

c. *Sentence combinations:* True concept formation through the uses of language, begins to take shape when the child learns the use of verbs and adjectives. Mothers note a complete new sense of mastery when the child begins to "talk in sentences". This is the period when children express ideas, often much to the amazement of their parents.

d. *Categorical language:* This is the level of language and thought development where the child learns to place things into categories. "Toys", for example, is a collective term. Colors, shapes, uses, sensory qualities, etc. are qualities under which things and ideas are classified. When the child reaches this point of development, he has gone far in his ability to master life situations. It is a point which is never reached by some severely disturbed individuals. Categorical thinking forms the basis for the Vigotsky concept formation test introduced by Kasanin. Categorical thinking is an intensive part of the crystallization in the mind of the child of the "meaning of things". Higher levels of this form of language-thinking development are correlated with greater abilities to sort out things, ideas, or events into categories. This phenomenology is coordinated with the sense of time, such as the sorting out of what was in the past, is in the present, or will be in the future. With categorical thinking, there is the application of an idea or concept to one item, followed by its transfer to all items of that category. At a higher level, the child begins to make generalizations.

e. *Symbolic language:* In this form of expression the child animates inanimate objects, identifies some objects with the characteristics of others, and can take any memory train or current happening and give it representation in play. Much of this symbolic thinking is conscious and part of the child's communication system, but this merges into unconscious symbolism, which will be discussed later under secondary perceptual thinking.

For the sake of completeness, we may pay heed to some later forms of language thinking. They bear direct relationships to the basic language structures which were just described and can be condensed under the term "abstract" thinking. Here again we can speak of levels of abstraction, inductive and deductive reasoning, etc. For the most part, these are intellectual capacities, which correspond to chronological cognitive maturations and individual endowments. Mention should be made of the generalizations and theories, which are constructed by the individual as an outgrowth of both the real learnings of actual events and their symbolic representations in fantasy. These generalizations are vital to ego development and will constitute a large portion of the substance of the rest of this presentation.

Let us go back to our toddler and look at the development of language from the emotional point of view. In the first place, there have been observations that speech is essentially an outgrowth of the necessity for the child to communicate his wants or needs. The fact implies that if all of his needs are anticipated, there would hardly be any motivation for speech whatever. Indeed, such cases of delayed speech have been described. From this we can say that the frustrations that the child has in his life situation stimulate his need for speech communication as a method for mastering his environment.

Freud had much to say about speech. He pointed out that the fixing of verbal symbols in the development of the child linked up with concept formation and represented a main road to objectivation. He showed, too, how speech plays a role in analysis by facilitating the patient's efforts to obtain a better grasp of physical as well as psychic reality. At a much later date he stated that speech brings internal events to consciousness.

Although "speech" and "thought" have been interchanged in the previous paragraphs, this is merely a device of convenience and not one which is truly valid, because in the child there may be entirely different "internal speech" from that which reaches the surface in motor activity. Then too, there are certain traits in ego development that may lead one child to be loquacious and another to be taciturn. From the point of view of mastery, speech can become an ego function on an autonomous basis or can be quantitatively overproductive or underproductive on a basis of secondary autonomy as a defense-adaptation to conflict. In other words, the child may learn to "talk his way out of a situation" as an act of aggression or remain very silent either as an act of defiance or in compliance to the command, "Children should be seen and not heard". As an act of defiance, loud speech may be a means of "making one's self heard." Kasanin * had such a case in analysis. The man spoke extremely loudly, but when he learned that this was his means of getting attention in a family where he was otherwise lost, he dropped the symptom. Other cases of overly quiet speech occur when the person is afraid to be heard.

Inasmuch as speech production occurs in this, the anal phase, the device of speech can take on the same quality as bowel function in which the organism either "holds back" or "lets go". Also, just as food itself can be either good or bad, words can likewise be labeled good or bad. It does not take very long for the child to be confronted with the concept of "nasty" words. Confirmation of this idea and traumatization of the ego can occur when the mother threatens—or acts on the threat—to wash the child's mouth with soap.

Imparting an emotional charge to certain words, as described in the previous paragraph, or by the association of other emotional events or attitudes to words, is of vital concern in the ego organization of the individual. Korszybski [40] founded the whole science of semantics on the postulation that human behavior is potentiated by emotionally cathected words.

Words can be both temporally and emotionally bound. For example, the word "mother" may connote a particular image or memory of mother stemming from a much earlier age period. Similarly, the word "father" can conjure up a picture of a fear-producing person long after any such reaction is called for in reality. Thus words can serve both as bearers of old emotional experience and as carriers of this experience into the living present.

late toddler phase

The phenomenon of speech brings us to the late toddler period. Here we can see that by being heard and noticed a new instinctual trait is

* Psychological structure of obsessive neuroses. J. Nerv. & Ment. Dis. *99*:672–692, 1944.

called into play and that is the one of display or exhibitionism. Before embarking further on this subject, let us mention two more phenomena of speech, persistence of infantile speech forms and stuttering. "Lallism" is the term often applied to the disturbed articulation of letters, particularly consonants. This may originate as pure mislearning, but its perpetuation may well have distinct emotional significance. As a display phenomenon where speech attracts attention as being "cute", or even where there is no need to talk differently, the disarticulation may persist in a libidinized fashion. Similarly, infantile speech may represent a regressive phenomenon, the defense of going back to when things were better, or as a defiance trait in the manner described in previous paragraphs.

Stuttering is a bit more complicated. There may be distinct differences between the stuttering of the toddler and that of the older child or adult. In the latter situation there is both a regression and an immobilization of speech expression resembling the motility conflicts that were postulated earlier as being present in arthritis. But actually is this conflict too different from that of the toddler who is trying to approach the world of reality? It is a known fact that two year olds who are subjected to any form of emotional strain are likely to evidence stuttering. The mechanism of the stutter phenomenon lies in the motor confusion arising. from the conflicting motivations toward loquacity and taciturnity at the same time. In other words, to talk may satisfy the need to release hostility or to display oneself for libidinal purposes and to remain silent may be a simultaneous motivation in order to avoid punishment or embarrassment. As a result, the words are spoken and reswallowed at the same time much in the manner of the ruminative process previously described.

A case illustrating the foregoing points is as follows:

J. stutters badly. This is not the reason he was referred to the psychiatrist. He was nineteen years old and suffered from depressions before college registration and examinations. It turned out that he had inordinate fears of failing. Yet his behavior had been such that he not only expected failure, but invited it. This is the masochistic picture which will be discussed later. But what we would like to bring out here is something else and that is, that he also had a fear of blushing and of speaking up before people.

His early history gives us some clues as to the relationship between speech and exhibitionism. As a toddler he was a cute little fellow with fiery red hair. He was the younger of two boys. Although there was evidence that mother had been a rather rigid disciplinarian in regard to feeding schedules and bowel and bladder training, her basic attitude was good. She was always so proud to show off her boys, particularly the little redhead.

It is not often that a single event can mean so much, but J. dated his troubles from the occurrence of an event when he was three years old. It seems that the family had been referring to a particular woman friend with a large nose as "eagle beak". One day at a bridge game, our patient said to the particular lady in question, "We all call you eagle beak." This caused laughter and embarrassment. The mother rebuked the child because of her own guilt and shame. She told him that he was not to say things like that, of course causing the child much confusion. But this was not the end. From that time on this incident became a family joke. The incident would be repeated over and over again amid gales of laughter with all eyes focused upon the patient. The more embarrassed he became, the more he would be teased and taunted. Even up to the present day he meets people who say, "Do you remember the story about 'eagle beak'?" The stutter appeared shortly after the original incident but did not become pronounced until later.

In therapy, a displacement of bowel function to speech became evident. Speech became a conflictual thing in which there was both a strong libidinal pleasure and great areas of forbiddenness leading to guilt and shame. The shame element was also tied up with urinary phenomena and competitiveness with his brother, which will be discussed presently.

In the previous chapter on infancy, there was described the phenomenon by which a basic impulse can become a basic threat. This seems to be the case with stuttering. The impulse to speak becomes involved with what will happen if one speaks so that the operation of "eating one's words" or holding back the impulse is but another example of the social conflict arising from the inhibition of expression of biological pressures.

Before we leave the subject of speech, let us mention another contribution by Greenacre [41]. It was her observation that some children who are not given the opportunity to release some of their feelings by speech have the tendency to seek discharge through the medium of action. Thus locomotion, which we described previously, and speech may have mutual interactions. This is in keeping with studies of the "acting out" behavior seen in later life, which is a defensive manifestation against either talking about one's problems or even thinking about them.

If we look at the over-all picture of the training and indoctrination that takes place during the toddler period, we can see that the child really wishes to cooperate with the parent in doing what is expected of him. However, he does this with the expectation either of maintaining the good things he has or of regaining the good things he has lost. Silverberg brings out a very important clinical point. He discusses the concept of "the broken promise". It is based upon the idea that "if I am good, I will be loved." He goes further to say that the toddler fantasies the idea of being returned to the breast. Certainly we can say that at least the child strives for breast equivalents in the form of some replica of the nursing situation. Failure to attain this anticipated nirvana causes the child to return to infantile forms of behavior, e.g. soiling, thumbsucking, etc. The outgrowth of the hope of regaining the nursing pleasures is the desire to be the favored child. Romm [42] has recently pointed out the universality of the phenomenon of the wish not only to be the favored, but to be an only child. Complications ensue with the birth of another sibling. However, this does not need to occur in order to make the child feel as though he is being displaced from his source of effortless gratification. A case in point is that of an only child just under three who burst into tears of anger when he was shown a picture of himself as a baby. "I don't like that baby. Get it away!"

The desire to be the only child, and the consequent feelings that arise when such an outcome is not forthcoming, leads to the feeling of suspiciousness. "I have been a good little boy and still didn't get what I wanted. What is wrong?" But there are other things which make the child suspicious of grownups. "What are the grownups talking about?" How such feelings can be intensified when the parents spell words or speak in strange or foreign languages! And what about the deaf child? I said in the first section that deaf children do not react to loud sounds. But this protection does not last very long. When real communication is needed, the child lives in a world of its own. The deaf toddler does not get the chance to auditorily feed upon or learn from his environment. I have spoken of this before in a previous publication [43].

The subject of learning in general has hardly been mentioned. We are obliged to carry our oral-perceptual theme to the point whereby we consider the process of learning as a swallowing of ideas or concepts. This makes "knowing" equivalent to "having" and "learning" equivalent to "getting" or "devouring". Here again our defense adaptations can operate to produce the child who is very hungry for new learnings or can result in the negation of this process. Thus learning difficulties may give the impression of feeble-mindedness when there is no organic basis for such a conclusion. Later, specific learning difficulties, such as reading or arithmetic disabilities, have their origins in such sources.

The toddler phase need not be a time of great conflict because there are so many new masteries and pleasures that the child can enjoy. Unless the disciplinary situation is very strenuous, the desire to return to the nursing situation is only a feeble background theme. But the feeling of suspicion or the feeling of doubt and indecision may lead in other directions. For example, the child may think, "What is wrong with me?" or "What does someone else have that I don't?" On the other hand, the feeling of self-esteem and the pride of accomplishment makes the nursing experience as such a less inviting situation. In this respect the little boy is somewhat luckier than the little girl, but not for long. The boy learns to handle his penis by himself and urinates standing up, "like daddy". The ability of boys to whistle better than girls may have its roots here. These accomplishments are accompanied by the feeling of pride. The ego traits which emerge from the mastery of the libidinal urges around the function of male urination are those of ambition and competitiveness. "I can do it better than you." On the perceptual level there is a coordination between vision and urination. The little boy can see where it is going. It is this learning which probably is at the root of the superior sense of direction exhibited by males over females who urinate merely by "letting it go" in only an approximate region. The mystery of how little girls urinate and in which direction the stream is directed is at the base of much male curiosity.

During the toddler period, a form of crying which is different in nature from the crying of the infancy period becomes manifest. Greenacre [44] has been particularly helpful in calling our attention to this. She has noted that "weeping" and urination are closely related phenomena. The awareness of urination as described in the previous paragraph presumably coincides developmentally with this other type of tear-shedding. It is her idea that the phenomenology of the attitude toward weeping corresponds to the same sexual differences which exist in urinary expressions. Boys control their urine so they must control their crying. It is her suggestion that parental prohibition of weeping is at the root of the symptom of enuresis. Statistically there are more boys than girls who wet the bed. However, her case material is scientifically very convincing.*

As we get on in the toddler period, we are now finding ourselves discussing sexual differences. Indeed, on the matter of urination, this differentiation first becomes manifest. As a result, two conflict themes emerge, "Is it better to be big or to be little?" "Is it better to be a boy or a girl?" These concepts have their beginnings in the late toddler period and are precursors to the next phase of development, namely genital libido. But as a toddler the true genital impulses are not yet established because of lack of maturation of this function and because of the struggle with the relinquishment of baby pleasures. This, of course, does not take into account the manipulation of genitals seen in infantile masturbation. More will be said about the excitations in the genitals in the next chapter.

It is toward the end of the toddler period that the child begins to have a secret life of his own, which he only partly reveals to his parents. It is this secret, unspoken life which yields the fantastic material that appears in psychoanalysis and which grown-ups are apt to disbelieve. They find it hard to believe that "children think that way." It is when some of this secret thinking or activity is unwittingly revealed to the parental eye that the child experiences the phenomenon of shame. It is akin to the wish to be swallowed up in order not to face the accusatory finger or eye. What it amounts to is a great sudden drop in self-esteem, or more specifically, in the feeling of being esteemed by an important external object. The feeling of shame is characterized by the desire to look away, to hide one's face and later to blush.

This later toddler period is the stage of development when the child first becomes conscious of the meaning of ridicule. The case of J. is illustrative. Parents sometimes laugh at things children do as a manifestation of their enjoyment of their children. Ridicule may often be a misinterpretation by the child. When no malice is intended, the child may feel that he is being disparaged and made a victim of derision.

---

* There are probably many other factors in eneuresis both of an erotic and a hostile nature. From the erotic side the warmth and moisture of urination probably embodies some image of the warmth of the maternal body and possibly the amniotic fluid. The "letting go" or expulsion quality can have the release quality of tears as described above, but what is more important is the displacement of rage or destructive impulses.

Teasing, which Sperling [45] pointed out to be somewhere between hostility and play, often has the effect of creating tension in the child. These methods of handling often lead to the feeling of being humiliated or experiencing the feeling of shame.

We spoke of remorse in connection with the need to undo certain activities, like a bowel movement in the wrong social setting. Shame is a more complicated phenomenon. It is as though the child were caught doing something that he or she was not supposed to be doing, with the full knowledge that it was forbidden. This is not exactly the same as embarrassment, which implies a discomfiture or discomposure when there is the disclosure of things not ordinarily exposed. It can apply later on to the discomfort experienced in the face of excessive praise. But shame is a more painful experience. It is a degree more disorganizing than remorse.

Children do not have an innate sense of shame regarding the excrements, nor regarding finding pleasure in erogenous zones. However, when there is punishment, ridicule, or humiliation attendant upon substitute gratifications like thumb-sucking or masturbation, these become shameful practices which the child then does secretly if he still feels the need. As to the body, nakedness is not at all an innately shame-provoking situation in the child. Shame can be looked upon as the reversal of pride. The little boy is proud of the penis which can perform those tricks. The little girl may not be this proud, but she has "nothing to hide."

Much has appeared in the psychoanalytic literature, since Freud's original contribution, concerning penis-envy by the girls and penis-pride by the boys as though the only sexual organ worth bothering about were the penis. There is much evidence to confirm this view. However, it has been largely described as a genital or sexual phenomenon. Our stress at this point is on the urinary or urethral aspects. It is true that this aspect is the precursor of the genitality which comes later, but exists as an important stage of development in its own right. Little girls seem to expect in their fantasies that mother will grant them a penis. Later they expect this from father, but at this point it is more urinary than sexual. Certainly the toddlers and even older children know a great deal more about urinary function than about sexuality. Closed bathroom doors or direct admonitions to "pull down the shades" or "keep your dress down" lend weight to the mysteries of the anatomy and functions of the human body. The element of fascination which was described in the last chapter becomes an important element in the establishment of the notions of envy and pride. The fantasies or ideas which are established are in relation to the emotional makeup of the child and the experiences that are taking place.

Many parents use shaming as a technique for controlling their off-spring. When they discover that the little ones can be made to feel ashamed, they are sometimes tempted to capitalize upon this power to accomplish their purpose. For some reason or other, this method does not seem to them as reprehensible as physical punishment or intimidation which may "break the spirit." In fact, parents are likely to consider shame as a virtue. The command is often initiated, "You should be ashamed of yourself!" As such, shame can become incorporated into the personality as a superego function. When ridicule is heaped on shame or when punishment is added to shame, phenomena such as fear of shame or erythrophobia may supervene. However, shame can be dealt with by the defensive-adaptive processes into secondary autonomous traits. At one pole, shame can be transformed through the process of reaction formation into the ego trait of boastfulness. This, of course, is a mock exaggeration of the autonomous trait of pride. At the compliant pole, shame is absorbed in the ego trait of shyness or bashfulness.

Two other ego traits show their beginnings in the late toddler period. Envy has already been mentioned and the other is spite. We shall consider envy in more detail in the Oedipal period, but this does not mean it does not occur sooner. Very young children envy the possessions of others and are envious and jealous of the favors accorded to others. This trait can be said to occur as a defensive adaptation to the conflicts arising from the inability to master the motivation for competition. If someone can compete for parental favors better than he or she, then the adversary is a target for envy. What the imagery consists of in the toddler may be hard to capture, but in most instances, if not all, it takes on sexual coloring.

Although we see penis envy as a fairly universal phenomenon in the girl, there is probably an equally strong basis for envy in the boy, which is based upon the process of giving birth to a child. Creativity has already been mentioned as an outgrowth of bowel function. The child gains a feeling of pride in producing something. This may be the forerunner of work-pride and the phenomenon of procreation. By identification with mother, or mothers in general, both boys and girls feel the role of the body as a source of creation. Little girls very early in their lives learn their effectiveness in this regard and little boys may perceive their relative inadequacies. This is often clearly demonstrated by observation of toddlers' doll play. It has been suggested that pride of penis or pride of urinary efficiency by the boys is a compensation for the inability to bring forth a child. Because of this motivation, which eventually develops into the desire for parenthood by both sexes, sexual pleasure and the desire to produce a child will be referred to in this presentation as "procreative impulses".

Spite, which like envy has developed as a result of the convergence of many forces that have operated up to this point, reaches its peak at a period when conflicts regarding loss in competition become threatening. Defiance or opposition are forerunners to spite. Here the child actually attempts to do things in revenge for failures to attain coveted favor. There is an undercurrent of anger both in envy and in spite, but it is more overt in the latter. Although the toddler does not show the violent rages of the infant, there are many forms of expression of displeasure which become apparent. The child may be cross, fretful, or querulous. He may be petulant, saucy, pert, or even insolent, but also he may sulk or show pique or sullenness. Pouting with the lips protruded almost suggests the oral response to the displeasure.

This pouting may resemble spitting or perhaps urination. But spitting in this case is like urination, which becomes a display in the overt language of the toddler. Here again the little boy is more fortunately equipped than the little girl. He may displace this interest in water play, especially the water pistol. Little girls, on the other hand, have a pert little gesture that says the same thing. We are all familiar with the little girl who flounces her skirts and shows her behind. This gesture is recaptured in the perennially popular can-can dance. It seems to say, "Kiss my bottom!" But actually it bears the implied concept, "If you come close enough, I will pee on you!"

One element of difference between boys and girls, which is for the most part culturally conditioned but perhaps to some extent biologically rooted, is the subject of crying or weeping. Greenacre's studies have been mentioned. From the biological point of view, control and direction of urination bear a close relationship to the shedding of tears. As a means of display, crying is a device to attract attention, but to use this for that purpose is less becoming for boys than for girls. "Boys don't cry." It is more or less tacitly agreed that girls are permitted to cry. It is their one weapon of aggression which boys cannot use. Besides, girls are expected to cry because of the lost or ungranted penis.

In addition to the male-female cathexis about crying, the phenomenon itself may be invested with other energy derivations or counter-cathexis. For example, as an act of defiance the child may not cry because he may have been punished for crying, e.g. "I'll give you something to cry for." Of course, these modifications of crying can occur much later in life as the case of the boy who cried while his father was dying. He was given the admonishment, "Don't cry, your father might hear you and it will make him worse." Father died anyhow, and as part of this person's neurosis he developed all sorts of physical symptoms including marked running nose and sneezing, which were crying equivalents.

The various traits we have been discussing are associated with ideas that run through the mind of the child. Some psychoanalytic writings suggest that the traits arise from the ideas or images; others believe that the images are formed from the traits. Selye's work [31] suggests that the adaptations arise from physiological sources. This would favor the thought that the imageries are superimposed. We shall discuss this concept further under secondary perceptual thinking.

It is during the toddler phase of growth that the child begins to think in terms of ideas which are capable of verbalization. It is a matter of great interest to psychoanalysis that first memories are generally placed toward the end of this period. This is the age of conceptual thinking. As many workers believe that all subsequent behavior is colored by the first memories, this toddler period is of utmost importance.

CHAPTER FOUR

THE OEDIPAL AGE

The age period when the genital impulses make their first profound impressions upon the child initiates a period in the life of the individual which is considered to be a most vital factor in the formation of human character and symptomatology. This is the period of the Oedipus complex, so named by Freud because of the famous Greek play in which the son slays the father and marries the mother. It is true that certain actual sexual excitations such as erections and genital manipulation are observed in infants and certainly in toddlers, but the procreative impulses, which can be clearly defined as such, do not become a predominant force in the personality until the age of three. When these impulses make their appearance, they remain in the forefront for about four or five years. It is these years, from age three to seven or eight, which will be the subject of this portion of the presentation.

It is a clinically observable fact that children at this age begin to operate on at least two distinct levels. It is as though they have one world in which they communicate their wants, needs, and ideas to persons about them, and another, a secret world, in which channels of communication with external objects is either partial or nonexistent. There is a great deal of variation in the relative importance of these two levels in different children, no doubt reflecting directly the mastery or lack of mastery of the problems that had arisen during the training and indoctrination period of the toddler phase. When there is already a large reservoir of "forbiddennesses", the excitations and curiosities of the Oedipal period fall naturally into line with the maintenance of a secret world. In this respect this world serves a self-preservative function and maintains a cherished but incomplete autonomy when the child is able to withhold a portion of his life from the outer world.

There are many factors which tend to promote the formation and perpetuation of the secret world. One factor which is of great importance is the fact that the world of the grownups is a mysterious, secret world into which the child is not invited to enter, nor with which is he permitted to communicate freely. Bathroom and bedroom doors are usually kept closed. Besides, the youngster is obliged to go to bed while the grownups are permitted liberties that he cannot enjoy. Coupled with this stratification of privilege that exists on these two levels, is the surge of speculative thinking that emerges from the awareness of stimuli from the generative organs. Just how the organism "learns" the relationship between body sensation and function cannot be adequately discerned. But certainly we can see that there is something which occurs in the economy of the three and four year old which directs him or her toward establishing a greater affinity with the parent of the opposite sex. This need not be in any way a source of tension in the child. The little girl who says, "I'm going to marry daddy" is only expressing the normal precursors of the ability to form a wholesome relationship with a mate. However, even though this idea may be expressed openly, another, hidden portion of the thinking apparatus contains the questions of what grownups do in their bedrooms and whether anyone is being hurt. Some children communicate their curiosities in this respect, whereas others are not prone to do so. Some children are extremely preoccupied with these questions, others do not show great concern, whereas there are those who do not dare make such revelations of interest, possibly even to themselves.

Actual manipulation of the genitals and discovery of sensations which do not directly require the presence of another person, no doubt contributes to the establishment of this secret world. Out of the need for attention and excitation, the child desires to have the parent touch or fondle the genitals. In order to get this type of stimulation, the child continues to secure contact with the parent. "Ride-a-cock-horse", "piggy back", or other games are subterfuges for obtaining genital stimulation. Still, the child will usually not openly admit that the game is for that purpose, except in unusual instances. In one case with which I am acquainted where a mother allowed her son to rub up against her leg at will, the child on one occasion said, "Boy penis loves mommy." Most other instances do not reveal such open frankness, particularly because the parent will not permit the child such unbridled liberties.

The forbiddenness of sexuality or the so-called incest taboo is not necessarily learned from lessons directly given in regard to sexual manifestations. It is true that when parents punish the children for touching their genitals or the genitals of other children (or even for looking at them), the cause and effect relationship of sexual pleasure or curiosity and humiliation or other reprisals can be established. But there are many instances where the child acts as though he had been punished for some type of sexual activity where the mother emphatically denies ever having in any way revealed an intolerance of such activity or interest. We do see in such instances a basic vulnerability from previous levels of emotional development (oral and anal) where other instinctual expressions were coupled with the alarm threats previously described. Such children establish their own taboo system by virtue of the fact that more basic primitive urges such as those embodied in the self-preservative impulses are called into play whenever a pleasurable inpulse from other areas is brought into the field of perceptions. This vulnerability tends to regard the impulse as subject to frustration and punishment, and the person to whom the impulse is directed as one who is capable of denying or punishing the child for having had the desire in the first place. It does not require much fear in order to make the child keep his impulses to himself and thus to maintain a secret world. More severe degrees of vulnerability, however, have results even beyond this dichotomy into the two worlds; the child even becomes uncomfortable within himself and he finds it necessary to subdivide his inner world. Thus, even this world becomes broken up into a world which he admits to himself and a world which he wishes did not even exist. This is the real unconscious of the organism. This phenomenon of relegating thought processes to the unconscious is the process of repression. As stated, it represents an attempt at renunciation of an impulse and denial of the complications or threats attached to it. If the atmosphere of the external world is not menacing, this need for repression is minimal.

A great deal more can be said about the concept of the inner world. Melanie Klein sees a relationship between this inner world and the child's awareness of the interior of his own body. She stresses the thought that even from early infancy the instinctual urges and emotions are reflections of "unconscious fantasies" about things that are going on inside the body. One need not fully agree with the highly conceptualized thinking and reasoning which she attributes to three or four months old infants; nevertheless, we must be mindful of her contributions concerning the awareness of "good things" or "bad things" inside the body. The awareness of such processes probably occurs as a result of secondary elaborations of internal sensations. Some of these will be discussed under secondary perceptual thinking. From the point of view of primary perception or derivatives of sensation itself which do not involve a knowledge of the meaning of things as in conceptual thinking, we can say a few words about the inner world. We have stated that the organism responds to sensations or perceptions from the outer world as well as to perceptions from the inside of the organism itself. There is evidence that there are some stimuli from the outside world which do not fully reach consciousness. But even more noteworthy, there may be a similar system in the interior of the body. It is this internal perceptual system which forms the pattern for establishing varying degrees of "innerness", which range from the deep unconscious to the inner-conscious secret world. Kleinian metapsychology expresses the concept of the inner world as a projection of the fantasy of the inside of one's body. Stimuli that intrude upon the inner world presumably have the same quality as a penetration into the inside of the organism itself.

The gap that exists between the inner secret world of the child and the shared world with external objects can be looked upon as a defense mechanism. As such this separation into the two (or more) worlds is to be considered a function of the ego. Perhaps the nature of the duality is essentially unlearned, as Klein seems to believe, but certainly it operates as a part of the cognitive portion of the human psyche, which in essence is the ego.

In order to understand the thinking processes of the child, we must penetrate his inner world and correlate this with what may be observed from his language and actions. Much can be learned from the child if we learn to understand his language. Play technique is such a language. He protects his inner world by projecting his thoughts onto something else. In spite of his safeguards, we have learned a great deal. Confirmation of observations of childhood thinking comes to us in our daily work with the analysis of adult patients.

masculinity-femininity

First let us discuss the matter of the psychological differences between little boys and little girls. There are both cultural and biological determinants for these psychological differences. Some observers feel that the whole matter is culturally determined. They favor the idea that there would be no differences in the thinking processes of males and females if they were brought up in exactly the same manner. One cannot deny the fact that encouragements towards certain "feminine" or "masculine" attitudes on the part of parents have distinct influences upon the child. The parent who begins with tying a ribbon on the bald-headed baby and says, "Isn't she feminine?" and repeats this attitude for a lifetime, can make a girl out of a potential All-American football player. Parental attitudes enhance the natural biological tendencies, and in some instances hinder them.

To pursue this idea further, let us take the interesting observations of Erikson [46] on the spontaneous play configurations produced by little girls as contrasted to those of little boys. With blocks and toys, little girls have a tendency to build low, flat houses with great emphasis upon the interiors and preoccupations with "keeping things out" and having things enter. Boys, on the other hand, tend to build towers, and if they build houses, show a greater interest in movement in a specific direction and purpose, a delight in knocking over the towers and an interest in entering houses or narrow spaces. Can we say that this is a conscious symbolism of the differing sexual interest of the little boy from the little girl? It is more likely that the symbolism is entirely unconscious, but reflects the general thinking processes and modes of behavior of the children at this age. The general theme seems to be that the little girl is aware of the inside of her body and has the desire to be penetrated, whereas the boy is aware of the outside of his body and has the desire to penetrate. Little children are interested in poking objects into body openings of pet animals as well as their own body openings. The preponderance of active poking seems to be more the "male" performance, whereas the being poked is the "female" performance. The fact that some males later do things that bear the hallmark of being female and vice versa is another entirely different subject which will be discussed later. The point we are trying to make now is that there is probably some internal awareness of body physiology and anatomy as a result of factors arising in the generative organs which result in an emphasis on things that are internal in the female and things that are external in the male. The stimuli to the perceptual system may also arise from the actual self-observation on the part of the child that in the boy the genitals protrude whereas in the girl there seems to be an opening that leads into somewhere. Inasmuch as excitations occur in these regions, there is developed in the children a state of tension which in the boy manifests itself as a wish to penetrate and in the girl as a wish to be penetrated. In the girls, the genital excitation is more likely to be diffuse than localized as in the boy and is attended with the same degree of indefiniteness as the relative directional qualities of the process of urination. The knowledge that boys have the equipment with which to penetrate and with it the knowledge that girls must wait to be penetrated, leads to the notion that boys are stronger than girls. These concepts are shared by both boys and girls. It is the basis for penis envy. Hormonal influences assist in intensifying these drives, as in the male the tendency is toward movement, activity, and aggression, while the female tends toward passivity and allurement.

As part of the wish to penetrate or the wish to be penetrated, there is at this age the motivation by the boy to establish an intimate affinity with the mother and the girl to establish such an affinity with the father. The origin of this desire for union springs from the original desire of the infant to be at one with the mother. In physiological terms it is an outgrowth of the desire to swallow or the desire to be swallowed. The intervening imageries that take place in the mind of the child probably differ to a great extent in different children, especially when the objects with which they desire to attain this affinity are already charged with emotions from previous stages of development.

In addition to the primary wish to penetrate or the wish to be penetrated by the boys and girls respectively, there is also present in many children, especially the girls, the wish to change the roles that they possess. In part this has to do with the relative effectiveness of males compared to females in the matter of urinary skill. The sequence seems to be that the little girl wants a penis first from mother, then from father. Finally this wish is replaced by the desire to have a baby with her father. Although some boys may be envious of the girl's ability to have a baby, it is only where there has been great interference with their own roles.

It is not clinically sound to state that the reason the Oedipal situation is established is because the mother is more seductive to the boy than to the girl and vice versa. It has been repeatedly demonstrated in case studies that the affinity to the parent of the opposite sex is present even when that parent was a hostile, rejecting, unloving person. The conceptualization in such an instance (by the boy) may be, "If mother doesn't love me, it's all daddy's fault!"

This brings us to the other leg of the Oedipal triangle, namely the desire of the child to eliminate all intruders who may block the way to the attainment of the union with the parent of the opposite sex. Sometimes the ideas connected with the destruction of the intruding person, namely the parent of the same sex and siblings, are openly expressed in various ways, but sometimes they remain hidden in the child's inner world. For many reasons, particularly because of the child's inability to cope with the parent of the same sex, the hostility is displaced to brothers and sisters, producing the picture of sibling rivalry. Figure 1 illustrates the principle of the Oedipal constellation.

Before discussing the many complications that arise from the Oedipal situation, let us emphasize the fact that this triangular configuration may manifest itself for two profound purposes. One purpose is to serve as a pattern for the ultimate gratification of the procreative impulses and the other is that it serves as a rescue station from tensions arising from previous levels of development. In one respect both manifestations represent forward progressions but in different ways, the former being a progression as a result of normal maturation, the latter as a result of desperation, an endeavor to be rescued from the frustrations of earlier levels. The rescue phenomenon is an exaggeration of genital expression as is the phenomenon of greed to purely oral expression. It is a case of the use of instinct to defend the organism against the frustrations of instinct. It does not mean, as some investigators have asserted, that children strongly showing this phenomenon are constitutionally endowed with greater amounts of genital libido. It does mean that the intensification of the Oedipal situation is a defense mechanism against anxiety. Bergler [44] particularly stresses the Oedipal configuration as a rescue station.

Freud has spoken a great deal about the primal scene. There is no doubt that many neurotics can trace their disturbed thinking to ideas which have emerged from the perception of the phenomenon of parental intercourse. Yet there are probably many children upon whom this situation makes a very slight impression. Actually, the entire Oedipal phase need not be a stormy one at all, if the child has mastered adequately the previous stages of development. It is only when strong conflictual ego phenomena still exist that there is difficulty in mastering this phase of psychosexual development.

As an accompaniment of the thought processes that take place in the inner world of the child, there is the phenomenon of masturbation. The

Fig. 1—This drawing represents an actual situation which was produced in play therapy with a child. The patient was a little girl who reacted to a situation in which both parents were lying side by side in bed by pushing mother out of bed and placing herself next to father. The child verbalized her hostile feelings to her mother and her erotic feelings to her father by projecting them onto the doll figure. This use of the third person is the familiar form of expression of the child and is characteristic of the medium of communication of play technique.

actual act of rubbing the genitals to the point of orgasm may not necessarily occur in all children. There seems to be a high correlation between the ability to obtain gratification out of the social communication between the child and parent and the lack of interest in genital manipulation. When the channel of actual pleasant communication is low, the physiological gratification of the genital area becomes more demanding.

If we observe children during this period, we may find that many of them show evidences of varying degrees of anxiety, ranging from mild tensions to severe forms of night terrors (pavor nocturnus). Stern refers to this as "Oedipal shock". He attributes this phenomenon to the inability of the child to handle the sexual excitations which cannot find discharge through orgasm. He considers the attacks of pavor nocturnus as the breaking through of sexual excitement during sleep that could ordinarily have been controlled or warded off during the day. This concept, of course, is in keeping with the original ideas of Freud. What it says in substance, is that the expression of the basic impulse gives way to the basic threat. This may not be the whole story. The basic threat is not only due to the inability to effect discharge of the sexual excitation because of ineffective organs, but because of the internalized parental images which forbid the free expression of the impulses. It must be remembered, too, that it is not only the sexual impulses that are seeking expression; the hostile attitudes toward intruders, who interfere with the establishment of affinity with the desired parent, are also trying to find their targets. Many workers, Finley [47] for example, consider hostility as the only factor which causes the child to feel disturbed.

Severe rage reactions or severe anxiety reactions must be looked upon as distinct complications of the Oedipal situation. These are the reactions that are ordinarily experienced during infancy when there is some frustration of instinctual gratification or when there is the apperception of threats from the outside or internal world. During the Oedipal age, the child is confronted with actual parental admonitions for various activities on the part of the child in direct continuity with the prohibitive commands which were issued during the toddler period. These prohibitive commands may include the restriction of both sexual and aggressive activities. Paradoxically, the children whose lives were not disturbing during the infancy and toddler periods have less cause for the expression of excessive erotic demands or excessive hostile expressions, hence they are further spared during this crucial phase of their existence. In contrast, the child who is already vulnerable from previous infantile conflicts or who is still in the throes of the defiance-compliance complex from the toddler period, runs into new troubles by virtue of his

(or her) expression of instincts and emotions which are not tolerable
to the parents. Unstable parents in particular are not likely to accept
their child's sexuality, both because of their own sexual conflicts and
because of their own rivalrous position with the child. This means that
the disturbed children are obliged to react to the introjected or internalized threatening parent images as well as to the real threats of the
actual parents who are administering their care. It is little wonder
that many children renounce their wishes to attain affinity with their
natural object choice, the parent of the opposite sex. Is this incest
taboo? Or is the child fearful of expressing itself freely to the parent
to whom he (or she) is drawn? Kinsey [48] points this out clearly
in his case histories of frigidity and impotence.

In addition to the Oedipal situation as we know it, that is, the child's
being drawn to the parent of the opposite sex and being hostile to the
parent of the same sex, there is an over-all picture of mother as the
kindly, warm, protective parent and father as the brutal, authoritative,
and forbidding parent. This may be true only in a paternalistic culture,
but then most cultures are paternalistic. It may be true because of the
quickly accepted fact that "boys are stronger than girls." As a result of
this phenomenology, there is often a shifting of allegiances and a revamp-
ing of imageries to suit the particular needs of the child. For example,
the toddler who has reason to fear and hate his mother for her over-
training methods, can shift his hatred to his father who may be a kindly
person who has never done him any harm. Or the little girl can combine
the thought of being hurt and being loved in the fantasy of rape.

In addition to the rape fantasy of the little girl (sometimes boys have
this fantasy) there is the classic punishment of mutilation of the genitals
or the castration complex. This in a sense is a punishment of the area
of the body which started all the trouble in this, the Oedipal period. The
presence of anxiety in the child at this age can be looked upon fairly
regularly as some manifestation or elaboration of the castration complex.
The actual phenomenon of being castrated is usually considered an act
of revenge on the part of the father for the boy's sexual and hostile
wishes. However, the imagery may be that of the mother carrying out
the punishment, but such imageries are involved with incidents of earlier
conflicts and will be discussed further under secondary perceptual
thinking.

the castration complex

The castration complex may become buried in a maze of displaced imageries. Take, for instance, the case of a young man who had many fears. One fear in particular manifested itself by a compulsion to sit on the aisle at the theatre. A first layer of associations revealed a fear of vomiting. He needed to get to the bathroom quickly. The fear of vomiting was not only associated with the humiliation and criticism that he felt when he vomited following asthmatic attacks as a child, but had deeper roots. There was disclosed a distinct relationship between vomiting and loss of masculinity, another fear which affected his personality. Further analysis traced his fears to an attack of whooping cough at the age of four years when he developed pains in his inguinal areas following bouts of coughing and vomiting. Inasmuch as at that period he had been subjected to a sexual intimacy of some sort with a maid concerning which he felt a great deal of excitement and fear of punishment in his genitals, the imagery then became one of a fear of loss of his genitals by vomiting them up. But this too has its precursors in awareness concerning things that lurk inside the body. This is the patient who developed the early infantile superego reactions at fourteen months, when his thumb was forcefully taken out of his mouth and he controlled his impulses by placing the thumb under his body. Vomiting then came to mean a getting rid of unwanted impulses as well as getting rid of the forbidding parent image.

As stated earlier, the hostility that a child may feel to a parent can be displaced to a sibling. In the same way the child can displace the retaliation that he expects from his parent for his forbidden impulses onto some created figure such as the bogey man or kidnapper. This leaves him free to share friendly communication with his real father. This fantasy is slow to be relinquished. But contrast this with the fantasy of Santa Claus, which the child relinquishes readily to say it is really father. This is because the child wants the father to be good, not dangerous.

Another manner in which the child manages his hostility is to merge his aggressive impulses with his sexual or erotic feelings. This is the process of libidinization of the aggressiveness. This produces the picture of sadism or pleasurable cruelty. In such a situation, the child actually derives gratification out of the expression of aggressive attitudes. The sexual aspect of the sadism may not be manifest, but can become so, especially later on, as a true perversion, but this is an exaggeration of the process in question.

It was pointed out that the child may not be comfortable in his sexual excitations, but this may not be nearly as potent a force for making him uncomfortable as he sometimes becomes when he cannot tolerate his own cruelty. He may fear retaliation from his larger and more powerful adversaries, or he may identify himself with the victims of his own aggressions. In such an instance, he may frighten himself with his own aggressiveness and rage, as the baby who scares himself by his own crying, may develop the reaction of guilt.

Let us engage ourselves with a few remarks concerning guilt. This is a subject about which considerable has been written in psychoanalytic literature. It is a phenomenon which emerges during the Oedipal phase of development. We can say categorically that guilt is a highly conceptualized form of thinking. Its precursors, however, begin on a perceptual level and merge into this highly complex mode of thought, which is characteristic of human thinking exclusively. The precursors to guilt are first anxiety, then suspicion and doubt, later disgust, remorse, and shame. All of these modalities can be exhibited by animals, but true guilt is a human trait. It is this quality which gives man a "soul", at least according to some philosophies, notably that of Descartes. Guilt is the force which operates within the individual and tells him whether he is doing or has done the wrong thing. It is a conceptualization which may be easily translatable into verbal form. The child learns to think at this age in such complex forms as "I deserve to be punished", or "I do not like myself", or "I should know better", "I am no good", "It was all my fault", or even "I can't trust myself". All of these conceptualizations show that the child assumes responsibility for his own impulses and passes judgment on himself in a self-derogatory way. It is as though the "I" is pitted against the "myself". When the two aspects of the self are not on good terms with each other, the child feels culpable or blameworthy. It may be superfluous to say at this point that the "I" in the aforementioned conceptualizations represents the internalized prohibiting parents. Let us add, however, that this "I" which refers to the internal critical portion of the ego, also derives energy from the child's own sadistic impulses which he appreciates as having come to him from the outside world and as being directed against him. The summation of these internalized prohibiting feelings constitute that portion of the ego known as the superego. The "myself" in these formulations represents the innate physiological excitations or instinctual drives plus the conflictual or defensive-adaptive ego reactions from the previous phases of development, which may no longer be considered good adaptations at this phase. For example, gluttony-anorexia from the oral stage or compliance-defiance, orderliness-messiness, or impulsivity-procrastination from the anal stage may pose serious complications to the child who must also deal with his genital impulses and aggressions. The autonomous ego traits such as self-esteem, patience, generosity, etc. not only cause the child no trouble during the Oedipal period, but help him master the problems he is facing. It is this emergence of the concept of guilt which prompted Freud to state that the superego is formed in the Oedipal period. Melanie Klein however, places the superego at six months, just as she places the entire Oedipal constellation in the first year of life. We showed in our discussion of the infant that there is formed a preverbal, perceptual superego which arises from physiological sources. The reaction to these "internal threats" is one of diffuse anxiety. These threats are not only of punishment but of the complete loss of self following loss of love or estrangement from mother. The true superego, however, although perceptual in a sense, as it incorporates the auditory impressions of the parental admonitions or the visual ones in the case of the disapproving finger or look, comprises memory traces that are essentially verbal or at least involve a verbal appreciation of the meaning of the parental command. As the parental teachings and other experiential learnings become incorporated in the self, the admonitions become "internal commands" which govern the discharge into action or feeling tone of the energies derived from the instinctual excitations. The intensity of the guilt reactions depends upon (a) the intensity of the instinctual expressions, (b) the intensity of the recent parental restrictions, and (c) the strength of the concomitant perceptual superego reactions from the pre-Oedipal periods. The readiness to internalize new commands from the external world is contingent upon a conditioning or pattern of "blameworthiness", which is an expectancy of something happening to the self as a fate or destiny to which the organism becomes attuned. As a denial of the pain of the expected punishment, the child may convert the whole procedure into a pleasure-gaining experience, thus libidinizing the guilt and making the child a masochistic individual. The conceptualization of the masochism transcends such formulations as "I expect punishment" or even "I deserve punishment", but may become "I need punishment" or "I desire punishment". There is usually some ultimate purpose included in the concept, such as "If I get punished I will suffer; that will make mother suffer too" or "If I suffer then my parents will love me". Or, "If I punish myself, they won't hurt me". All of these masochistic concepts bear the traces of libidinization as a defense mechanism. These conceptualizations thus become tied up with the pleasure motive so that the child may learn either to be prepared to pay a price for having had pleasure or to pay a price in advance before he has the pleasure.

As to the punishment itself, the imagery that the child develops is distinctly colored by the child's awareness of his own body. This means that the visualizations of catastrophes to the self would be different in boys from girls. This is essentially true, but to some extent boys have some of the same imageries that girls have and girls the same as boys. Mention has been made of the castration complex. What is most important is the emotion that accompanies the images. The primary reaction that the child experiences stems from the realization of the power that the parents actually possess. Inasmuch as the parents, more or less, have powers of life and death over the child, the fears attendant with the punishment may reach extreme proportions. Castration fears are particularly geared to the thinking of little boys. The boys have the protruding genital which is in a vulnerable spot for being hurt. Girls, on the other hand, center their fears on the inside of the body. They have the fear of being empty or of not getting filled up. With this fear is the feeling of longing or of being abandoned.

The concept of guilt, which is essentially an inner apperception of a painful situation accompanying a need for renunciation of instinctual gratification, can itself be subject to defensive manipulation by the child. For example, he can project it outward by saying, "It's your fault, not mine". He can deny his action completely by bald-faced lying; "I wouldn't do such a thing", or he can assume the guilt of others by acting as though the action was really his fault when it really was not. The greater the degree of sensitivity or alertness to perceptual alarm signals the child manifests, the greater is the degree of emotional response to the guilt concept. Inasmuch as higher levels of ego organization are correlated with increasingly complex levels of conceptual thinking, we are now prepared to show how concept formation acts as a defense mechanism. Denial of guilt or direct lying is a highly organized form of thinking. At a still higher level of abstraction is the concept of rationalization by which the child is able to offer a logical explanation for something he inwardly regrets or for which he feels he should be punished. This sets the stage for intellectualization, which, as a defense mechanism, represents the uppermost level of cortical activity. The type of ego organization depends, of course, on the nature of the events that occur as life moves on, although the sequence of events and their consequences leave their mark. The passage of time itself needs further discussion in the study of the growth of the ego.

During the toddler period the child developed an awareness of the sense of time. This awareness plays an important role on a new basis during the Oedipal period. Anal functioning is essentially bound with time as a discipline. Disciplinary threats or rewards are part of the memory traces accompanying the differentiation of past, present, and future. During the genital phase when intense feelings are brought to the surface, the meaning of time assumes intense and symbolic values. The passage of time, for example, can be either friendly or unfriendly. As a friendly point of reference, the passage of time can be associated with the happy ending so ardently sought after in the kiddies' stories; also, "time heals things." On the other hand, time can be an inexorable foe, as in the case of the unhappy children who say that they are afraid to get older because that means they will be closer to death.

It is at this stage of development that the child is able to establish the sequence and duration of events in his life. This form of conceptualization is the property of man alone. Meerloo [49] and Bonaparte have made great contributions in our understanding of this aspect of human behavior. It was pointed out that the sense of reality and the sense of time are synonymous. To give every event its temporal place is indeed a function of the well organized psyche. As such it represents a well mastered ego function. In the presence of anxiety or depression, however, this mastery of time sequence becomes distorted. The past can become the present, and the future a menacing threat. Because the past is already known, bad as it may have been, it can still be a lesser threat than the unknown future. This fear keeps the organism from ever fully enjoying the present. The symbolism of past and future generally can be looked upon as mother and father respectively.

Let us recall what was said about the infant regarding the primary motivation for sameness and the primary motivation for change. At this stage of development these tropisms become tied in on a conceptual basis with the concept of time. "I want things to be the same", or "I want things to change."

The past, which represents tradition, nostalgia, and security, is a return to mother, her breast, and her uterus. This is the phenomenon of regression. The future represents adventure, reality testing, and experimentation. This is progression. It is the flinging of oneself into the fray with Father Time. This progression may be exaggerated in extent or intensity as a defense against current anxiety, but as an orderly approach to reality, it represents a maturational phase in the growth of the ego. It goes without saying that the more happiness the child has had in the past (mother) the less danger looms up in the future (authority).

secondary perceptual thinking

Events which occur during the Oedipal period seem to have a great deal of bearing upon the future ego organization of the organism. Traumatic events, such as the loss of a parent, parental quarrels, or witnessing scenes of mutilation or pain, may color the memories around the Oedipal situation to such a degree as to make the whole period a tragic era. Because of the tensions which have been accumulating up to this point, a period is reached in the later portion of the Oedipal age in which the stage is set for the denial of the passage of time by returning to the imageries and memory traces of the past "when things were better" or by taking chances on the future by spurting forward into unexplored levels of growth "when things will be better." The motivations for seeking a change of the environment or a change in the reactions to the outside world follow the lines of the biological reactions to the stresses of the life situation. The general adaptive syndrome of Selye sets the stage along biological lines. The imageries of the body processes that accompany these adaptations seem to arise as a consequence of the physiological changes but proceed on psychological lines. It is the stimulation of these new imageries which is the basis for fantasy formation.

The fact that the child must look forward to the time when things will be better or that he feels he must look backward to when things were better, suggests that things are never perfect as they are in the current present. This leads to a very important concept in regard to human behavior. It is a principle which perhaps applies to all biological as well as psychological processes. The concept is that the organism is always in some sort of disequilibrium which seeks to stabilize itself. Homeostasis is the term which is applied to both the biological and psychological state of attainment of this equilibrium. The implication which is offered is that a true homeostasis of the organism is never reached. It has been said that the only real homeostasis that the organism attains is death itself.

In some measure, growth itself is part of the conflict of life. Mastery of the Oedipal situation affords a major challenge for the growth experience. Some authors, in describing the phenomenon of emotional development of the organism, seem to suggest that childhood is a sickness from which one must be cured. The emphasis in this presentation is upon the healthy aspects of ego growth. Psychopathology is but a complication to the growth process, which unfortunately occurs much too often when the life situations interfere with healthy growth. Allen [50] has been stressing this point for many years. He looks upon all human relationships as being inherently capable of affording the child this growth experience.

French [51], in a recent publication, has called attention to this phenomenon of growth as an "integrative" process. He emphasizes the ability of the organism to make compromises and adjustments to conflicting instinctive motivation by affording the organism a type of thinking which will satisfy both needs. For example, a boy may direct his hostility to a younger sibling who is an interloper for the love of the mother. To act in an aggressive fashion against this sibling may alienate the mother who is so fond of the younger child. The boy then acts in a protective way to the sibling to deny his aggressive aims, to win the mother's love, and to show the mother that she need not be so solicitous of the younger one. When such a happy solution cannot be found, the child may be subject to the "disintegrative" process. This means that there is no current solution for the conflictual situation and some measure of disorganization of the individual takes place. The disorganization that takes place during the Oedipal phase is a result of the conflict or confusion of instinctual motivation. In later chapters of this book other conflicts will present themselves, but at this stage of development the conflict of motivation remains the paramount issue. As such, the Oedipal age stands out as a period of crisis in the life of the organism.

In the consideration of the integrative or disintegrative processes, there are stimulated thought processes and imageries based upon memory traces and wishes which constitute the fantasy life of the organism. These fantasies or what will now be referred to as secondary perceptions may be of the nature of the unsolved conflicts themselves. One aspect of the action of secondary perceptual thinking is to motivate the organism to repeat over and over again a similar life situation in thought or action. Freud called this the "repetition compulsion". It presumably serves the purpose of affording the organism a chance to solve the conflict.

Other forms of secondary perceptual thinking may exhibit differences in the thinking processes from the actual life situation because they contain solutions or near solutions which enter into a framework of imaginative thinking. As such there is developed a secondary or reparative mastery, through the use of magical thinking, of the conflictual or traumatic situations. All of the elements in the thinking processes, the instincts, the external objects, the outcomes of the instincts whether they are discharged, repressed, or displaced, and the ego traits which operate toward both adaptation and conflict, are capable of representation in dream, reverie, play, or artistic creation. These representations are subject to the distortion known as symbolism which both protects the organism from his own critical faculties and gains some release from the instinctual conflicts. The reason that fantasy is referred to here as a form of perceptual thinking is that the thought processes are converted to nonverbal form since they are, for the most part, pictorially imaginative. As such they appear as images or "imageries".

From the foregoing we can say that fantasy formation includes (a) imageries which either have returned from the past or have not been fully repressed, (b) imageries arising from current happenings, and (c) imageries from the way things might be in the future. In this presentation, all the elaborated images are referred to as secondary perceptual thinking. This type of thinking may be subject to the distortions of perception referred to as symbolism. Freud pointed the way for an understanding of how concepts or ideas can be converted into perceptions that are representative of the original idea. This is, as stated, the language of the dream, reverie, play, drawings, as well as the psychic language of the body. The symbolic return of past memories can of itself serve as a source of trauma for the child. It is this device which is a part of the process for perpetuating a neurotic pattern.

All of reality becomes colored by the elaborations of the organism through the process of secondary perceptual thinking. Although this process presumably serves the organism as a defense against anxieties, the child may also become victimized by his own imaginative processes. Secondary perceptual thinking gives the child (and later the adult) a distorted picture of reality. His reactions to the outer world come from projections outward from this process going on within his inner world. Just as the child at this age acts in the belief that the images on a motion picture screen are living people, so does he react to the outer world with the images that emerge from his own inner world as though they actually existed in reality. And just as the movie being shown on the screen from the projection room may have been made many years previously, so have been the recordings in the human brain. The real outer world is not appreciated for what it really is, because the organism overprints the inner world onto the outer one. This makes the apperception of reality the combination of the current sensations plus the images that have been projected outward.

Because of the various levels of regression or progression, integration or disintegration, the character of the secondary perceptual thinking shows great variability of structure. It is this variability in structure or type of secondary perceptual thinking which gives us a great deal of insight into the establishment of a therapeutic approach to each type of thinking process. Emphasis is here given to the "process" rather than the "content" of the fantasy. There is a correlation between the content and process, but the main emphasis in understanding the nature of a given psychopathological process is on determination of the depth and nature of the secondary perceptual thinking. It may be said without question, in classifying these fantasies, that the more malignant forms embody greater degrees of primary perceptual imagery, the memories of actual sensation, than do the more benign fantasies which are based on higher levels of conceptual thinking. With these thoughts in mind, the author would like to present for consideration a classification of secondary perceptual thinking as follows: (a) archaic, (b) ruminative, (c) sado-masochistic, (d) organizational.

Let us discuss each of these in some detail. But before doing so, let us be mindful that each of these forms of secondary perceptual thinking represents an attempt on the part of the ego to deal with the conflicts arising from the Oedipal situation. Clinical experience has confirmed

Freud's original notions that the Oedipal triangle is the main constellation of the neurotic conflict which stirs the organism into emotional turmoil. This turmoil sets in motion all sorts of defense mechanisms and adaptations, which vary from one person to the next.

It must be clearly understood, too, that the imageries surrounding the Oedipal conflict have a direct correlation with the interaction or interpersonal relationships of the parents. It is only when the external objects are sufficiently stable to carry out their normal roles as father and mother respectively that the thinking of the child becomes uncolored by the complicating secondary perceptual thinking. When parental attitudes are such that they convey to the child concepts in the minds of the parents regarding their own unsolved problems from their Oedipal age periods, there is produced an altered mental imagery in the child as to the roles he is obliged to play. Thus, a rejecting mother can force a child to seek refuge in the father, who then becomes a mother-like figure to the child. Conversely, the strict, disciplinary mother can become a father figure when the father is ineffectual or absent from the home. In the secondary perceptual thinking, the father can appear as a nursing father (the oral-phallic fantasy) and the mother can appear as a punishing figure (the phallic mother). Both of these imageries can be further distorted by symbolic representations.

Each of the four types of fantasy formation which are being described does not exactly occur in a pure form in any one person. Portions of each type may exist in any person. For purposes of description, however, the classification has rather clearly demarcated variables. A feature of secondary perceptual thinking, which particularly complicates the adjustment of the child to his future reality, is the acceptance by the organism of the existence of the fantasies as though they were realities. In other words, when the child pictures an action, it becomes a literal truth. This lends to a type of "literalism" which is entirely out of bounds from reality testing.

Archaic thinking represents a return to consciousness of the imageries associated with the infancy period. It is essentially a return to the nursing and teething situations. This implies a wish by the child to return to a period in life when there was a protective union with mother. It can even extend to the imagery of return to the intrauterine state. If this were purely a pleasant return, the emotional overtone would be the state of bliss or nirvana that accompanies the merging of child and mother. This is the basis of ecstasy, and can find its expression in religious and aesthetic experiences. Lewin [33] has pointed out the universality of the breast memory as a basis for the dream or symptom picture of many forms of neurosis. He has postulated the concept that the dream is projected on a screen which represents the image of the breast (or bottle).

Of particular concern in the study of the archaic form of secondary perceptual thinking is the addition of the disciplinary elements that have been incorporated by the child into the original perceptions of the nursing situation. For instance, the child may imagine the approach of a large round object, which represents the breast as an enveloping and smothering organ. Lewin refers to this as the Isakower phenomenon. This reaction seems to exist, but it may be an overwhelming "juggernaut" reaction containing elements of all parental authority including that of the father. The phenomenon of the mass approaching the mouth, which appears in children as well as adults as a dream or in some delirious or febrile state, has been fairly definitely confirmed to be a true memory of the breast. Sometimes the archaic imagery may even represent some antecedent imagination, which may or may not have actual memory traces, and that is the phenomenon of either being born or being within the uterus. Such pictorial representations as passing through narrow passageways or being saved from water probably have their origins in such projected perceptions.

As stated previously, the primitive superego contains elements from the child's own sadistic impulses, so that the nursing fantasy can appear as a biting or devouring breast. Also in the imagery of the archaic thinking processes appear the pictures of mouths, ears, and eyes. These are characteristic of the oral-perceptual level of psychosexual organization in which the organs that participate in the reactions are represented in the imagery. Inasmuch as such thoughts as wishing to devour or fearing to be devoured are manifestations of early infantile thinking, they appear in the regressive fantasies of the Oedipal period.

Archaic thinking includes the infinities of space and time characteristic of the infantile thinking forms. During illness, particularly in the delirium of a high fever, the child (and later some adults) have dreams which are characteristic of the archaic thinking forms. Such a recurrent dream which was reported by an adult as having occurred for the first time as a very young child is as follows:

I am a little figure at the corner of a large billowing blanket. It was a tremendous frightening power which threatened to engulf me. It was infinity itself— both in space and time. It was as though it would go on forever. I felt helpless. I tried to overcome it. I had a pin in my hand and wanted to pierce the bulge of the billowing blanket.

The Oedipal constellation, consisting of the erotic manifestations to the parent of the opposite sex and the sadistic manifestation to the parent of the same sex, is colored by the oral-perceptual residual elements from the infancy period. If the sex act is tied up with hostility, the penis can appear as a biting or devouring organ, the vagina may appear as a mouth with sharp teeth. The actual act of coitus can appear in the imagery of the child as one parent devouring all or part of the other. I have referred to these condensations as the "edible complex". The accompanying emotion of such fantasies can be that of overwhelming anxiety. The oral antecedents which are fused with the castration complex of the Oedipal period have been well described by Fenichel [52], Lampl-de Groot [53], and De Monchy [54].

An interesting case in which the wish to devour was used by a child in a very literal way was reported by Diamond [55]. It is the case of a rather disturbed woman in analysis who reacted to a type of imagery which was set in motion at the age of five years. It seems that this child was subjected to some peculiar handling by a psychotic mother. This mother both seduced the girl sexually and terrified her in many ways. On one occasion the mother performed some sort of a ritual sacrifice involving both sexual excitation and threatened mutilation, and the child went into a trance-like state, in which she pictured herself as physically devouring her mother. This was a thought which grew out of hatred that she was not able to express. From that time on, the patient acted as though her hated mother was actually inside her physically.

The actions of the child which are governed by the feeling that the person of someone else is inside the body in a literal sense are not far removed from the whole subject of incorporation and identification. Just as food is ingested and assimilated, so does the organism take in and make part of itself the impressions gathered from the important persons of its environment. Literal incorporation, however, is an outgrowth of secondary perceptual thinking. Other literal fantasies, which Klein claims to occur at the age of six months, are probably formed during the Oedipal period when secondary perception operates. Such fantasies as fearing mother because of all the bad penises inside her body which were left there by father require a good deal of conceptualization on the part of the child. They are derivative of many thoughts, including instinctual, superego, and defensive reactions.

A good example of the influence of the early perceptual superego in archaic thinking form was offered by Erikson in a case discussion of a schizophrenic youngster. The young man reported a frightening dream of seeing objects that looked like the letter "H". The arms of the H's moved like scissors. Associations led to the idea that these H's were actually the representations of the mother's harsh biting voice which had terrorized him as a very young child.

Archaic thinking is accompanied by all the primitive emotional reactions that are exhibited by the infant. Inasmuch as an outer world is not fully appreciated by the infant, this form of fantasy life presents quite a gap between the child and the external objects. Thus, *archaic thinking* is associated with varying degrees of withdrawal from reality, presenting the picture of detachment when the infant is overcome by overwhelming anxiety.

Because of the fact that the infant is unable to distinguish that which is outside the body and that which is inside, archaic thinking is fraught with the device of projection. A schizoid patient in analysis revealed a method of thinking which had been part of his life from very early childhood. One day he reported for his hour in great distress. A few days previously he had been severely chastised by one of his instructors. When the incident occurred, he went into a decline, walked out of class, and, according to him, was "away from things". He walked into a restaurant and was startled by the expressions on peoples' faces. Everybody seemed to be looking at him. They all had ugly, distorted faces. He was terrified and could not sit down to eat. It was explained to him that he saw in those people the anger and ugliness he felt within himself. The symptom did not recur. What the case illustrates is the use of projection and with it the tenuous hold on reality which is exhibited in archaic thinking.

Let us now turn to *ruminative thinking*. This form of regressive fantasy represents a return to the thinking of the toddler period. The characteristic feature here is the oscillation between the forces of gratification of instinctual demands and compliance with parental authority. Whereas in the training period the edible-inedible or clean-dirty theme predominated, on the Oedipal level these become attached to sexual or hostile feelings. In other words, in order to ward off the anxieties associated with masturbation or sadistic feelings, the child buries himself with preoccupations on the lessons he was taught during the toddler phase. The oscillation may take the form of an attraction-repulsion theme which later on can have the moral-immoral quality or be associated in a magical way with a life-death theme. The magical quality here has bipolar quality with good or bad magic operating. The child who is given to ruminative thinking builds up all manner of superstitious imagery. By the magical gesture of doing certain things, all will be well. The castration threat can be averted by such a thought as "If things are all right externally, they will be all right internally".

When the organism is pulled in two directions at once, every act can be subject to this type of thinking: "Is it right, or is it wrong?", "Am I good or am I bad?", or, to help with the Oedipal conflict, "Would it have been better if I were a boy?" Ruminative thinking has a peculiar repetitive quality. It is as if the child repeats over and over again a pattern of action or thinking that things will not change and the imagined catastrophe will not happen. If there is a doing, there must be an undoing, or a not doing; other thought contents can be, "Shall I do it this way, or that way?", "Shall I do what I want to do, or what I must do?", "I should not be doing this, I should be doing something else." The suggestion has been offered that the thinking process itself has a masturbatory quality. Certainly it occurs frequently as a masturbation substitute, but unlike masturbation, there is no gratification and no discharge. It more closely resembles the child playing with his feces.

The conceptualizations of the ruminative type of thinking are associated with the compliance or defiance of the internalized parent images. The conceptualization process is further complicated during the Oedipal phase by the attempts on the part of the child to work out his affinities with parent persons who are not in agreement with each other. When there are arguments or hostilities between the parents, the child may be torn between compliance or defiance to one parent, then to the other, first on an external, later on an internalized basis. "If I love my daddy, my mommy will punish me. This will please my mother, but will anger my father." It taxes the adaptive ingenuity of the child to adjust to these pressures. Hence, he resorts to the magic of trying to find a formula for adaptation. The ruminative thinking is the persisting awareness of the external worlds now internalized into an inner world of quandary. There is no real solution because the internalized parents are "foreign bodies" within the organism. In other words, when the child reacts in a ruminative fashion, he admits the existence of conflicts with the internalized parents and thus is far from being a free agent. This makes the child turn to the world of things instead of people. The process can go on even further to the point of actually experiencing these internalized conceptualizations, yielding an hallucinatory experience.

A good example for the establishment of ruminative thinking as a fixed form of mental activity was furnished by one of my patients. A young woman in analysis, whose problems centered about many obsessive thoughts concerning doing things or the way she looked, reported the onset of her symptoms from the time of life corresponding to her Oedipal age. Although there were many factors in her development which could be considered pathologic, particularly the chronic tense atmosphere that existed in the home, a single event stood out which colored her adaptive or, more correctly, her maladaptive thinking processes. At the age of four, she slept in the same room as an uncle of whom she was very fond. He always slept in the nude. Both she and her uncle were awakened one night by loud screams from the next room. Her mother and father were having a fight. Her father was trying to push her mother out of the window. As the uncle got out of bed to go to his sister's defense and hurriedly put on a robe, the child was transfixed by curiosity over uncle's naked body and showed little concern for her mother. She was obviously torn between two very strong simultaneous impulses. This event fortified a previous one of an almost similar nature. Her older sister fell off a fence and lay screaming on the ground. Another uncle came rushing out of the outhouse pulling up his trousers. Here, too, she had been fascinated by the interesting sight of her uncle in this intimate position and her concern, or lack of concern, about the head injury of her rivalrous sister. Her entire life has been characterized by indecisions, doubts, and fears.

When ruminative thinking becomes the defensive agent against the emotional reactions arising from conflicts in the Oedipal constellation, the pattern of *any* action leading to gratification or satisfaction becomes disturbed. Either action becomes completely inhibited, or it leads to this sequence: action—remorse—exoneration, or—propitiation. Even in the adult who suffers from this type of thinking, the normal life pattern

becomes contaminated by obsessive thoughts which intrude themselves
between the wish for pleasures and its fulfillment. These obsessive
thoughts may take any form, but the source of energy for this con-
tamination is derived from anal sadistic libido. A feeling of guilt
following pleasure by this mechanism is replaced by a feeling of
disgust. It is as though the individual becomes concerned with the
naughtiness of defecation to avoid the guilt for sexual pleasures. A
dream fragment from such a patient is illustrative: "I was at a carnival,
having a wonderful time. I went into a 'phone booth and noticed I was
all covered with feces. I knew I could not go out there among the
people. I felt bad. I had to clean up first before I could rejoin the
people." Children with strong ruminative thinking processes are not
happy children. They are often beset with thoughts that they cannot do
things correctly, that they are not loved, that they are not clean enough,
or that they are not good enough.

Although the ruminative form of perceptual thinking is a regression
from the Oedipal conflict situation, it can be said that in some respects
it is a stopping point in preventing a more complete regression to the
helplessness or autistic thinking of the archaic type.

I wish to call attention more to the process of ruminative thinking
than to the actual content. Although it may have a masturbatory quality
there is often contained within its expression painful rather than pleasurable affects. Thus there is not only a delibidinization effect but there
may be in its place a self-condemnatory or self-punishing result. As
such it is "autoaggressive" or "autophagic" in its effect. It leads to the
merry-go-round type of thinking so characteristic of the adult obsessive
neurotic. Whereas in the child, ruminative thinking serves the purpose
of protecting him from more disturbing external reality, in the adult
it often prevents the individual from enjoying a pleasurable reality. In
the child this form of thinking is intensified when new emotional insults
are added in his daily life. I have stressed this point in my work on
play therapy. It was pointed out that when a child shows a repetitive
pattern of play in the therapeutic sessions there are probably new
traumata currently operating in the home.

The clinician will recognize the archaic form of secondary perceptual
thinking as being the kernel of the schizophrenic process and the manic-
depressive process, and the ruminative form as being the kernel of the
obsessive-compulsive process. I wish to call attention to Kubie's [56]

differentiation of the neurotic or psychotic "process" vs. the neurotic or psychotic "state". In the latter instance, the total personality or ego dissolves into the secondary perceptual thinking with little or no preservation of autonomous ego structure. It is beyond the scope of this presentation to enter into the discussion of the psychopathology of the various clinical entities. Suffice it to say that during the Oedipal age, severe forms of thinking disorder can be crystallized. It is these crystallizations which can later form the patterns for the severe forms of mental disease which the organism may suffer if decompensation sets in under the pressures of living. On a lesser level, the so-called schizoid personalities, depressive characters or hypomanic or obsessive-compulsive individuals have the roots of their neuroses in these imageries.

Let us move on to a discussion of the *sadomasochistic* form of secondary perceptual thinking. Although the imageries in this type of thinking have their origins in infantile physiology and perceptions, the difference between this type of thinking and the archaic or ruminative forms is that sadomasochism is not necessarily regression from the Oedipal situation, but may be an integral part of it. It must be emphasized that this is a distinct form or process of thinking that can be differentiated from the other forms. Still, archaic or ruminative thinking may be present in a person who also exhibits some sadomasochistic fantasy formations.

Sadomasochistic thinking contains more integrative elements of thinking than the other forms which are essentially disintegrative. Let us emphasize at this point that both the integrative and disintegrative functions are attempts on the part of the organism to deal with the conflicts that are raging at that particular period. During the Oedipal phase the conflict is, as stated previously, primarily one of motivations or instincts. The imageries that emerge as the result of the realignment of the instinctual forces may serve the organism well during the particular phase in question, but can lead to difficulties later because of the violation of the general principle of progressive ego growth.

Sadism was described as a libidinization of the impulse to hurt an external object. Out of this impulse arises a wish or plan to carry out such an objective. Imageries which lead to the annihilation, torture, death, or humiliation of pertinent persons may exist in direct or disguised forms. The ego may find it too intolerable to direct the cruel thoughts (or actions) to the true objects and may displace the wishes onto related or symbolic figures. The weapons of attack may be the original anatomical equipment, namely the teeth to devour or the excrements to poison or besmirch. But these can be fortified with the finger nails or fists or, through the acquisition of experiential knowledge, with knives, guns, and fire.

In the young child the sadistic death wish may not be as meaningful as it is to the adult. For him death is a fairly reversible phenomenon. Children play "cowboys and Indians", "gangsters", or "war" and perpetuate acts of extreme cruelty in effigy but do not expect their casualties to remain dead for very long. Similarly, they can talk of deaths of members of the family without any apperception of its permanence. The guilt or anxiety factors arising from the expression of the sadistic impulses are lessened by virtue of this concept of reversibility. Furthermore, if the cruelties are perpetuated in fantasies distantly removed from the realities of the actual lives of the children, they are much more tolerable. For example, the unrealities of interplanetary warfare or the shootings of the pioneer days on the frontier are out of the scope of the child's living present, hence completely devoid of threat in any way.

The fear of castration or mutilation may lead to retaliatory wishes on the part of the child against the feared perpetrators. The boy may fantasy the emasculation of his father; the girl may wish to rob the inside of the mother's body of all her babies, or she may wish to steal the penis of her little brother. Actually, the sadism may have many meanings. The child may develop this type of thinking as an outgrowth of the guilt factors previously described; such a concept implies the desire to force the external object to inflict a punishment or rejection in order to expiate the guilt.

Another concept involved in sadistic thinking is that of forcing the parents to give attention in any form, which seems to some children to serve as a substitute for love. In this respect, the gratification of exhibitionism can be added to the phenomenon of aggression in such a way as to produce a most obnoxious child.

Masochism can be similarly tied to exhibitionistic or genital impulses. The display of suffering in order to create an effect on others is a familiar mode of thought-action. Through reaction formation the child may picture his own death or suffering as a way of punishing his parents. "If I die (or am sick), then you will be sorry."

The fantasy of being beaten, as originally pointed out by Freud in his famous case report "A Child is Beaten", embodies many of the principles of the masochistic imageries. Berliner [57] has been particularly helpful in pointing out that masochism is an ego process and not a primary instinctual expression. The pleasurable quality of even the true sexual masochism is now considered a defense mechanism against the feared pain. Involved in the masochistic picture is the strong superego which releases the guilt feelings. By means of the process of reaction formation, the guilt feelings can convert the sadistic or hostile impulses into the wish to suffer. The sadomasochistic patterns of thinking are the precursors of the action patterns of children (and later adults) who act in the manner of "biting the hand that feeds" or "kissing the hand that beats".* Accident-proneness and the belief that one is destined to be always the loser have their origin in this form of thinking. Bergler stresses this point. The child uses the self-punishment to gain a point of agreement with the parent which will serve as a bridgehead in establishing an affinity: "We both agree that I'm a bad boy."

The *organizational* form of secondary perceptual thinking or fantasy formation is the most benign form of this type of thinking. Whereas the other forms are essentially retreats from the current reality, the organizational form represents an approach toward reality. As such, it contains mostly elements of the integrative and progressive forces of the ego. In this respect the child prepares himself for the world that is still to come. He prepares himself to cope with new situations because he knows what trouble he is already having with the present ones.

* The above formulation can be considered an oversimplification of a really very complicated process. I am particularly partial to Berliner's [57] contributions on masochism which describe it as an ego phenomenon. This is in direct contrast to Freud's original idea that masochism is a direct expression of an instinctual impulse. Masochism in such an instance becomes predicated upon the existence of the "death instinct" which has been questioned a great deal by many observers. Although the death impulse is referred to many times in his book, it is not considered a primary or specific instinct. It is generally regarded here as an outgrowth of the aggressive impulses of the organism or as an expression of the self-preservative impulses which signifies a surcease from pain or return to the mother. In the latter respect, death and sleep are equated. For more detailed studies of masochism, the reader who is already well informed on the subject is referred to the many writings of other authors, including Bergler, Bonaparte, Reik, Reich, and others.

Although many observers have reported interesting clinical studies of the imaginative processes of individual children, there are no statistical studies on the preponderance of the various subtypes of this kind of thinking. A few will be mentioned.

In general, the perceptual processes are an attempt by the child to visualize himself in situations similar to the world of adults. Whereas in reality children appear small and grownups are large, they cope with this inequality in their play by reducing the outside world into a miniature model. In this way the big-little ratio is reversed and therefore less frightening, since the child is larger than his representatives of the world. Although the child can almost hallucinate the presence of imaginary siblings or playmates, or convert a chair into a rocket ship, there is at all times an appreciation that these represent a deviation from reality. This is the difference that exists between the normal organizational or planning type of fantasy and the archaic or schizophrenic forms where reality appreciation may be at a very low point.

A child of three was playing with his imaginatively created brothers one day, but when his mother entered the game realistically as though the child were dealing with real persons he became annoyed and said, "Mother, this is only make-a-believe; mothers are supposed to be real."

All the little problems or big problems that the child has in working out his Oedipal situation can be dramatized in thinly disguised or more symbolic form. No attempt will be made in this presentation to discuss the various kinds of symbols the child (or adult) uses. There seems to be a process in the brain which converts some of the emotionally charged concepts into less understandable percepts. The more pathology that exists, the greater is this distortion from realistic representations.

We are all familiar with the castles-in-the-air or Walter Mitty type of organizational thinking. It is an outgrowth of the little child who is planning to enter or surpass the world of grownups. While such thinking may be entirely normal in the child, to whom it is an approach, it becomes pathological in the adult who uses it as a form of escape. As Thoreau [58] said, "We can build our castles in the air if we later build the foundations beneath them."

The organizational type of thinking, when associated with self-esteem and autonomy, leads to a direction in life and a hope for eventual mastery of the problems of being a child. It is an aid to the problem-solving that is part of our lives and helps the child to build up a reservoir of experience. Furthermore, through the medium of such thinking, release is afforded for the physiological expression of some of the resentments or fears of daily living. A child can dramatize actively some of the things he experiences passively. The play of the child burying the fire engine with blocks after he was scared by passing fire trucks, is a case in point. This kind of autotherapy also occurs in dreams.

In a recent book, Wolff [59] offers an interesting idea concerning the formation of dreams which seems to fit the general theme of this book regarding ego growth. He stresses the "synthesizing" function of the dream: the dream fuses reality and imagination, past and present experiences, and future expectation into one unit. It represents an attempt on the part of the organism to solve the conflict of his needs.

It can be seen from the discussion of the four forms of secondary perceptual thinking, that the adjustment or ability to handle reality depends upon the quantitative as well as qualitative ingredients of the thinking processes. The well functioning or mature ego in the Oedipal phase has a minimum of archaic thinking forms. To express this differently, there is less of the primary, preverbal, perceptual superego and more of the conceptual, verbalized, organizational type of thinking.

There are distinct qualitative differences in the organizational mode of thinking between little girls and little boys. It was suggested that these differences arise from the inner awareness of the parts of the body that differ in the two sexes. The boy can aim his urine, and he wants to look into or go into things. The girl is less direct and more attuned to be receptive than intrusive. Play and daydreams serve to express their individual needs as well as to repeat in miniature or effigy the world of grownups. When the planning fantasies are contaminated by emotional conflict, the fantasy formation may take on the character of plotting or scheming through the process of reparative mastery and secondary integration. This type of thinking carries on into later stages of development; in fact, it is part of the makeup of all normal persons. Every contribution to mankind existed at one time in somebody's fantasy. However, the fantastic imagery which has arisen in the mind of the child up to and including the Oedipal period serves to act as a reservoir for the unconscious stimuli which influences the behavior of the adult.

To carry this theme further, it can be stated that the imagery which is associated with secondary perceptual thinking, forms the basis for hallucinations, delusions, and other forms of distortion of reality perception. "Imagination" is an important part of the development of the child. It represents something which is created by the organism out of the memories of perception of the past and not only serves to prepare the child for new and anticipated pleasures but also to extrapolate for him future dangers or catastrophes which do not exist in reality. Secondary perceptual thinking thus furnishes the "overprinting" which makes the current perceptions serve as stimuli for reactions which are entirely unrelated to reality or are exaggerations in degree of responsiveness. As pointed out, when these overprintings are involved with archaic and magical thinking, the apperception of true reality becomes less distinct. The lack of appreciation of reality and the indistinct boundary of the ego are probably similar phenomena.

Out of the learnings and masteries that emerge at the Oedipal age, the autonomous ego traits of object-love, courage, and self-assertion are developed. Such masteries can occur only when there is a direct pipeline established with the previous masteries of earlier levels on which the ego traits of trust, reliance, and security were established and later followed by patience, generosity, autonomy, self-esteem, creativity, pride, ambition, and competition.

When there are conflicts on the Oedipal level, the ego adaptations or secondary autonomous traits which emerge from the disturbed thinking processes may produce children with open belligerence or covert jealousy, or with compensatory bravado or displays of inadequacy. This polarity may produce the trait of dominance or its opposite, submissiveness.

The dominance-submissiveness theme of ego organization is the major emphasis of Adlerian [60] psychology. Adler explained all of the complexities of human behavior on the variations of this type of thought process. It is an outgrowth of, or adaptation to, the conflicts which arise in the Oedipal age. It had its origins in the early power drives or feelings of omnipotence which the infant employs in his motivations for survival. In an attempt to attain mastery over the external objects who have thwarted the procreative impulses, the child strives to attain a position of ascendency. In this manner he hopes to maneuver himself into a preferential position. This desire usually manifests itself by displacement of a domineering attitude toward siblings and playmates even though the internal organizational thinking contains the imagery of the mother-father triangle. As a fixed pattern of performance, the ego trait of dominance represents a preponderant concern with the attainment of personal goals in preference to compliance with the demands of the external objects.

Recessiveness or submissiveness is the obverse side of the coin. Some children relinquish their goals in favor of the real or projected demands of the external objects. The ego adaptation of recessiveness may arise from the fear of being dominant, just as dominance may arise from the fear of being dominated.

On the more pathological side, when the life situation or parental attitudes militate against the mastery of the Oedipal triangle, the imageries resulting from each or all of the types of secondary perceptual thinking may be further subject to repression or what Freud termed "the secondary process". It was pointed out that the child sees reality by means of the real perceptions and the superimposed secondary perceptions. This may be so disturbing that not only will there be a retreat from reality, but there may also be a retreat from fantasy. The suppression of fantasy may lead to feelings of emptiness, boredom, or apathy.

On the other hand, the Oedipal triangle can be shifted in such a way as to distort its configuration beyond recognition. Klein pointed out that it is inherent in the Oedipal fantasy to have another fantasy exactly opposite in character to the main theme. The reversed Oedipus fantasy, where the boy is drawn to the father and the girl to the mother, probably has its roots in the original polarity of function or direction of each of the physiological body processes. Body areas can be pleasurable or painful, body function can be friendly or unfriendly. Thus genital impulses too can have a bipolar quality. By adaptations of the compliance-defiance theme or the dominance-submissiveness theme, the seeds for a reversal of the masculine-feminine roles can be established.

Homosexuality is thus a defense adaptation to conflicts in the Oedipal age, whereby homeostatic equilibrium can be established through a reversal of the Oedipal triangle or the assumption by the organism of a type of secondary perceptual thinking which involves a change of role from the wish to penetrate to the wish to be penetrated or vice versa. The culmination of this type of ego adaptation, however, involves many layers of conceptualized thinking which finally result in this reversal of the procreative impulses. It contains many elements of guilt and fear, regressions to infantile pleasure zones and an attitude of perverseness. "If you want me to be a boy, I'll be a girl", "If you expect me to be big, I'll be a baby." *

On the more unconscious level, the homosexual attitude is accompanied by archaic thinking forms which combine the procreative impulses with gastrointestinal, or more specifically oral-anal, imageries. Ideas can be present in boys as well as in girls in which passive sexual union and pregnancy are involved with the functions of eating and defecation, such as oral impregnation and anal birth. Such internal perceptions are not centered around the normal heterosexual affinity; in such instances, rather, the external object is the parent of the same sex. The deeply seated regressive thinking processes which involve the oral and anal orifices lay the groundwork for the formation of the so-called sexual perversions.

At a higher level of abstraction, the concepts dealing with a homosexual adaptation may be one of the following: "If I act as my mother does, I will be able to control my father", or "If I am a boy, my father will love me", or "If I am a boy, I will be able to destroy my mother."

Some homosexual adaptation probably exists in all individuals, because all children have two parents, but when there is a wholesome balance of instinctual gratification and mastery of the demands of society, this need not be a very potent factor. As one well adjusted three year old said, "Mommy, I've got it all figured out. Boys like girls and girls like boys and that's the way it is."

* This is but another example of the way the human mind can operate in opposites. Such a reaction should not be a great surprise when we examine the physical operation of the brain. The author is indebted to a neurologist friend (Dr. Edward E. Shev) for calling attention to the correlation of brain physiology and thought processes. The image as recorded by the human eye, for example, is inverted and reversed. The left side of the brain controls the right side of the body. The upper part of the brain controls the lower part of the body. For this reason it should not be difficult to understand why a given phenomenon of human thinking may be a direct expression of a reversed motivation. Reaction formation and other changes in direction of motivation or ego trait integration have their origins in the power of the organism to set up these reversals as defense maneuvers.

CHAPTER **FIVE**

group relations · reso-
lution of the oedipus ·
identification · ego de-
velopment in latency ·
late latency

LATENCY

As we move in our developmental scheme from
the age of six or seven, we enter a phase which Freud [61] termed the
"latency period".* He applied this term because in his observation overt
sexual activity was no longer discernible on the surface, but in some
way was driven underground only to return later at puberty. Various
students of human behavior have disagreed on the exact duration of
the latency period or whether it exists at all. There are some like H.
Deutsch [62] or Redl [63] who speak of a latency period and a preadolescent period; others speak of early latency and late latency as two
distinct stages. In Bornstein's [64] article, "On Latency", she describes
two stages: one from five and a half years to eight years of age and a
second from eight to ten years of age. Her description of the early stage
of latency corresponds to what I have called in this book the late
Oedipal phase. She particularly stresses the guilt factors and defense
mechanisms, which were alluded to in the latter portion of the last
chapter. The present chapter will roughly correspond to the second
stage of latency as described by Bornstein, but it will go further to
include the prepubertal period, sometimes referred to as "late latency".

I see no need to quibble over terminology as long as we understand
what age period is under discussion. The term "latency period" has now
become so fixed in the literature that there is no need to introduce new
terms, nor do we need to categorize this period with sharply defined
limits. We do know that there are distinct behavioral changes in children
at about the ages of six and seven, and there are further differences

---

* In "Three Contributions to the Theory of Sex" he states that latency begins
at five years of age.

later on. Let us here examine the facts as we see them and proceed from there to the activities of the minds of children of these ages.

Limiting ourselves now to the sexual interests or activities of the child, we need first to draw a behavioral picture of how he acts in all spheres, at home, in school, and among his friends and playmates, before we can obtain a good correlation with his thought processes. As I pointed out in the previous chapter, the inner world of the child may be very different from what we see on the surface. Furthermore, with a now growing reservoir of unconscious thought processes, there is a great deal that can be said about the dynamics of this little understood phase.

Freud pointed out that the latency period is a purely human phenomenon. There is no evidence that animals demonstrate anything comparable to this stage of development. Moreover, there are many cultural groups described by students of anthropology which show no evidence whatever of a latency stage. Another circumstance which casts doubt upon the truly organic or physiological aspect of a latency period, is the lack of evidence of any hormonal changes in the body. Endocrinologists have investigated the possible changes in hormone balance by making biological assays of the estrogenic and androgenic substances in the body. It is beyond the scope of this presentation to discuss all the experimental literature; the preponderance of evidence, however, points to the fact that there is no true physiological latency period. The entire responsibility for the existence of this state in the human organism would seem to rest, then, with the social or cultural influences.

Even though the seven year old has already made some contacts outside of the home with playmates and has been attending school for one to four or five years, his (or her) main libidinal interests have, up to this point, centered within the home. The Oedipal triangle, which is depicted in the play configuration shown in figure 1, certainly concerns itself mainly with father and mother as external objects. The latency age shows a change of emphasis from interests within the home to interests outside of the home. The picture would not be complete unless we described the performance of the child in each of his social settings, the home, the playground (or street), the school, and the church. Here again we shall note that there are distinct differences in the behavior and thinking between the boys and the girls. For example, it is quite characteristic for boys to tease or torment the girls; whereas girls are quick to run for help and hence are considered "tattle-tales". Each makes sport of ridiculing the other.

At home there seem to be decided changes in the behavior of the child at this age. Whereas the youngster may formerly have functioned as a well coordinated unit in the family constellation, he may now become a bit opinionated and critical of things about his home. Even the magic of the parent figure becomes somewhat shaded. An otherwise polite child said in all seriousness to his mother, "You are really too dumb to be a mother!"

These children are truly "in-between". They are no longer small enough to be cuddled or fondled and are not old enough to appreciate family affection on an adult level. Girls may be a bit more affectionate, but the boys shy away from overt gestures of tenderness. This is particularly true in the presence of people other than the family. They show a general tendency to pull away from the adults in the home. Their self-sufficient attitude makes it difficult to establish any real line of communication with them. They are busy with interests of their own and resent any intrusion by the grownups. Parental admonitions, scoldings, and disapproval do not seem to register upon them as keenly as they did formerly. Hence they are likely to exasperate the parents in matters of discipline.

As to their own interests, the latency youngsters begin to value certain objects, like collections of pictures, junk, shells, or other items. Often this begins with having two or more of something they like, and subsequently they want more and more of them. Boys seem more interested in collecting than girls, but girls do this too. They collect dolls whereas boys may collect stamps, or pictures of fighters, or airplanes.

Other interests such as the radio, television, movies, and comic books furnish an integral part of the life of the " 'tweenager". These media furnish the vicarious thrills for excitement and adventure which are so bound up with the developing character of youngsters. As part of the fantasy life of these children, they enjoy stories which show clear-cut demarcations of "good guys" and "bad guys". Although these interests may have some deleterious effects, such as competing with other activities like homework, chores, and outdoor play, by and large they furnish the children a good deal of pleasure. With good planning these programs are potentially an excellent educational source. Actually the

nature of specific shows and comic books to some extent stems from
the demands of the children themselves. As Bender [65] has stated,
these sources comprise the folklore of our day.

In our present state of mechanization and congested living, television,
and to a lesser extent the radio, occupy a good share of the youngster's
time. Although parents seem to object, they usually welcome the chance
to keep the kiddies busy so that they will not be under foot demanding
attention or getting into some sort of mischief. Furthermore, mothers
are often happy to see the children engage in some sedentary relaxation
in order to get some rest following strenuous play. Some children, however, utilize these forms of recreation to engage their total attention to
the exclusion of outdoor play and school work. These children are
usually ones who utilize the imageries of the television or radio to
fortify their own internal secondary perceptual thinking on an escape-
from-reality basis.

Another observable activity on the part of the latency period child is
an awareness of, or concern about, his or her own body image. The
boy begins to worry about his height, the size of his muscles, and his
physical skills. The girl becomes concerned about her clothes, her hair,
and the time when she will be permitted to wear lipstick. Although these
interests are presumably geared to a level of competitiveness with, or
display to, other members of their own sex, the implication of attracting
the interest of the opposite sex is quite obvious.

This brings us to the discussion of the actual sexual interests in the
latency period. Freud stated that there was no observable sexual activity
in this phase. The article by Alpert [66] certainly dispels any such
notion. Kinsey's studies of the sexual activities of children as well as
the histories of people who recall their own childhood sexuality, certainly belie the notion that the latency period is one devoid of sexual
interest or curiosity.

One case in point is the description by Levy and Monroe [67] in *The
Happy Family* of the two little boys who were never around the
house because they were so busy playing out of doors all day. A little
girl their age came to visit and since the boys protested that they did not
like girls and would have nothing to do with her, they were relieved
of any responsibility for her entertainment. When she came, however,
they stayed around the house all day to torment her. They pulled her
pigtails and seemed to make life quite miserable for her. No doubt

she enjoyed the attention as much as the boys enjoyed denying that they were really interested in her. After all, they could have gone out to play!

Actually, the sexual interests of the latency period children are quite open, at least in our present day culture. They at least "talk a good game" of sexuality even though they do not actually engage in such activity on anything but a superficial scale. Group activities such as kissing games at parties are about the extent of the actual overt activities of the children, but their talk may sometimes extend to greater lengths. In the company of grownups, some girls will talk freely of their "boy friends"; boys, however, are apt to be a bit more reticent. Some children who have older brothers or sisters are likely to be a bit more daring in describing their interests. When the boys resort to the "wolf-call" or "pinups", it is mostly imitative and not based upon any genuine intense sexual urges. Boys are more likely to state, "What good are girls anyway?" or girls may say, "Boys are an awful pain!"

Boys are concerned about not being considered "sissy". This refers to either the male-female conflict or the big-little one. "Sissy" can refer to either. It means moving down the social scale with loss of self-esteem. Girls, on the other hand, though they pursue the boys, have a tendency to imitate boys. It is as though being masculine or acting "as if" they had a penis will enable them to move up the social scale. Not all girls act this way. Some do an about-face at this point and exaggerate femininity in such a way as to deny that femininity is really second best. They are the frilly "girlie-girlie" females who flaunt their feminine wiles but who are often fundamentally cold in their boy-girl relations. The manner in which the child perceives himself or herself in a sexual way at this age period is but another step in the establishment of a "sexual identity". More will be said on this subject later, especially in the discussion of the period of adolescence.

At the beginning of this chapter the statement was made that during the latency period the libidinal interests of the child shift from the inside of the home to interests outside of the home. Let us return to this aspect of the subject for a more complete discussion. The child in this age often finds people outside of the home more interesting and engaging. He or she may flaunt other parents' virtues as a basis of comparison with their own parents. "Mrs. So-and-So lets Mary do it", or "Mr. Smith takes his son to the ball games." He may even become

a bit ashamed or embarrassed by his own home. This may be a revela-
tion of his guilty feelings because "this is the place where naughty
things take place."

Organizational fantasies that he (or she) does not really belong to
that family, that he was adopted or that he is a long lost prince are
common at this age. The Cinderella fantasy is another typical defense
reaction. This turning away from the parents to other parent images is
part of the search for other symbols with whom the children can
identify. The entire subject of identification will be discussed more
completely in this chapter.

group relations

Another vital ego development at this age period is that concerning
group relations. Trotter [68] many years ago postulated the theory
that the human organism was motivated by a "herd instinct" which
caused him to seek others of his kind for a sort of mutual protection.
Freud [69] accepted the concept of a social instinct but considered it
more a "horde instinct" by which man congregates in a group that is
led by a chief. From the facts as we see them, we cannot entirely dismiss
Trotter's original ideas, especially in the formation of the gang where
the youngsters are able to use the group as protective coloring for
their own impulses.

Before the latency (or prepubertal) youngsters have a group feeling,
that is, during the Oedipal age, the schoolroom orientation is purely a
teacher-pupil relationship. This corresponds, of course, to the parallel
relationships of parent and child in the home. By the time the child
reaches the third grade, however, the emphasis begins to shift to a
pupil-pupil relationship. Finley [70] has been instrumental in stressing
this point. The youngster finds greater comfort in his association with
his peers than he obtains from the grownups.

Before we engage ourselves with the thought processes of the children
at this age period, there are a few more latency period observations
that are worth noting. This is the age of secrecy. The children become
interested in secret codes and languages in order to communicate with
each other and to keep out the prying eyes and ears of the grownups.
It is as though they find a comfort in each other by which they enjoy

their mutual disrespect or fear of parent figures. Not only do they seem to be sharing guilt for actions or thoughts which may be unseemly to the authorities, but they also use the group or club as a medium for sharing pleasures. Out of this stratification of the "gang" arises the concept "we" versus the concept "they". These words carry a great deal of meaning to children at this age period and can be charged with all sorts of affect ranging from indifference to extreme suspicion.

From the point of view of display or exhibitionism, the group can serve both as a medium to hide and as a medium for being noticed. The truly shy child delays joining the group, hence is not a subject for discussion at this point. However, there are some youngsters who can dilute themselves in a group and vicariously enjoy the aggressive or exhibitionistic acts performed by the group as though they were his own exclusively. This is, of course, the spirit of the mob.

Although emphasis is made here of the formation of groups and interests outside of the home, it must be remembered that there have been precursors to these activities from much earlier age periods. As soon as the child "goes out to play", which may be the late toddler or kindergarten period, some group activity is set in motion. As I stated in a previous publication [71], "Even if the home affords the child all the gratification he needs, if this were to take place to the exclusion of contacts outside of the home, he would be woefully unprepared for the vicissitudes of our complex society."

As pointed out in the previous chapter, play of the child may take the form of an approach to the world of adults, but there are also forms of play which satisfy certain basic needs of the child. Playing with dirt, making mud pies, and digging holes, may have symbolic meaning. But when two little boys build a fort or castle out of sand, then make rivers (sometimes with their own urine), there is an interchange of feeling that transcends the activity itself.

The focal point which begins the formation of friendship or play group is first the activity itself. Girls may gravitate to playing jacks or hop-scotch whereas boys prefer kick the can, cops and robbers, leap frog, and hide and seek. These sexual differences of activity reflect differing degrees of motility between the two sexes. Skates, flying kites, riding a bike, or hunting polliwogs are both for individual or joint enjoyment. Actually little excuse is needed for the formation of a tentative group. To give it structure in the form of a club in no way alters inter-relationships within the group. Louis Redmond [72] captures the spirit of the boyish club delightfully in his "What I Know About Boys":*

> The formation of a Club calls for four Boys: one to think of the idea,
> one to approve of it, one with a nickel for dues,
> and one who is not to be admitted under any circumstances.
> Reasons for Clubs are: (1) to discuss the idea of forming a baseball team,
> (2) to discuss the idea of building a fort,
> (3) to discuss the idea of getting out a newspaper, and
> (4) to discuss the idea of forming a Club.
> The duration of a Club is about three days, at the end of which time
> the excluded member loses interest in trying to join.
> The Club then instantly falls apart of its own
> weight and becomes four Boys with a nickel.

There is a remarkable homogeneity for the spontaneous group. The boys or girls try to find, as close to their homes as possible, one or more persons as nearly like themselves as possible. This phenomenon has a quality of objectivizing the self in a living image of oneself. As such it is essentially a derivative of what has been referred to as primary narcissism or love of oneself. It is a continuity with that which is familiar. And what is more familiar than one's own body image? When the child finds one or more children nearly like himself, he obtains a sense of comfort from being in the presence of a carbon copy or mirror image of himself. However, there are enough differences to cause the mutual reinforcement of some characteristics or the elimination of others. All these tend to render the group more homogenous as it consolidates. This homogeneity gives the child a new pattern of behavior which has been termed a "group identity". This is but a step in the search for a permanent identity which takes place to a great extent during the latency age period. Emphasis is being made here on the "search", not on the actual attainment of a true identity. The motivating force which draws the youngsters together to form a group, whether it be a true instinct or a derivative of other instincts, gives the child a great deal of gratification and support when it is successfully accomplished. The force itself, which has been referred to as the "herd instinct" or the "horde instinct" or the "social instinct", has been

* Reprinted, by permission, from Coronet, August, 1952. Copyright 1952 by Esquire, Inc.

described as a centripetal [73] or a sociocentric [74] motivation. When the group is established, its effect is essentially the same in nature as the relationship that had occurred during the infancy period. Instead of the mother-infant affinity there is a group-child affinity. This affinity then becomes a re-enactment of the relationship with the mother. In fact there is much evidence to offer that the group represents a symbolic extension of the mother. As such, it carries with it the same sense of "belonging" which was originally established in the infancy period. The meaning of the group to the child can be gleaned from the observation of the child as well as the reported imageries of patients in analysis.

The mother symbolism of the spontaneous group offers itself for study in patients who have difficulty in relating themselves to the group situation. Many observers, notably Melanie Klein and Lewin have pointed out that the "claustrum", or closed space, which is symbolically connected to crowds or groups of people, is a direct memory trace of the union-with-mother theme. When there is fear of the group, we sometimes find that there is some fear connected with the establishment of union with mother. Corresponding to the drawing away from mother, there is a drawing away from the group. This force can be likened to a "hermit impulse" or to a centrifugal or egocentric motivation. It represents a regression to older reaction patterns that have afforded the organism a certain amount of survival value.

Although the secondary perceptual thinking was colored by disciplinary elements, the imagery of the following case excerpt should throw some light on the point which is being made: A Marine veteran who suffered from severe social anxieties and marked archaic fantasies in his thinking processes, reported the following thoughts: "Even though I felt scared when I was in the Service, in some way I felt protected. It was like the Marine Corps represented my mother. The individual men represent fathers. It is like a thought of being inside my mother, and my father's penis comes in there to frighten me".*

* The above case is the one which has already been referred to in Chapter 2. It is the one in which the imagery of mouths and eyes appeared. The above mentioned type of fantasy is typical of the kind described by Melanie Klein as existing in all infants on an inborn basis. It is her idea that severe anxiety has its origin in infancy when the baby wishes to be inside the body of the mother and fears that he will encounter the dangerous penises which were left there by the father. Inasmuch as this case could very well serve as a point of departure for the applica-

If the group can be a symbolic representation of the mother, then we are on safe ground in postulating from this that when there have been pleasurable or gratifying experiences with the mother, which have established the autonomous ego traits of trust and reliance, then the child is able to respond to friendship and the group situation. A friendly group then becomes the equivalent of a loving mother. Rangell, in his discussion of the psychic significance of the "snout" or perioral region, points up this concept. He shows how children who felt deprivations on the oral level feel unanchored in the complex social and interpersonal relationships and need to be supported. To carry over Silverberg's see-touch-swallow theme into the group situation, we can see that by projection there is the need to be "taken in" by the group and to be noticed and accepted by it. This is the feeling of "belonging" as applied to the group.

The dependency or reliance upon the group has a distinct overlap quality with the Oedipal phase of development. There is no point at which there are not observed evidences of both of these processes going on at once. As the Oedipal situation fades, however, the training and indoctrination period emerges in the group. Here the principles of sportsmanship and fair play are given an opportunity to develop. Mastery of the discipline of the group helps the child attain a status of ego autonomy, which enables him to adjust to basic forces of group or community living. It is comparable to finding his place in the tribe. Through the group relationship, the child begins to learn the principles

---

tion of the basic theory, the author entered into correspondence with Mrs. Klein about it. She kindly consented to read a rather lengthy summary of the protocol on this case. The author is extremely grateful to her and to her associate, Dr. Rosenfeld for their comments.

There was no disagreement regarding the basic handling of the therapy. There is only the difference of opinion on the one comparatively minor element of theory which is that of the innate "unconscious fantasies". The theme of this book, which seems to be the one most widely accepted among academic psychologists as well as psychoanalysts, adheres to the concept that the reactions of the infant are on a basis of pure primary perception and that fantasies, such as the one under discussion, are a later construction based upon known anatomical concepts. For calling attention to the concept of the persistence of infantile anxiety, Mrs. Klein is deserving of all the accolades that can possibly be offered. To postulate, however, that the fantasies are present at birth and that the proper stimulus in the life situation only acts to bring them forth is another story.

of honest rivalry, courteous relations, and graceful acceptance of results. Concomitant with the gratifications that the child obtains from the mastery of the challenges and threats of the group situation is the feeling of attachment or cathexis to the other members of the group. This leads to a new ego trait which can be termed "group loyalty". The trait of group loyalty is a manifestation of allegiance or alliance with his peers which may transcend many other interests, often those of the family; yet it is an observable fact that when a child has had family loyalty, it is easy for him afterward to develop group loyalty. However, an intensification of this feeling of group loyalty on a defensive-adaptive level may show many exaggerations of this feeling of solidarity. For example, one group of youngsters can be very close with several loyal constituents, but will show uniform hostility to other groups or other individuals whom they do not desire to take into the group. A younger or weaker child may be "ditched" by the established group, just as many animals, notably birds, destroy the sick or injured ones of the flock. In such a case the one who is left out is not permitted, for a time at least, to participate in the ego gratifications of the other group members.

Let us distinguish between the spontaneous group which arises out of the companionship and mutuality of interests that children have for each other, and the artificial or organized group. Here there is an adult leader who acts as a parent figure. In such a situation the typical family constellation repeats itself in such a manner that not only is the leader either an authoritative or protective parent but the members of the group are rivalrous siblings. The changed orientation from the pupil-teacher to the pupil-pupil relation represents a change of emphasis from this organized or Oedipal-like pattern to the picture resembling the spontaneous group. The theme which is being offered in this chapter is that this change of emphasis is a growth phenomenon. One is reminded of Trotter's statement that the human organism seems to follow the embryological changes from a unicellular to a multicellular organism in the sphere of social relations.

There are many points of overlap between the psychology of the spontaneous group and that of the organized group. To return to the spontaneous group feeling which develops during the latency period, we see a few interesting items. For example, whereas children act at home as if they were free and independent agents, outside the home they are actually quite enslaved by the mores of the group. If it is not fashionable to get good marks in school, then to get good marks would be a threat to being accepted or loved by the group. The same is true about particular items of clothing. The styles or "fads" change so rapidly and differ so markedly from one part of the country or even from one neighborhood or school to another that no attempt will be made even to mention them, but it is characteristic of the prepubertal period to find boys dressing so similarly to other boys and girls to other girls that their outfits almost constitute self-imposed uniforms. To wear something different, especially if urged to do so at home, marks the youngster as an outcast, a "square", or a "sissy".

There emerges quite naturally out of the spontaneous group situation a stratification of the youngsters into leaders and followers. Even further, there develops the single leader who is accepted as such by the others. In studies of leadership conducted by Shaskan [75] and his co-workers, there is some question as to whether "leadership" as seen in unstable groups is the same as the true leadership that develops in prepubertal youngsters as a positive autonomous trait. Actually the true leader is one who can either take the role of leader or can subordinate himself without protest to another's leadership. On the other hand, there are pseudoleaders who make their presence felt in groups and are persons who show strong exhibitionistic and aggressive tendencies with the conflictual ego trait of bossiness producing the bully or domineering "tough guy" youngster. Thus leader and follower can be reflections of the sadomasochistic form of secondary perceptual thinking. The pseudoleaders have a preponderance of the sadistic forms whereas the perpetual followers may be victims of the masochistic forms. In ego terms the dominance-submissiveness theme is put into operation in the group situation.

It must be remembered that the groups as well as the individual youngsters within the groups are subject to various cultural influences. These influences are those of color, race, or religious affiliation as well as economic or vocational stratification of the parents. Although the influence of the parents may be felt in the groups, there may also arise conflicts between the groups and the standards set by the parents. Even if certain practices may endanger their health, such as not wearing a hat on a rainy day, if the "fellows" do not wear hats, that is the way it must be. The same can apply in varying degrees with unsocial or delinquent behavior. A quotation from Tannenbaum [76] is illustrative:

> The criminal career tends to begin in a gang where the differentiation between play and crime is not sharply drawn. In fact, at first this distinction may not be drawn at all. It is play, one kind of play, to go robbin'. Games themselves, of course, are derived from the folkways and the mores of the environment; the opportunities for play and mischief as well as the materials for it are also to be found in the environment. The difference between going robbin' and playing robbers is not so great after all.

Tannenbaum goes further than most sociologists in ascribing all criminality to the group phenomenon. He states that the criminal is a group member and the group, not the individual, is the source of the crime problem. I have been interested in this question. In working with military offenders during World War II, I studied the nature of so-called "psychopathic personality" [77]. It may be of interest to note that not only were group relations mentioned in that study, but it was shown that there were no wholesome identifications with parents of the same sex, nor were there any close relations with parent figures. The conclusion was drawn that these people had an arrest of development in the latency period.

resolution of the oedipus

It will be noted that the groups and friendships that have been described in the latency (and prepubertal) periods have consisted of relationships between members of the same sex. We can say then that the principal external objects are the isosexual contemporaries. The question then arises, "What happened to the Oedipus complex?" This question is of importance in understanding the growth of the individual ego as well as affording insight into the method by which the organism finds his place in relation to the society in which he lives. Our discussion of the behavior of the child in the latency period up to this point, especially as it concerns his interest in becoming a member of a group, has been essentially descriptive. We shall return to this subject from the dynamic point of view after we have discussed the thought processes surrounding the Oedipal triangle which belong to this age period.

It is true that the Oedipal situation as described in the last chapter does not play as prominent a role in the life of the child at this age as previously, but there is a great deal of doubt as to whether it is ever eliminated. On the contrary, the forces which operated, namely, the erotic impulses to the parent of the opposite sex and the hostile impulses to the parent of the same sex, continue in some form through the life-time of every individual. Freud pointed out, however, that in the latency period these forces are at a low ebb. He pointed out very clearly that the Oedipal triangle undergoes some kind of reorganization at about the age of six or seven years. He offered the theory of repression, which has been the cornerstone for the understanding of many phenomena of human behavior. Although repression is essentially a defensive process, it is in keeping with the facts to look upon the passing of the Oedipus as a form of mastery rather than merely an outcome of surrender. Accordingly, for purposes of exposition, the subject will be discussed from two points of view: (a) as a phenomenon of repression and (b) as a growth experience.

Freud in his paper "The Passing of the Oedipus Complex" was of the opinion that the Oedipal age comes to an end by virtue of the repression of the erotic impulses toward the desired parent. He recognized that there may be some question as to the acceptance of this idea and offered his arguments so convincingly that he felt there need be no quarrel over this concept. The force of the repression was based upon a continual countercathexis which served to keep the impulses from reaching con-sciousness. This force is a derivative of the anxiety arising from the threats of castration emanating from the avenging father. This would suggest that the more anxiety the child has, the greater or more complete will be the repression. In such a situation one would think that the child would quickly relinquish his sexual wishes toward his mother in order to keep in the good graces of his father and thereby lessen his own tension. This obviously is not the case because clinically where the anxiety or guilt is greatest, the Oedipal situation is most pronounced. Silverberg in his discussion of the resolution of the Oedipus complex makes the statement that the renunciation or collapse of the genital wishes toward the mother "may be gravely doubted, since such collapse and disappearance of impulses are never seen as a response to fear and anxiety in other settings, and since, clinically, such total absence of unconscious Oedipal impulses is never encountered." This clinical fact that the Oedipal situation is more intense in the presence of great anxiety can be accounted for by factors described in the previous chapter on secondary perceptual thinking and the defensive use of the sense of time. Because of the intense fears, the child is unable to look forward to the normal unfolding of the future; instead he retreats to the imageries of the past, which are already fraught with the dangers from both the pre-Oedipal and the Oedipal periods. Thus, not only does all time seem to stand still, but also fears become intensified. Such children become the adult neurotics who live in the present as though it were the past. Thus, the organism moves away from a three-dimensional time sense of a past, present, and future, to a two-dimensional one of past and present.

There is no disagreement about the existence of repression of the Oedipal impulses, but it is doubted whether this is on the basis of anxiety alone. Redl, who has made extensive contributions toward an understanding of group psychology, stresses the point that in the latency (or preadolescent) period there is a disorganization or "loosening" of the childhood personality. He implies a "breakup" of the Oedipal constellation. To quote him directly, " 'Growing' into an adult means leaving behind or destroying some of what the child has been and becoming something else in many ways."

An example of the beginning of the resolution of the Oedipus complex is revealed in a story which came to my attention. Without going into detail about the possible dynamics of the situation, here is the story. A seven year old girl stood with her father next to the lion cages at the zoo. After watching the lions pace back and forth for a couple of minutes, the girl turned to her father and murmured pensively, "Say, Daddy, if one of those lions escapes and eats you up, which bus do I take to get home?"

Inasmuch as "successful repression of the Oedipal situation" or "breaking up of infantile personality reactions" depends upon a good adjustment of the child rather than a poor one, the entire matter becomes very complicated. Certainly there is a distinct change that comes over the child during this period. It was pointed out in the previous chapters that growth and differentiation proceed out of frustration of the impulses. We can say quite definitely that the Oedipal situation was of necessity doomed to frustration from the very start. The child obviously cannot possess his mother libidinally nor can he destroy his rivals much as he would like to. The forces which made it obligatory that he relinquish his impulses are derived from the same sources that prevented unbridled instinctual gratifications in the previous stages of development. These forces can be very strict and forbidding or mild and reasonable, depending on the actual severity of the parents themselves, the imageries surrounding previous traumatic experiences, and the reaction to the child's own projected hostility. These forces become internalized or introjected and constitute the true superego or conscience of the child. Freud several times has made the statement that the superego is the heir of the Oedipus complex. By this he meant that the prohibitive forces against the Oedipal impulses remain a stronger force at this age than the impulses themselves.

The superego as we know it is essentially an unconscious force, but before it becomes unconscious there is a mode of thinking which is entirely conscious to the child. As had been pointed out in the general theme of this presentation, the organism reacts in a "perceptual" manner when there have been traumatizations at the oral (perceptual) level of organization and in a conceptual manner (verbal, or with an understanding of the "meaning of things") if the trauma were at a later stage of development. Thus a child who has attained a measure of autonomy and self-esteem will react to the Oedipal situation in a manner that is both reasonable and factual. The case of Little Hans, the most frequently quoted of Freud's early cases, is illustrative. After he "worked through" his anxieties concerning the Oedipal situation, he accepted the reasonableness of his impulses by granting his father the right to enjoy his mother as Hans would enjoy his own mother. At a later date, many years later, Hans did not remember these ideas. They were repressed because he had mastered his impulses after his fears had subsided and could deal with his feelings "conceptually". The author has had the experience, as have many other therapists, of having worked with children and seeing them later as adults, who have not only "forgotten" the things they talked about but have just about forgotten the therapist as well. This would suggest that when the Oedipal situation is heavily charged with emotion the "normal repression" does not take place. Freud gave to us the clue that the appearance of the strong Oedipal feelings represented a "return of the repressed", hence are not the true original strivings, but a phenomenon of a return to consciousness of that which has been strongly denied. This is more in the nature of the secondary perceptual thinking described in the last chapter. This "return" may also be repressed only to reappear at a later date in adolescence or beyond.

In the preceding chapter, mention was made that the Oedipal situation may become intense as a rescue phenomenon from the conflicts arising during that age period. The same idea applies to the delayed resolution or mastery of the Oedipal fantasy during the latency period. The former represents a progression, the latter a lag. The persistence of Oedipal thoughts can therefore be looked upon as a defense mechanism. Although the imageries and somatic perceptions are essentially genital, there are distinctly oral-perceptual colorings from infantile memory traces. By the same token, all the secondary perceptual thinking of the archaic, ruminative, sadomasochistic, or organizational types may exist as overprintings in the life of the child at the latency age. In addition, new conflictual situations, which arise from the current life or from the complications of past conflicts impinging themselves upon the present, cause the past flames to continue to burn and new fires to be kindled.

Many psychoanalytic writers have followed Freud's lead in pointing out that as the resolution of the Oedipus takes place in the latency period there is a strengthening of the ego. Take for example the statement of H. Deutsch: "All the dynamics, all the drives in this period of weakened sexual urges can be used for the development of the ego." This suggests that there is a redistribution of energy within the organism. It is this type of thinking which stimulated Freud to suggest a different set of instincts which he called the "ego instincts" and which are related to self-preservation and nonsexual aims. Anna Freud [78] states that in the latency period the "ego assumes superiority, directs the actions of the child, establishes the reality principle and effects the first real adaptation to the exigencies of the outside world."

Szasz has stressed this point and has already been referred to in the text. This "character" is an outgrowth of the mastery of the impulses. Hendricks [14], it will be remembered, suggested that the "impulse to master" is a basic instinct of man and thus leads to a sense of gratification within itself. Whether we agree with this instinctual concept or not, the autonomous traits of courage and assertion, which are outgrowths of such learnings by the child, not only give new pleasure values but also help the child further to master his genital strivings.

In a sense we can look upon the mastery of the Oedipal situation as a form of weaning. It is but another stage in the progressive weanings of the organism, which began with the act of birth itself, followed by the weaning from the breast or bottle, later the relinquishment of the desire to put anything in the mouth, and finally the indoctrination of the where and when of bowel and bladder functioning. The impracticality, by virtue of parental taboos and forbiddings, of carrying out all the wishes to see or be seen, to penetrate or be penetrated, leads to the necessity for this new weaning. Each of these weanings represents a major crisis in the life of every individual. It must be remembered that the forbiddenness may not be due to the very specific prohibitive commands concerning sexual matters, but simply due to the fact that the parent is in general a forbidding person and will not permit very many demands of any kind to be expressed, or even further may prevent the child from even daring to express his wishes if they seem out of line.

There is one conceptualization, which seems to be very common in the mind of the child, dealing with the resolution of the Oedipus complex. It has been the experience of many therapists, including myself, to have heard some such formulation several times by children as well as by adults in analysis. The idea consists of a depreciation of the mother, presumably because she is willing to put up with the no-good father. Having thus devalued his mother, the boy is willing to relinquish her to the father. In fact, sometimes this is a way of punishing the mother. The conceptualization may be as follows: "If my mother loves my father, she cannot be so much. So if he wants her, he can have her." In the female the reverse picture prevails. "My father is not worth having if he prefers a person like my mother."

It may be that many children expect to have all their impulses gratified or at least they operate as though there were some sort of reward for their "being a good boy." When it becomes obvious that "being loved" does not mean getting everything in the world, a sense of feeling that a promise has been broken may set in. The reaction to this feeling of frustration may be one of the following: (a) the thought processes of the child may be figuratively represented as a perpetual pounding on the door of the parental bedroom demanding admittance, an aggressive quest for love; (b) the imagery may result in a symbolic continual vigil outside the parental door like an abandoned puppy, a passive, watchful waiting for love; (c) the child may say in effect, "To hell with you, I'm going out to play", a relinquishment of the incestuous object.

The first two forms represent patterns of the delayed resolution of the Oedipal triangle. The first form may produce the picture of an angry, disgruntled child. As to sexual manifestations, they may not be directly exhibited in the home but as Alpert [66] and Buxbaum [79] have shown, many children show decided sexual interests during this period. Certainly they talk a great deal about sexual matters but their goals are diffuse as they cannot reveal their true interests in the home and are not ready to bring these interests to fruition outside the home.

The second group is composed of the isolated, shy children who are concerned with their problems, are not free to join the group, and are not happy in their homes. It is this group which furnishes the most frequent referrals to the Child Guidance Clinics or to private psychiatrists. It is when there are many unsolved problems from earlier childhood that the feeling of despair or fear becomes intensified at this point. Children who may have functioned fairly well may return to older ways of behaving. They may bite their finger nails, stutter, show evidence of facial tics, or return to wetting the bed. On a less disturbing level, they may resort to magic formulas to counteract their tensions by compulsive acts. Stepping in the squares and not on the lines may be a magical ritual for avoiding punishment or rejection, or for neutralizing the hostile wishes. It is actually of the nature of the ruminative thinking process. On the libidinal level there may be regressions from genital interests to anal, or urethral ones. It is as though the child were saying, "I will make so much fuss about the bathroom that you won't know what I want to do in the bedroom." The ruminative thinking in the group situation, fixated as it is in the anal period, may accentuate the feeling of isolation. It is as though the child feels himself to be the "unclean one" or the "dirty one". The imageries or substitute instinctual expressions may be of an even more archaic nature than this. For example, the child may react to a group of his peers as though he were being devoured.

As to the third group, the ones who relinquish their parental ties and reach out for the group, it is important to understand their thought processes. As stated earlier in this chapter, the children pull away from both of their parents. They are not as demanding of intimacy or display of affection, nor do they fear the authority of the parent as much. In his "Totem and Taboo", Freud spoke of the dethroning of the father and its relationship to the family pattern and the patterns of society. He refers to his own previous statements again in "Ego Psychology" [80] when he speaks of the group or "horde" consisting of individuals who are too weak to proceed alone after getting rid of the father. This leads to a regressive state in which the group joins for mutual protection and dependency. To some extent this concept applies to this stage of development. Children in the latency period join their "fellow sufferers" in their mutual compassion for each others' problems with their respective parents. A patient reported a dream: "I read an ad about 'lower back pains cured forever.' I thought it was a quack, but I went down there anyway. As I went into the place, I saw a group of fellow sufferers who had just been in the doctor's office. They had wincing, agonized looks. I went into the office, the doctor looked at my back and then looked at my testicles. He said, 'We've got to put your testicles in traction.' He attached some weights there and I put my pants back on. Then I went out and stood around with my fellow sufferers."

There was more to the dream, but the point worth illustrating is the "identification" with other members of the group. The term "empathy" would be better than identification. The foregoing dream clearly illustrates the castrative theme and the mutual understanding of the other victims. This interchange of understanding may also extend to the point of engaging in some form of sexual activity or in sharing feelings of hatred against grownups or rival groups. This type of identification is related to the "primary" or perceptual processes of the infant. We have said that perception incorporates the outside world, but identification as it appears here is the appreciation of something on the outside which resembles something one experiences on the inside. This is the essence of perceptual communication which operates in the formation of the group.

identification

There is increasing agreement by students of human behavior that the process of identification is one that goes on throughout the lifetime of the individual. During latency, however, this process proceeds at a very rapid rate because of the new persons and situations which enrich the life of the child. It seems pertinent that we should discuss the subject of identification more fully at this time. Reich [81] and Jacobson [82] have recently emphasized two lines of identification, namely archaic (primary) and post-Oedipal (secondary). We shall discuss these two forms in the light of the general theme of this book, namely perceptual and conceptual thinking.

The primary or archaic form of identification is essentially on an oral, perceptual level and has been discussed in the chapter on the infant. However, it must be remembered that the process of mimicry and imitation can go on throughout life. When that which has been imitated becomes a part of the self, it becomes part of the ego and constitutes a primary identification. As pointed out earlier, this is a primitive form of defence against too much excitation or threat. On a more conceptual level, the conflictual ego traits of defiance or compliance play decided roles in the process of identification. An adaptive type of behavior embodying the defiance theme would consist of, "I want to be the opposite from my father (or mother)." Thus the burlesquing or mockery of parent figures can become so thoroughly incorporated within the framework of the organism as to give the child a quality which resembles the opposite or reverse picture of the parental representation. This has been termed "negative identification" or a "negative identity".

Both the positive mimicry or its opposite serve the organism as defense mechanisms. During the Oedipal phase, when the conflicts on the sexual theme were greatest, the parental identifications are changed to suit the exigencies of the situation. Thus, mother identification of an archaic nature, even if it has served the organism well, will become displaced or overshadowed by the new identifications at this level. Holmer [83] has introduced a useful concept in this respect that helps us to understand better the whole subject of post-Oedipal identifications. He pointed out that such identifications can be either imitative or substitutive. The substitutive is more clearly related to destructive or hostile impulses, but the imitative has a good deal of admiration mixed with emulation. What is being stressed here is that even though these identifications may have either of these meanings, the fact remains that *they have meaning*. As such they belong to concept formation and conceptual thinking. In other words, the girl may arrive at a solution to her Oedipal situation by arriving at the formula, "If I am just like my mother, my father will love me." This is imitative. If a boy concludes, "If I do as my father does, my mother will not need to notice him", there is contained a note of hostility. Under this category will also fall Anna Freud's contribution regarding identification with the aggressors. "If I am as terrifying as my father, people will be afraid of me." There is also the identification with the victim, embodying compliance and masochistic imageries. "I will become what you want me to be, though I shall suffer." All these conceptualizations not only operate in the child-parent relationships, but afterwards become transferred to the group, as for example, "If you can't fight 'em, join 'em."

Before discussing the internalized or introjected images arising from the group situation, a few more words should be said concerning identifications arising from the parental setting. The parent figures serve as prototypes for the manner of performance in dealing with the instincts in terms of the reality in which the child circulates. Out of these prototypes the child develops a "home identity". This home identity, which forms part of the "ego identity" described by Erikson [10] can be considered a merging into the ego of the perceptions and concept formations that are stored in the superego. This identity then bears distinctly the imprint of the parental figures. It is a satisfactory adjustment as long as the child remains within the orbit of the home.

When the child moves outside the home circle, the acquisition of traits which are considered acceptable by the group repeats the process of perceptual and conceptual thinking which had taken place in the identification with parental prototypes. At first the identifications are automatically imitative. It is easier to swim with the current than against it. The child is quick to perceive what will be accepted by the group and takes on that which will make him most like the others. The standards of the group are passively accepted. The only choice that may exist may be among groups or cliques.

ego development in latency

When the latency or prepubertal youngster is accepted by the group, the same experiences are duplicated that existed on the one-to-one relationship with the parent figures. The reaction of the child to the group, when there is some fear of not being accepted or loved, is the phenomenon of social anxiety. This condition, which is equivalent to the anxiety of the infant, transposes the parent-child fears into the group-child fears. Thus, the group represents a threatening parent by virtue of the summation of the collective egos of the members of the group. A preponderance of social anxiety may exist when a child moves into a new neighborhood and is obliged to meet an entirely new group of playmates. The burden is often made a good deal greater by the hostility of the group toward acceptance of a new member. In such an instance, the group puts the new youngster through a trial period, which roughly corresponds to a new training and indoctrination period characteristic of the toddler phase in the family setting. This is the precursor to the initiation ritual. Failure to make the grade intensifies the feeling of difference from the group, thereby amplifying the social anxiety to a point at which a lasting trait of self-consciousness is produced. Actual differences such as religious, racial, or age discrepancies, or marked peculiarities of body image (too fat, too tall, or crippled) can add fuel to the flame of social ostracism or isolation. This feeling of isolation causes the youngster to seek out other children whose ego identities are most similar to his own. Shy children either find no companions or can only relate themselves to other shy children. Aggressive ones seem to find others like themselves.

Although some children feel isolated by the group because of the emotional tensions which they experience, there are some who experience genuine surprise in finding themselves accepted by others. In fact, a small amount of this feeling is quite universal because of the expectancy of hostility from strangers or strange experiences. It is only when the child successfully masters the group situation that he feels free to enter other groups later in life with greater confidence. On the other hand, if this feeling of expectation of rejection persists, it is either because there have been bad experiences in the early group relationships or because there is an ingrained feeling of rejection because of the frustrations in the home scene.

There are some children who, by force of circumstance, were not given the opportunity for obtaining the growth experience of group relations. This isolation may be due to the pressures of parents who do not allow their darlings to be contaminated by the neighbors' children or to actual invalidism or chronic illness which causes the children to be forcibly separated from their peers. A case which will be discussed in more detail in the next chapter showed many complications because of an enforced quarantine for three years, from the age of six to nine, because of suspected tuberculosis.

Because of prolonged dependencies and tenacious adherence to the libidinal parental figures in some sensitive or vulnerable children, the problems of group adjustment are not only reflected in the failure to fit into the group, but present new complications within the home. For example, the youngster who cannot cope with the other children and comes into the house weeping because he is being "picked on" or because the boys "ditched" him, taxes the powers of the parent as to how the matter should be handled. Inasmuch as the problems of such children are already reflections of the inadequacies of the parents, oftentimes new problems are created or old problems are accentuated. If a parent teases or punishes a child who is already the butt of jokes in the group, he reacts to the loss of love not only from the group but also from the parent as well. On a more mature level, when the parent says "Go fight your own battles!" the child may be confronted with the alternative of facing the danger of the group or losing status with the parent. If he wins in his struggle with the group, he can also attain stature with his parents. The most tragic situation ensues, however, when the child is beaten or taunted by the group and then is beaten or humiliated by the parents because "he does not get along with other children."

Through the establishment of some reciprocal relationships with others who are like mirror images of themselves, a freedom to express unsolved elements of their personalities may be gained. Aggressive attitudes that sometimes would not be tolerated at home become displaced to the group situation. As these aggressive attitudes reveal themselves in the peer situation, a give and take exchange takes place to such a degree as to create a new disciplinary situation entirely different from the parental scene. It becomes necessary to develop a tacit group law or code in order to keep the reciprocal relationships functioning. This, then, becomes a new standard of performance which furnishes the basis for internalizing a new set of concepts which can be termed the "group superego". The merging of the group superego into the ego, or in simpler terms the mastering of the group conscience, creates the group identity referred to previously. When there is an inability to attain the same station in the group that had been attained in the family, the phenomenon of social anxiety supervenes.

When the child defies the standards or demands of the group situation, he will be subject to the same type of superego reactions that occur in the family settings. There are special characteristics, however, of the reaction to the group situation which render the reactions slightly different. For example, the reaction of disgrace is characteristic of the group. This reaction has its origin in the reaction of shame but it carries with it certain conceptual elements like "losing face" or status in the group. At a still higher level of abstraction there is the superego reaction which we call dishonor. This implies not only loss of credit to the self and to one's own reputation, but can also refer to the guilt that one holds for bringing blame to the group.

These superego reactions in turn operate to modify the behavior of the youngsters to an extent which transcends anything the parent can possibly accomplish. Parents have very little influence at this point, but group approbation or disapproval is paramount. A case of group pressure on a child at this age period is exemplified by the following instance: Sally was eleven. She was not getting along with her mother. One day the mother invited Sally and her friends to luncheon. Sally's behavior was such that it was necessary for her mother to reprimand her. When the mother's back was turned, Sally stuck out her tongue at her. The entire group turned on Sally. In a body they spoke to the mother. They said, "We don't like the way Sally behaves; we are going to give her a bad time. We stick together." Thus we can see that the need for being loved by the group can invite the group to act as though it were a disciplinary parent. As such it forms a frame of reference for external controls which, when suitably mastered, become incorporated into the reservoir of internal controls that are a necessary part of good ego organization.

Another identity which begins to emerge at this age period is that of religious or church identity. Here there is a displacement onto a higher level of authority, the doctrines of morality and ethics as defined by the church. Feelings of guilt may become fortified by the reinforcement of parental authority by religious teachings. The entire pattern is essentially more like the home identity than the group identity. If a parent or priest says, "If you are not good, God will punish you", he is not introducing anything new but merely extending the parental eye into all portions of the child's life. By virtue of the home identity the diety can appear protective as well as primitive. The imageries may extend from God equals the good father or good mother, to God equals the angry or bad father, the devil equals the bad father, and to the concept of Heaven and Hell as representative of mother and father respectively. Out of these teachings, however, there sometimes emerge identities which are quite unlike the identities of the parents. For example, when one or both parents are of another religious affiliation than that of the training of the child, then the church identifications may produce a superego structure quite unlike those of the parents. This discrepancy must be reckoned with later in the establishment of the true identity during adolescence. However, usually the religious identity of the child is the same as the religious identity of the parents, so that a sense of belonging to a group includes the home and all members of that church.

The child who has successfully mastered the home situation (and church situation) finds little difficulty in adjusting to the spontaneous group situation, as previously pointed out. In fact, he finds within the group setting an opportunity for releasing and mastering new skills and interests. Learnings and experimentation take place out of the mutual stimulation and curiosities of the members of the group. The use of tools and equipment by the boys and sewing and knitting by the girls are growth phenomena and learnings that often occur out of imitation and competition. The spirit of adventure so characteristic of this age period becomes kindled out of the mutual inoculation and challenges of the youngsters toward each other.

As a continuance of the establishment of the concept of "object love", which had developed in the Oedipal age, the investment of libidinal cathexis in others leads to the autonomous ego trait of group loyalty. This loyalty becomes intensified with specific members of the group so that intense reciprocal relations can be established with one or more close "buddies" or "pals". These reciprocal relations form the bridge between the sexual object-love in the home and the ultimate reciprocal love relations in the selection of a mate. The stirrings of the latter situation during this period have already been mentioned. Body perfection and proficiencies along selective lines have as their underlying purpose the future influence upon a member of the opposite sex.

The latency period is the age for grudges. Children at this age period often get into some sort of argument with one of their peers, and they then stop talking to each other for long periods of time. During the period of estrangement there is usually a complete boycott of any communication. The boycott may extend to other youngsters who remain friendly to the adversary. In addition, the child who harbors the grudge tries to induce his friends to ostracize the child in question or his whole group. These grudges or antagonisms usually continue long after the reasons for the original feud have been forgotten. The grudges are often perpetuated endlessly because neither party wishes to appear as though he or she is surrendering to the other.

From another direction, the latency period youngsters often usher in an intense friendship which had begun with an argument or a fist fight. The acute rivalry situation which more or less runs into an impasse often results in a reconciliation or intensification of friendship after the battle. This reconciliation of two rivalrous peers furnishes the prototype for the ultimate reconciliation and identification of the child with the parent of the same sex.

late latency

As an outgrowth of the skills and interests arising from the latency and prepubertal period, the youngsters select new adult prototypes with whom they seek to make new identifications. This is the phenomenon of hero-worship. Extreme forms of hero-worship can be considered pathological at later stages of development as it may indicate a marked submissiveness and vicarious gratification out of being associated in fantasy with a person who can do the things that he or she cannot do, but at this age period for the boy to have pictures of the prevailing home-run king or the girl to choose a famous actress as her heroine are not at all out of line in a wholesome ego growth. These new identifications or "introjects" serve to overshadow some of the earlier parental identifications. As such it serves as a defense mechanism against some of the painful internalized parent memory traces. Let us not forget that some of the "mother introjects" were good or loving mother memories but others are bad or punishing mother memory traces; the same applies to the good or bad "father introjects". The newly acquired identification symbols thus serve further to help master the Oedipal triangle by giving the youngsters new objects to emulate. To say this differently, the new external object accompanies the enrichment of the superego from other sources, thus rendering the child more independent of the actual parents.

Concurrent with the establishment of new identifications and the acquisition of interests and skills in the form of hobbies and other learnings, there emerges a "work identity". This working interest may or may not resemble that of the parent of the same sex. At earlier ages the work identity may be of the fantastic variety deriving its imagery from the organizational thinking of the Oedipal age. These are the unrealistic occupational interests such as being a pilot or movie star. As the child moves closer to puberty, an autonomous ego trait of initiative or spontaneous selectivity of work or hobby interest seems to come into being.

During the later portions of the latency period, complications may emerge out of conflicts that arise out of the different orbits of identification in which the child operates. Mention has been made that the child brings to the group situation (in the early latency period) attitudes and imageries which have developed within the home. Later on the reverse takes place. The child brings into the home situation attitudes and values he has acquired outside the home, particularly those from his or her relationship with the group. When there are differences between the two orbits, a clash is inevitable. Certainly there are bound to be differences out of the implied criticisms of the youngsters by the parental figures. In this fashion the grownups are looked upon as the nonconformists. They are of the "old school", they are considered "squares" or "fuddy-duddies". It is this very thing which dictator nations have employed to invalidate the parental teachings or even to cause the children to act as informers against their parents. In our culture, scenes at dinner tables, clashes over homework, television, or bedtime are manifestations of the search for a level of independence. At this point a vicious cycle of parent-child antagonism can lead to many unpleasant moments. When the conflicts are such as to foster a state of continual tension, adaptation may result either in having the child's spirit broken or in maintaining prolonged warfare. These conflicts in the home reflect themselves in turn upon the group situation. Mastery of such conflicts through the processes of secondary autonomy result in ego traits which are at either pole of the behavior scale. As it shows itself in group relations, instead of normal leadership, as described previously, there may be the trait of bossiness or bullying, the defensive nature of which is clearly apparent. On the other hand, there may be varying degrees of subordination or shyness in the group as a survival compromise. Some children have a greater proclivity for gregariousness than others. This is the trait which leads to neighborhood clubs or gangs. This gang or club gregariousness may be the trait which leads the child ultimately to become a mobster or chronic "joiner". Both of these have traits in common, though the social significance has entirely different meanings.

Because many children carry into the latency period unsolved problems from the Oedipal situation, they approach puberty with all sorts of conflictual ideation. These ideas or conceptualizations, which were given added meanings in the group relationship situation, can result in the accentuation of the polarity of the big-little or masculine-feminine identities. "Big" or "masculine" can be exaggerated in the minds of the youngsters to the point where they show a trait of impertinence or brashness while the counterpart, "little" or "girlish" may lead to meekness, docility, or self-effacement.

To recapitulate some of the things which were said concerning the thought processes and ego growth during the period of a child's life from the Oedipal age to the onset of puberty, we can see that this is a period of transition. Just as in any other transition, there are overlaps and swings from one base to another; there are representations of the little boy or girl as well as harbingers of the approaching adolescence. Indeed, parents are well aware of the vacillation of these children who one moment are so grownup and the next moment so babyish. The babyish behavior bears the residuals of the unsolved problems surrounding the early parent-child relationship or home identity, the more grownup behavior bears the earmarks of the anticipation of things to come, or a new identity.

The shift of interest from the Oedipal triangle to the group situation is a manifestation of a redirection or redistribution of libidinal impulses from parent persons to the group. The failure to make this adequate shift is associated with manifestations of painful emotions, such as anxiety, shame, or guilt, as well as expressions of actual sexual activity. The sexual expressions either may be the direct continuity of the libidinal impulses to the parent or may be a third layer effect (Bergler) as a denial of the repression of the Oedipal impulses by the use of the primary motivations. As such, it is a manifestation of the "repetition compulsion" which Freud showed to be an attempt on the part of the organism to solve a problem which has repeatedly proved too much to handle. On a more autonomous level the sexual impulses may show direct expressions of boy-girl affinities almost as an imitation of grownups. Little girls talk of their "boy friends" or boys of their "girl friends". Their main sexual activities are kissing games at parties and perhaps a little dancing later on, mostly in groups.

The main consideration yet to be mentioned is the direct influence upon the child of the culture and mores of the society in which he lives. This culture has been defined by his friends and their parents, by the school, by the church, and by special organized groups such as the Cubs, Brownies, and later by the Scouts as well as club or camp groups.

All in all, this period of transition is one in which the child has really not found himself (or herself). In other words, he has still not found an identity of his own. In the words of a song, "In-Between",* popularized by Judy Garland, the ego organization of the latency period is summarized:

> Fifteen thousand times a day
> I hear a voice within me say,
> 'Hide yourself behind a screen,
> You shouldn't be heard, you shouldn't be seen,
> You're just an awful in-between'
>
> That's just what I am; an in-between,
> It's just like smallpox quarantine.
> I can't do this, I can't go there,
> I'm just a circle in a square,
> I don't fit in anywhere.
>
> I'm past the stage of doll and carriage,
> I'm not the age to think of marriage,
> I'm too old for toys
> And too young for boys,
> I'm just an in-between.
>
> I'm not a child—all children bore me,
> I'm not grown-up—grown-ups ignore me.
> And in every sense, I'm just on the fence,
> I'm just an in-between.

This does not mean that all children are necessarily confused at this period of their lives. Many children have worked out some of their family conflicts by repressing the genital impulses and coming to terms with their hostile impulses through identification and redirection of their feelings through sublimation or reaction formation. These are the children who seem to show evidence of a calmness that had not been present previously. They go to school, have their friends, and enjoy their special radio and television programs, and seem becalmed in all ways. It is this relative tranquility which prompted Sullivan [84] to make the statement, which many may question, that preadolescence is the most untroubled period in the life of the individual.

---

* "In-Between" words and music by Roger Edens. Copyright 1938, Leo Feist, Inc. Used by special permission copyright proprietor.

ADOLESCENCE

The latency period was described as one in which there is a minimal amount of obvious sexual expression. In the pubertal and adolescent age period, the reverse situation prevails. This statement is so universally true that we can speak of this period in reference to genital sexuality as the *age of manifestation*. Many writers in the field of dynamic psychology have referred to this phase of development as a reactivation of the Oedipal situation that had been repressed during the latency period. It seems preferable to consider this age, as Spiegel [85] does, a period which is a new phase of development and not merely a duplication of an earlier age. In the discussion of the thought processes and ego growth during adolescence, it will be necessary to refer to the anatomical and physiological changes that take place in the body and the reactions of the organism to these changes and to the altered relationships in the home, with the group, and with individuals of the same and opposite sex.

Let us first mention the anatomical changes. Here, of course, we find the accentuation of the physical and physiological differences of the body producing the necessary developmental maturations which render the organisms capable of carrying out the procreative function. Thus the boy or girl goes through the process of growth which changes him or her into a being more closely resembling an adult. The maturation of the girl with breast development and onset of menstruation may be a bit more dramatic than the voice change of the boy, his growth of hair on the face and the increase in size of his penis. The growth of pubic and axillary hair is not essentially different in the two sexes but is a marked difference from the previous hairless state. Growth of physical stature is rapid, with the girls getting the edge at first, but later being superseded by the boys. This earlier development has led many workers to believe that girls are more sexually precocious than boys. In the narrow sense of genital sexuality this is not true, as will be mentioned shortly. It is true that anatomically one can consider the secondary sexual characteristics of the female as true sexual manifestations because the changes are distinctly perceived both by the self and the outside world, but as to real sexual information, traditionally the youth has more knowledge than the maiden.

Although the tempo of subjective sensual excitation varies in the male in contrast to the female, there is a surge of stimulation of the organs of procreation by virtue of the outpouring of endocrine products into the bodies of both sexes. These surges of excitation motivate the organism in very pronounced fashions in order to attain the goal of finding a mate. The manner in which the organism handles these excitations differs in the male and the female and is contingent upon the masteries of all the previous levels of development of the organism. The latter point is of extreme importance because the behavior and emotional state of the adolescent becomes a highly complicated tangle of motivations when the surge of sexuality overtakes the organism when he is not yet ready to handle it. Thus the adult motivations which are conditioned by the developing endocrine-gonadal organ systems may be set in operation when there are still unsolved problems and conflicts from the earlier age periods. These overlaps cause the adolescent period to be such a crucial one in the development of the organism. Let us put aside for the moment the complications that arise during this period and turn our attention to the normal or average adolescent as he or she develops in our present day culture.

To describe a normal adolescent or "typical teenager" is not an easy task because there are so many differences among them. Still, there are a few characteristic features. The average wholesome adolescent welcomes the secondary sexual changes that are taking place and is impatient to shave or to wear a brassiere, as the case may be. There is a growing degree of emancipation from parents which differs in a sense from that of the latency period. During the latency stage parents often seem not to exist, whereas in adolescence there is more or less open overthrow of parental authority. Adolescents may flaunt the enjoyment of first freedoms of the grownup world by wanting to stay out later in the evening, by selecting their own bedtime, by earning their own money and spending it as they choose. They like to express more individuality of dress than they showed previously. Similarly, the teenager likes to feel that he is exercising some choice over the courses he takes in school or what he expects to be when he grows up. He avers that he wants to get away from the "stuffiness" of the older generation and breathe new air in some distant place. He may change his ideas regarding religion, often questioning the tenets of his parents in regard to the church. He is also likely to become "intellectual" if his intelligence is of a sufficiently high degree to warrant the exploitation of his learning powers or else he is likely to engage himself in some form of mechanical or physical betterment. These devices are part of the process of attempted mastering of the surges of sexual excitations by covering up or redirecting of interests. Other forms of emancipatory strivings may be seen in flaunting their imitations of grownups by puffing on a cigarette or taking a drink. A typical, less drastic, but more teen-age emancipation is drinking coffee or "Coke", instead of milk.

The typical healthy adolescent is aware of his sexual maturation and does not fight it. In fact, he not only accepts his body changes and sexual urges, but is often psychologically ahead of his physical and endocrine growth. The happy teenage male whistles at the picture of a "pin-up" girl and anticipates the role of manhood. In like manner, the teenage girl looks forward to womanhood. As my thirteen year old son remarked, when asked the definition of a teenager: "A teenager is like people." The adolescent has contempt for the preadolescent, a wholesome respect for his contemporaries, especially those of his own sex, and an admiration for those a little bit older. As part of the maturation process there develops an acute awareness of the opposite sex. The intense polarity of this feeling will be discussed later.

There is another type of adolescent who is less fortunately constituted than the one described in the previous paragraphs. There is the teenager who shows a lag in the acceptance of the new role that has been thrust upon him. This type of boy or girl is more secretive about the changes that are taking place. The boy may hide the fact that adult sexual manifestations are appearing, the girl may wear clothes that deny her beginning breast development. These denials are part of the conflict situation that arises out of the lack of acceptance by the organism, particularly the superego, of the instinctual urges that accompany the development of the secondary sexual changes. These are the youngsters who show evidences of emotional tension during their adolescent years. It is as though they are driven forward by the strong libidinal drives but are held back by equally strong counter forces. This conflict leads to the picture of the moving vehicle with the brakes on. It is this kind of tension which leads to the severe emotional crisis of this period. These are the adolescents who are still struggling with unsolved problems from earlier periods, the ones in whom sexual development has overtaken their emotional development.

It has been said by many observers that puberty initiates a reliving of the Oedipus complex. Indeed, there are numerous adolescents whose Oedipal constellations had never been resolved before the onrush of gonadal maturation, so that the incestuous object relations and the true mating impulses merge into one phenomenon. It is this situation which has led H. Deutsch and others to state that adolescence gives the individual a "second chance" to work out his Oedipal conflict. It is true that there is even in the most wholesome or normal adolescence the parallel between the Oedipal triangle and the normal boy-girl affinities that will later lead to marriage. Just as the three year old, who said that he had it all figured out that boys like girls and girls like boys, was talking out of his own feelings toward his mother, so does the adolescent youngster find his interest drawn to the opposite sex in a pattern which was initiated by the original Oedipal theme. This does not mean that the boy who finds his mother in some girl is still hopelessly bound up with his mother, but rather, as Alexander [86] says, it is an indication of the fact that he is breaking away from his mother.

In addition to the mastery of the Oedipal situation, the ability of the adolescent to mingle freely with members of both sexes is contingent upon his or her mastery of the social situation in the latency period. The child does not move freely from the incestuous objects to the non-incestuous objects without previously having gone through the phase of socialization described in the last chapter. Without the ability to form social contacts, sexual excitations remain a solitary experience, which may in turn intensify the isolation from other human beings. Successful group relations set the stage for establishing channels of communication with people outside the home. First, of course, communication was with contemporaries of the same sex, but in adolescence contemporaries of the opposite sex become objects of vital interest.

On a purely descriptive level, the adolescent youngsters show exaggerated or overevaluated interests (Freud) in certain members of the opposite sex. A boy or girl may single out a particular classmate as an object which is valued more highly than anyone else in the world. This affinity may be kept a deep dark secret and exist only in the fantasy life of that particular youngster or can be a matter of giggling conversation to one's friends. In the more outgoing youths, it becomes a matter of public knowledge. The general trend in the early adolescent period is for the object of this attention to profess a lack of interest in that person but to prefer someone else. The someone else usually turns out to be interested in someone else, and so forth. This round-robin type of heterosexual interest plus disinterest indicates that early in adolescence the youngsters seem to show a fear of, or reluctance toward, establishing a reciprocal affinity. A higher degree of this reluctance exists in those young people who have known disturbances in their social relations and, of course, as was pointed out, in those who still have guilts and fears associated with their incestuous object relationships.

In addition to the sexual and social orbits through which the adolescent operates, there is the educational or occupational orbit, the religious orbit, and the orbit of the home. Each of these contributes to the establishment of the "ego identity". It is at this stage of development that the ego crystallizes into the identity which becomes the true self of the person. Erikson's definition of this identity suggests that there is a correlation or sameness of the perceptions of the inner self with the perception of the person in the minds of others. The ego identity is not merely a summation of isolated orbits of operation but is the coordination and integration of all these factors. However, before we attempt to synthesize these various identities or orbits, let us focus our attention on each of them separately. Our emphasis here will be upon the thought processes and emotional concomitants of the essentially normal teenager. Later our attention will be focused on the complications that arise where this synthesis or integration of the various identities does not take place.

sexual identity

As I pointed out in the chapter on the Oedipal age, the male and female thinking processes are essentially directed to the concept of penetration and being penetrated respectively. Although this idea roughly corresponds to the notion of active vs. passive, Freud pointed out that the female is in a sense active but with a passive aim. Although there are many points in common in the sexual developments of the male and female, it is safe to say that at no time in the history of the organism is the "male identity" so completely at contrast to the "female identity" as during the period of adolescence. This point will be clarified later.

The onset of menstruation and the development of breasts seem to have a profound effect on the girls, even the ones who had maintained a strong masculine or tomboy attitude during the latency or prepubertal period. The girls do not have too much orientation or interest in regard to the actual act of intercourse. They become interested in the phenomenology of having babies much more than the actual act of impregnation as an end in itself. Although some awareness of sexual tension takes place, there is not a high measure of masturbatory activity in the adolescent female who has not experienced local sexual stimulation by another person. Kinsey has shown by his questionnaire method that in spite of the prior anatomical development of the female over the male, the actual interest in sexual matters in the narrow genital sense is much delayed in girls as compared to boys. Sexual feeling as determined by the number of orgasms that appear through masturbation or in sleep does not develop to any great extent during female adolescence. The Kinsey figures show that age twenty-five is the average point at which true sexual pleasure is experienced by the female. This leaves adolescence as a period of comparative anesthesia on the part of the female. If there is some masturbatory activity, it is purely of the clitoral type. This does not mean that girls do not engage in all forms of forepleasure of sexual activity. Kinsey here points out that the curve of sexual actions on the part of the girl corresponds to the curve of sexual feeling of the male. Thus the girl behaves in a way which is altogether contingent upon the level of sexual feelings of the boys. Necking and petting are activities which the girls gradually move into with varying degrees of resistance but with the initiative usually invested in the boys.

Some girls show more hunger for the attentions of the opposite sex than others. When overtly displayed, the phase of being "boy crazy" is manifest. This may lead, in a certain percentage of cases, to actual intercourse. Often this act is performed when the girl shows a strong attachment to a boy who takes advantage of the situation. If the act is not based upon true affection but is accompanied by some contempt or aggression, he "gets away with murder" and leaves the girl to her own devices. In instances like this there may be severe reactions on the part of the girl in the form of defiant promiscuity or defiant aloofness. Severely disturbed girls, on the other hand, can become promiscuous sexually as a defense mechanism against deep-seated oral frustrations from the infancy periods. In any case, there seem to be differences in the reactions of the girls who have had sexual experience in early adolescence or in the prepubertal period in contrast to those of teenage girls who are still virginal. Freud mentions a "coarsening" of sexual behavior in girls who have had such early experiences. According to Bühler and Hetzer [87], even girls who have been seduced or raped have reactions to sexuality which are not the same as the girls who have not had such experiences. It has been said that the dormant sexual feelings are "awakened" by the actual act of intercourse and thereby launch the girl on a career of sexual action. It is as though there is no need to maintain the barriers once actual penetration has been effected. Carrying the sexual identity into the social scene, the behavior of the teenage girl can be characterized as "vulgar" at one extreme or "decent" at the other. The so-called decent girl is to be distinguished from the "prudish" or frightened girl and from the unfeminine, potentially (or actually) homosexual girl. The wholesome, "decent" teenage girl is not repressed in an obvious degree about sexual matters as a matter of factual knowledge; she has no particular fears but chooses to emphasize other matters of a broad sexual nature rather than the narrow concept of the act of intercourse itself. Her main interest is directed toward object choice. As such it is coupled with ideas of marriage, a home, and children. She is satisfied to learn all about sexual matters after she is married.

There is much more to be said about the sexual makeup of the adolescent girl, but for the time being we will consider the sexuality of the adolescent boy. In contrast to the girl, the boy becomes acutely aware of sexual manifestations in realistic perception of localized organ excitation. Although erections may have occurred much earlier than the pubertal period, the phenomenon of increased pleasurable excitability and orgasm does not become an integral part of the life of the boy until the onset of puberty. Usually orgasm coincides with the maturation of the generative apparatus to include ejaculation. However, this need not be so. Some boys experience orgasm before they are able to ejaculate semen. Others have their first orgiastic sexual experience initiated by the phenomenon of nocturnal ejaculation (emission). With this awareness of orgasm sensation and function, there is an intensification of the desire to experience the actual act of penetration or orgiastic release. Freud postulated that sexual tension itself is a rather painful process that accelerates to a point where more and more pleasure is demanded to a point of discharge of the excitation. This drive for release not only is the root of the universal masturbatory activity of the boy, but motivates him to seek new fields to conquer with the girls by breaking down their resistance to his advances.

This awareness of the actual physical manifestation of erection and the motivation for orgasm leads the adolescent youth to look forward to, and finally experiment with, intercourse with an experienced woman or prostitute. The actual act of intercourse becomes for him an act which raises his self-esteem or his esteem in the group. Masturbation, on the other hand, is looked upon for various reasons as a sign of "weakness" in contrast to intercourse which is a sign of strength regardless of whom it may be carried out with as long as it is a female of the same age or older.

Freud pointed up the fact that feelings of guilt or "weakness" in regard to masturbation are due to the incestuous fantasies accompanying the act. It was pointed out that many adolescents have a great deal of unresolved attitudes concerning the incestuous love objects. Sexual excitation occurring when the external objects are still predominantly within the home intensifies all of the fears and guilts that had occurred during the Oedipal age. But aside from these fears, which are greatest in the youngster who has carried over many conflicts from the past and least in the contented teenager with well mastered preadolescent problems, there are probably other factors implying the "weakness" of masturbation. The suggestion is offered that the concept of penetration is intimately tied up with the concept of masculine strength vs. masculine weakness. Probably the penetration of the nonincestuous object carries with it the feeling of success that was denied the child when he was obliged to relinquish the incestuous external objects.

In spite of the fact that the adolescent boy usually wants to go as far as he can with the female, he still expects to be refused. If the girl is too available, he may take advantage of the situation or he may not, but he is likely to feel contempt for the girl as a reaction to his own feelings of guilt. This leaves him free to idealize the "pure" virginal girl, who does not have an interest in sexual matters. This virginal object becomes overevaluated as a partner. The libidinal forces which motivate this object choice draw energy from the cathexis or love of the unsullied mother, who in fantasy has not been touched by man, hopefully the father.

From what has been said about the attraction of the two sexes for each other, we can see that there are some forces which operate to bring the boy and girl into close affinity, and there are other forces which seem to drive them apart. What is quite unmistakable is the discrepancy between the inner or fantasy world of the youngsters and the establishment of a real or lasting personal reciprocal affinity. It seems to be the general rule of adolescence that there is a reluctance or fear of establishing this reciprocity of genital libidinal interchange. In the boy in particular, there is a marked dichotomy between "sex" and "love" with implications that sex is associated with hostile or unclean ideas and love is devoid of such baser feelings, but the forces that interfere with the establishment of the reciprocal affinity have deeper roots. The dirty or unclean sexuality contains admixtures of anal libido, and other cases of fear reactions are orally constituted. The boy or girl may be fearful of forming an attachment because of his or her own hunger for love. This hunger is projected onto the other person when some reciprocal feelings are evidenced. The imagery then becomes of this nature: "I know I want to swallow you, therefore I think you want to swallow me!" The result is a desire to escape the situation.

This desire to escape the situation seems to be more prevalent among boys than among girls. It is the fear of getting "roped in" or ensnared.

Perhaps the feeling is greater among boys than among girls because of the greater degree of vulnerability present in boys as a result of the imageries of the castration theme and the vagina as a biting organ. It is as though the boys feel they have much to lose and the girls have something to gain. Furthermore, the males have a greater degree of motility and assertiveness than females, hence feel able to move on to new pastures which do not seem to impose such threats. The fear of being "roped in" is quite descriptive of the fear of losing this motility. Coupled with the greater degree of motility is the more precocious development of genital excitability in the male. Although boys may have discovered their genitals as far back as in infancy, the height of excitation with orgasm reaches its highest level during adolescence. Kinsey's figures show a sharp curve upwards from fourteen to eighteen years of age. The latter point represents the top of the curve of sexual activity in the lifetime of the male, from which there is a steady decline to old age. This is in sharp contrast to the female who shows no real genital interest at the period of the male's greatest sexual capacity.

There are a few other factors of the sexual identity of the male and female adolescent that are worthy of mention. Not strictly sexual is the body image identity. The body image awareness was mentioned in the preceding chapter on the latency period. During adolescence the changes that take place in the body image give new meaning to the concept of the body ego. Greenacre and others have revived Schilder's [88] contributions regarding the importance of the body image as a factor in the idea of one's own identity. In the male, the concept of strength and muscular development, especially of the chest and shoulders, is a paramount feature of the male identity. The female identity is characterized by softness and breast and hip development, with the curves so characteristic of that sex. There are also masculine and feminine gaits, gestures, and voice control. When there is an identification with the opposite sex by either sex, as in the homosexual, the exaggeration or burlesquing of these body image traits is especially noteworthy.

The masculine identity is associated with aggressiveness or sadism, as though the male is expected to hurt or to be capable of hurting. This may be part of the residual primitive impulse of males fighting each other for the mate; also phylogenetically it was necessary for the male to subdue the female. This identity of the "cave man" masculine figure is one which in the female fantasy is both attractive and frightening. The "cave man" role may represent a libidinization of the hostile or sadistic elements in the male ego organization; sometimes the male dramatizes this role by exaggeration. The original source of excitation for this genital sadism is derived from the oral sadistic or biting impulses. It now operates in the direction of subduing and penetrating the female.

On the female side, the concept of passivity and suffering may reach a high point of organization. H. Deutsch has stressed the point that masochism is part of the normal development of the female. I do not believe that masochism is a primary motivation in the female; rather, it is an outgrowth of female physiology. The phenomenon of menstrual bleeding, cramps, and the awareness of the pain of defloration and childbirth makes pain or suffering an important concept in the thought processes of the female. Thus masochism becomes a secondary development and renders the female passive. The original source of excitation for this genital masochism is derived from oral sucking impulses. As the sexual impulses become manifest, the masochistic and passive position of the female becomes libidinized. This phenomenon merged with exhibitionistic or display impulses becomes a pertinent element in female ego organization. Here let us note that a kind of displacement has taken place. Some of the oral impulses are imparted to the vagina. It is as though the female has two mouths.

The contrast between the male sexual identity and the female sexual identity during adolescence presents the picture of two charged electrodes of opposite polarity. Out of the attraction of these two poles to the other there is produced a change in each of the partners. It would be jumping ahead of our story to talk about the real situation of human mating, but the finding of the mate and the decision to perpetuate such a union marks the end of the adolescent period. The point that will be emphasized in later pages, which we can anticipate now because it points up the theme of the sexual identity of the organism, is that the female learns about genital sexuality from the male and the male learns about home, marriage, and children from the female. This is accomplished by the identification of the male with the female and the female with the male. Possessing two parents of opposite sexes, who have been prototypes for this incorporation of the identity of the sexual partner,

facilitates this process. It is this entire tempering of the adolescent sexual
identities which prompted the statement made earlier that the greatest
contrast between male and female identities occurs in adolescence.

social identity

The foregoing section dealing with the sexual identity of the adolescent has been largely concerned with the biological factors involved
in the growth of the ego. In this section we will be more concerned
with cultural and social phenomena. Although there was a good deal
of allusion to conceptualization of the biological phenomenon, we can
say that a great deal of the sexual identity was based upon perceptual
thinking. In the social scene conceptual thinking plays a more prominent
role.

During the latency period the emphasis was placed upon becoming
amalgamated into a homogenous group. During adolescence the groups
have a tendency to break up into subgroups, and in addition the motivations for individuation begin to appear. Inasmuch as there are now
strong forces operating in the direction of finding a mate, it becomes
necessary to become more individualistic in order to be noticed. Furthermore, with selectivity taking place in the choice of suitable social relationships with members of the opposite sex, there is an acceptance of
one's own individuality as differing from that of others. Herein lie
the elements of competitiveness and rivalry. Too much individuality of
personal appearance or behavior may render the adolescent too far
out of line with his peers and calls for retrenchment or facing ostracism
from the group. Group opinion is still extremely strong. If a boy shows
a girl some special attention resulting in his being ridiculed by the
others, he is likely to cease his attentions. A simultaneous struggle goes
on in the adolescent with his or her becoming familiar with the changing
body image and changes in emphasis in the social situation. The changes
that occur in the body image or sensations may not keep pace with the
organizational or integrative powers of the organism so that the teenager
may appear as an awkward, self-conscious individual. In the social
situation particularly, the comparison of these changes is most noteworthy. During the latency period a homogeneity of group relations
was fairly well established. During early adolescence, however, this

balance is often destroyed because the pace of physiological development may vary greatly in different children. Take the matter of stature
alone. The too tall girl or the too short boy may present real social
problems of acquiring an integrated social identity.

In the quest for a social identity the teenager seeks to correlate the
sexual identity, to which he is becoming accustomed, with the idea
that others must change their estimation of him. In other words, the
way the youngster sees himself must come to terms with the way others
see him. This process is sometimes a rather turbulent one particularly
when the youngster has not been prepared for the changes and considers
himself or herself different from the others in the group. As a result
of the gap that has been established at this point in the life of the
adolescent between himself and his parents, the uncertainties of the
developmental processes either lead to a burdensome secrecy or a sharing
of intimate information with a special friend who is going through the
same process. In this respect girls are somewhat better off than boys.
Because of menstruation, girls are aware of biological functions early
and in our present day culture generally have had some instruction from
their mothers, older sisters, or teachers. Of course, if menstruation comes
as a complete surprise, the resulting imagery may be quite devastating.
Boys, on the other hand, get very little instruction on the details of
masculinity. Josselyn [89] makes the point that the adolescent in our
culture struggles blindly with his problems. "Manhood" in particular is
described in very intangible terms. The initiation rites of graduation,
confirmation, Bar Mitzvah only vaguely describe the concept of the
approaching maturity. As a result, standards of maleness or femaleness
become more or less established by the merging of the composite social
identities of the group.

The merging of the social identities constitutes a force of social pressure which is an outgrowth of the original groups in the latency period
but with new evaluation of what is "acceptable" or "unacceptable". The
group may condone or reject the behavior of any individual member
who is reacting to his own internal changes. When there is approval,
the adolescent gains courage for his thoughts and actions. The group
can still be symbolically the protective mother. When there is rejection,
the individual may leave the group and seek a new one, or he may
find it necessary to deny some of his impulses in order to maintain

acceptance. There is in addition, within the group itself, competition and rivalry. The youngsters use the group as an area for boasting and exaggeration.

Although there still exists a large measure of isosexual group relationships at the adolescent period, the merging of male and female groups becomes part of the social scene at this age. Here the problem of being acceptable or unacceptable to the opposite sex is another factor in the social identity. For example, there may be social acceptance by the group of the same sex and lack of acceptance by the opposite. The converse of this may also be true: a girl, for example, may be very popular with the boys but unpopular with the girls. Such a situation may result in many complications, especially since girls of this type may be acting out some neurotic need by purposely alienating the girls while being seductive to the boys.

The social identity of the male as contrasted to that of the female adolescent is further complicated by the marked discrepancy in maturation. This tends to make heterosexual relationships even more awkward. This situation corrects itself in later adolescence when boys develop very rapidly. During later adolescence the boy takes exhibitionistic pride in displaying his girl friend just as the girl does in displaying her boy friend. The good-looking girl friend, therefore, serves as an added means of obtaining self-esteem and as such can represent a phallus in his unconscious. Similarly, the girl who receives attention from a popular boy no longer misses a penis, but obtains pride and self-esteem from her external object.

By and large, however, the real acceptance of one's social identity must stem from the group of peers of the same sex. It is the group superego which later becomes "public opinion". To be rejected by a group, like a club or sorority, works serious hardships on some youngsters. Such a rebuff may be based purely on artificial cultural lines such as religion or economic or social status, etc. This rejection can serve to accentuate feelings of inadequacy that may have been present from conflicts and confusions of previous age periods. On the favorable side, many youngsters who are endowed with good-looking faces and bodies, who have good intelligence, and are not handicapped in other ways, find ready acceptance into groups, thereby enhancing their social identities.

Reference was made to the concept of social anxiety. This anxiety stems from the feeling of being different or estranged from the group. The inner sensations may be expressed as feeling fearful or embarrassed, but more specifically may appear as feeling "stupid" or "bored" or "speechless". It can be expressed in physiological terms as being castrated. In fact, when the unconscious processes of such persons are revealed, the fantasies of castration or being swallowed by the group are prominent. Being on display brings into focus the exhibitionistic wishes and fears of such persons. Fear of saying the wrong thing or doing the wrong thing may have its roots in the fear of "letting go" either tears, urine, feces, or flatus.

The imagery of the social anxiety exhibited by the adolescent may be qualitatively the same as that of the latency period children who had trouble in getting into the group situation. During adolescence, however, there may be an intensification of the previous difficulties. In fact, the anxiety may become a manifest reaction during this period inasmuch as the unconscious processes which had been dormant are called into play in the social situation. Such items as the reluctance to urinate in the presence of other boys may have existed from the Oedipal or latency age, but often become manifest symptoms only after the onset of pubertal masturbation. On the social scene, such youngsters may find it difficult to recite in class, to appear on the dance floor, or to accept social engagements. These asocial tendencies are, of course, the manifestations of shame and guilt. They are coupled with the fear of being looked at, of blushing, and of ridicule. The whole situation is often perpetuated when the somatic reaction of shame becomes converted into the disorder of facial acne. Thus the adolescent bears the hallmark of his sexual feelings and is further subject to the social pressures created by the display of this condition. Sometimes the sexual problem is displaced onto ideas concerning the size of one's nose, or the look in one's eye. These can be very serious reactions to the original conflicts or confusions of the instinctual motivations.

On a less serious level there may be varying degrees of unsociability by both boys and girls. In this respect there are also cultural or regional differences as to the degree of sociability shown by the adolescent youngsters. In one California high school, for example, there is an almost complete absence of active sociability on the part of the boys toward the girls. School dances, where the boys are expected to invite the girls, are almost completely unattended. Dances where the girls invite the boys, however, are crowded, successful affairs. Furthermore, it is not stylish these days for the youngsters to exchange dances. This may be purely local, but there is reason to believe that there are some cultural changes in the relative position of males and females during adolescence in our current society.

As a reaction to the presence of social anxiety, the social identity of the adolescent can assume many forms as a result of the defensive and adaptive aspects of the ego. Homeostasis can be sought for in manners that are asocial, antisocial, or supersocial. These adaptations call into play the various ego reactions that have been operative from the previous developmental periods, e.g., compliance-defiance, dominance-submissiveness, gregariousness-isolation.

The social identity of one adolescent can be that of the "sap" or scapegoat who is the butt of all the jokes or tricks that the group can think up; another may exhibit inoffensive "cockiness" or bluster; and a third may have a chip on his shoulder all the time, ready to fight on the slightest provocation. These are reactions to the painful aspects of social relations. Other reactions to social anxiety may be the chronic search for "fun". Here we see the use of artificial media such as alcohol and, rarely, marijuana to get "kicks" out of life situations. It is this type of reaction which considers adolescence the period of wild abandon, e.g., "flaming youth", "sowing wild oats", etc.

Although there is a great feeling of emancipation in the adolescent, there is still a great need to be accepted by groups, but at this age the groups must reflect some conceptualized meaning. Either there is a search for social stature, which one gets from belonging to a particular club or fraternity, or there is an identification with a particular cause or movement. On the socially acceptable side we find the Christian Endeavor or youth movements and on the socially unacceptable side the "fast crowd" or delinquent gangs. The particular social identity which the teenager chooses bears a high correlation with some organizational forms of secondary perceptual thinking from the earlier levels of development, e.g., to be an explorer can be carried out in the camping experience; to be a pilot, in racing hot-rods.

Even though the social stature of the teenager coincides with his or her acceptance of the particular pattern of the group, e.g., special "teen talk" or articles of clothing, there is still special social stature for some individuals. The special penis-display quality of being the outstanding athlete, the drum majorette, or even having the best grades, carries with it particular ingredients for the elevation of social status and thereby promoting one's self-esteem. Other acceptances and nonacceptances by the group lead to a sensitivity on the part of the individual toward the coordination of his own idea of himself, and his "reputation".

occupational identity

The concept of work or doing work has already been alluded to in various ways in some of the preceding pages, but as an important aspect of the personality, work itself begins to come into prominence during adolescence. Bartemeier has stated that the beginnings of the child's attitude to the work situation stem from the process of eating. Certainly anyone who has fed a plate of solid food to a baby or has watched this being done realizes the pride of accomplishment which comes when the food is "all gone". The pleasure of the mother, of course, is the signal which denotes the goal of accomplishment, but there is no doubt that a good deal of gratification comes to the child from the doing of the task. This feeling of accomplishment is the accompaniment, too, of the task of producing a bowel movement. We have not yet mentioned the gratification that the child can get out of doing actual tasks which fit into the general pattern of useful work. This work activity stands out in sharp contrast to play activities. The implication here is that work refers to doing something for somebody else, whereas play is for the gratification of the self. They both involve the exertion of energy but the goals are of a different character. This does not mean that these two aspects of childhood behavior do not have many overlapping features which will be discussed, but for the moment let us see what has been happening to our teenager along these lines.

The doing of a job or some constructive work fairly well reflects the emotional level of communication that the child presents at that particular level of development. Thus the ego traits of defiance or compliance, impulsivity or procrastination, may be demonstrated in the way the child hangs up his things or puts away his toys. That he may be willing to do a favor for the neighbors but is too tired or just "forgot" to do a chore for his parent may reflect other ego attitudes. If the over-all picture of "work habits" were followed in all its ramifications, it would reveal a great deal about the ego organization of a particular youngster. Some children keep themselves busy with all sorts of useful work; others are lazy and uncooperative.

During adolescence there comes a realization that work is an essential part of the means for survival in the realistic world. Adolescents are confronted with the question of what they hope to do to make a living. Earlier in their lives the fantasies may have had decidedly unrealistic qualities. The Oedipal age youngster had his wild ideas of what being a grown man or woman would be like. The latency age had other ideas. The boy may have been a pilot, a cowboy, a policeman, etc. The girl was a nurse or a dancer, or perhaps just a mother. These things do not seem too real to the growing child, but they are not any more unreal than the world of grownups in general. But in adolescence this unreal quality of the occupational or work identity is greatly modified. The sexual urges toward maturation as well as the recognition that one's own body image is approaching that of the adult motivates the youngsters to take stock of themselves and begin to think on what place they will take in the general scheme of things. Coming as it does with a good deal of impetus at this time, there is to be expected a good deal of confusion as to direction of the occupational urge. This confusion is manifested by many teenage youngsters, especially boys, where occupational choice seems more a pressing necessity.

Ginsburg [90], who has done much to call attention to the psychodynamic features of work, divides the adolescent work interests into two stages. The early period, about fourteen or fifteen years of age, is the period of self-evaluation and the second period, beginning at about sixteen years, is the period of concern with the life plan. During the period of self-evaluation the youngster takes into consideration the assets or liabilities that he possesses for the arrival at some sort of occupational self. It is at this phase of development that there is likely to occur an incompatability between tentatively established interest and the commensurate skills or physical development to carry out this interest. The use of tools, the preoccupation with hobbies, and the imitation of friends all enter into the process of taking inventory of the occupational possibilities. Added to this process is the one of identifiction with the father. Years ago it was a foregone conclusion that the son followed the occupational line of the father. To some extent this is true today. But by virtue of the dissatisfaction of the parents with their own occupational lots in life, which may well be a reflection of the culture in which we live, the boys are often discouraged from entering their father's work. A hostile attitude to the parent may likewise result in a negative identification by which the youngster is drawn to something very different from the occupation of the father he hates. On a less pathological level the need for emancipation from, or devaluation of, the parent as part of the severance reaction from the dependency positions motivates the teen-ager to exercise a degree of self-determination in his choice of occupa-tion. Add to this the tendency of individuation as encouraged by the schools and we can see that the occupational identity of necessity goes through a period of flux.

This period of self-evaluation and self-determination brings with it a changed attitude toward school work. Although girls seem to show better study patterns than boys and as a result may get higher grades, the concepts of acquiring useful knowledge and doing things that may prove of some worth become an increasing consideration for boys. Actually girls gather better grades by more application to assigned tasks rather than through better intelligence. From the physiological or id level the need for girls to surpass boys scholastically reflects the imagery, by displacement and compensation on an intellectual plane, of the rela-tive disadvantages of being without a penis.

The desire to save money also motivates adolescents to do some work. Boys may get great satisfaction out of being able to earn some money by cutting leaves or shoveling snow or washing cars, and girls by being baby-sitters. These work identities bear close relationships to the ultimate life patterns of the respective sexes. Girls take some pride in being able to take the responsibility of caring for the neighbors' children. Even though boys wouldn't disdain such activity, there is a tacit admission by both boys and girls that this is a job which is more efficiently performed by girls. Washing dishes or clothes, though effectively performed by boys, is still considered "girls' work". Mechanical dishwashers and clothes washing machines seem to be changing this pattern somewhat because of the boys' interest in machinery. What stands out here is the clear demarcation that exists between the male work identity and the female work identity. Many girls, of course, imitate male work patterns. Boys, on the other hand, almost universally disdain the female work pattern. A normal adolescent boy would rather be dead than be caught

doing embroidery. This attitude is, of course, overdetermined and suggests that the vulnerability to castration is very close to the surface. It
is as if the penis is still not firmly attached and requires assurance and
fortification from the school and work identities to maintain the
masculine self-esteem.

Late adolescence sees the preparation of youngsters for a serious life
plan. Whereas formerly children may have had objective anxiety when
their homework was not done, i.e. they feared the actual disapproval of
parents or teachers, or they had superego anxiety because they felt
they deserved punishment, the older teenager, who is more emancipated
from parental authority, may feel that to neglect his homework would
lessen his chances for getting a good record for college. Thus his work
identity has an ego preservative quality and helps him toward building
the foundation for his goals.

The occupational goals of the adolescent brings us to a point where
our discussion involves the concept which Freud described as the "ego
ideal". The patterns of performance which were originally demanded
by the parents, teachers, other adults, and the group, constituted models
of action and thought which influenced the child's thinking processes.
As these became internalized, they constituted a part of the superego.
From the superego there emerge pressures which become materialized
in the imagery as idealized identities. This type of thinking was described
earlier as the organizational form of secondary perceptual thinking
where it became a defense against the Oedipal conflict. During adolescence the idealized identities can become much more realistic in terms
of the accurate knowledge of the person's skills and interests. The true
ego ideal may become attached to a real person. This is a process which
goes on for a lifetime. I might even be accused of such an idealization
of Freud because his name has appeared so often as a reference source.
As Adler stated when he was accused of describing the inferiority
complex because of his feelings of inferiority to Freud, "This only proves
my point!"

The occupational goals and the ego ideal are not meant to be
synonymous terms, but one can hardly speak of the former without
referring to the latter. Freud introduced the term "ego ideal" to mean
the picture of the self as the organism would like to be. This involves
a highly conceptualized process of thinking in the adolescent because
it is the amalgamation of many autonomous ego functions and defense

measures. The ultimate goal is survival from (a) the personal point of view, (b) the group point of view, and (c) the point of view of the world at large. To visualize an ego ideal involves the incorporation of experiential items plus an appreciation of the time sense or reality principle so that not only does the future become something for which the organism must prepare, but also the organism is afforded some choice or selectivity as to how he or she will care to live it. The motivation for survival in all aspects of the personal and interpersonal relationships is embodied in the concept "success". At a deeper layer than meets the eye, the dethronement of the father, the successful competition with siblings, and the out-distancing of the members of the peer-group constitute the elements which move the adolescent toward attaining his occupational identity. Identification with the parent of the same sex includes the consideration of following the father's occupation.

Although the youngsters have been generally bombarded throughout their childhood by platitudes and slogans regarding their future lives, it is only in late adolescence that these begin to take effect. Success stories which appear in the movies, on television and radio, or in story books have their influence upon the establishment of the work identity. Not only are these sometimes unrealistic from the point of view of practicality but they can be the source of considerable conflict later on. Inasmuch as the youngsters who are most disturbed are most likely to defend themselves with fantastic occupational goals, their problems become intensified by the inevitable frustration. Furthermore, the promises that sometimes emerge from teachers and clergymen that hard work and study will always be the open sesame to success, may also lead to unrealistic goals. Counsellors have sometimes not taken into consideration economic or other cultural factors in encouraging some occupational choices. This unrealistic attitude is more likely, however, to arise from the teenager himself who wants to carve a niche for himself in the complex world he is to face. It seems to be an axiom in America with its residuals of the frontier and industrial expansion, that everybody has a chance for reaching the top. Vigorous motivation becomes apparent either to go far in school work or to get out to work. Where there is a good deal of impetuosity, the "quick buck" or lazy dollar becomes the watchword for the adolescent who cannot withstand further frustration in his goal for self-determination. In such an instance the acquisition of wealth becomes the road to attainment or realization, without too much consideration for the obstacles on the way.

The life-plan or ego ideal which sets the stage for the crystallization of the work identity receives many environmental or cultural pressures. On the masculine side we have already alluded to the concept of being self-supporting but there are other motivations that have prestige value for the attainment of elevation of self-esteem and masculinity. These values are not necessarily the ones arising from the adolescents themselves, but from the family, friends, and teachers. Conflictually, the life-plan may create a disturbance between the imagery of the prestige-bearing occupation and the imagery of what that work entails, e.g. "I think it's great to be a doctor, but I can't stand the sight of blood."

As to the female work identity, there is a close correlation between this and the sexual identity. Specifically, the concept of marriage embodies both the sexual and the occupational identity. Although in actual operation the female work identity is a vicarious or complementary identification with the husband's occupation, yet in our culture the concept of a "career" appears as distinct and apart from marriage. The motivation toward a career for the female can be considered a phenomenon of our present day culture and a defense against the possibility that marriage may not come along or an ace-in-the-hole against the eventuality that the marriage may fail. By and large, however, the adolescent girl thinks of a career which will bring fame or fortune merely to satisfy repressed instinctual conflicts, e.g. exhibitionism. Conflictual ego traits, such as orderliness, may motivate the girl to be a librarian or bookkeeper. The concept of being a housewife, or more acceptably a homemaker, as a career in itself is often looked upon with disfavor because it seems, on the surface at least, to many girls as an admission of the inability to compete with the masculine world. Others turn to a career because of the fears of marriage and childbirth. It is the well integrated adolescent girl who can accept an identity as wife and mother as a career to be anticipated and not merely one to escape into as a means of getting away from a troubled home situation.

Cultural pressures which encourage girls to seek theatrical careers are acutely operative on teenage girls. The glamour and money of stage and screen and the adulation of the throngs present enticing ego ideals for many girls and even boys. Inasmuch as many unstable people are attracted to the theatre, cultural values, quite different from those of society in general, may be established. For example, at one famous school of the theatre, young girls who are found lacking in talent or other requirements are told: "You haven't got what it takes. Go home and get married." Often the girl feels that marriage is second best and that she falls below the standards of "success" as a womn. Of course, in the theatre as in all branches of human endeavor, there are many gifted, stable people who are worthy of the emulation of our adolescents.

Poverty may have extreme influences on young people. Some react with an exaggerated motivation to acquire money. This becomes, to them, life's main challenge. To others poverty becomes the standard. Not only do these persons fail to achieve any other mode of living but would feel guilty and uncomfortable in any other setting. In the latter instance, to rise above the parental economic level would do violence to the incorporated parental images.

Work success, or at least the establishment of a work goal toward the attainment of this success becomes an important ingredient of the ego. As such it is motivated by the external environment which becomes internalized as part of the superego. (This component will be more completely formed later in the stage of adult life.) As a teenager, true occupational identity is not fully achieved. This is a trial and preparation period. Nevertheless, the influence of many ego traits can converge to establish an occupational identity which can presage the adult work pattern. An attitude of creativity or workmanship, perhaps originating in play or hobby, can carry over to satisfy other demands.

On the psychopathological side, the concept of "failure" may be the destructively motivating theme that militates against the development of a satisfactory work identity. It does not necessarily mean that school failure is a harbinger of work failure. Often the opposite is true, especially when the gratifications of remunerative work exceed the gratification in the scholastic sphere. However, there are some youngsters who are under the influence of strong masochistic drives which force them into positions of chronic failure. Those teenagers who are overprotected, the drifters and the procrastinators, present pictures of inadequacy in many ways, including the inability to make a choice or to prepare for making a living. They cannot accept ultimate responsibility. They postpone any crystallization of an occupational identity. Such youngsters have not only failed to cope with the problem-solving that is required in reality testing, but have given very little thought to the concept that they have the capacity for mastering the future. It is for that reason that they not only do not establish any goals but cannot come to grips with the notion that they have the capacity within themselves to attain those goals. Furthermore, they may rely upon the magical omnipotence of their parents to take care of them.

Finally, the work identity in relation to defense mechanisms against anxiety or depression should be mentioned. We may deal with youngsters who find it necessary to keep busy all the time. This activity may not be to please somebody or to get gratification out of a task accomplished, but merely to relieve the tension that would occur if he or she did not maintain a work activity. As one person expressed himself to the author: "I must work to avoid emptiness." Some people manage to leave some task undone for this reason. It probably represents a way of avoiding temptation or of getting out of the way of parental authority.

religious identity

The adolescent's attitude towards religion offers some interesting material on the operation of the thought processes. All of the emancipatory and anxiety reactions may have their repercussions in the attitude toward the church.

Let us first return to the period of puberty when the beginnings of adult sexuality were first evident, a stage at which a deeply religious attitude may develop. It is at this period that the youngsters become initiated into manhood and womanhood through various residuals of tribal initiation. The ceremonies of confirmation and Bar Mitzvah, the latter described so well by Arlow [91], give indication of union with adult society as well as sanction by the highest authority, God, for their sexual maturation. The early teenagers may have a great interest in religious matters, may be very diligent about their prayers and attendance at church or Sunday school. This acceptance of the religious attitude on the part of the youngsters is a response to a parental authority by submission, as a device for relieving the guilt for the libidinal and hostile impulses which are brought out at this period. The feeling of "badness" or sinfulness is one which has long been established in the Oedipal or pre-Oedipal stages. Erikson suggests that this feeling of sinfulness had its origin in the oral biting stage of infancy when the paradise of union with mother was lost by the aggression against her, viz., original sin and the Adam and Eve story. Prayer and atonement become the means by which the organism renounces his or her impulses and assumes the position of being a suffering penitent. These attitudes, when further fortified by new admonitions and threats, tend to fortify the punishing superego.

As adolescence proceeds, the organism can move in either of two directions. Either the religious identity becomes one of integrating or incorporating the teachings of the church or there is a complete turning away or denial of the church doctrine. In either instance the social identity of "I am a Presbyterian" or "I am a Jew" does not change even though the ego attitudes or religious identity, as we shall call it, may show great fluctuation.

When the superego forces which operate to deny the libidinal impulses are such as to cause a repudiation of the sexual identity, a state of asceticism, prudery, or prissiness may supervene. It is at this stage that many teenagers decide to go into the ministry or to enter a convent. Many more give thought to this goal, but do not go through with it. This ascetism or self-denial may last in some instances for a lifetime, especially if it is fortified by identification with parents who have similar religious identities. However, in more instances this is merely a stage of ego metamorphosis.

There are instances when the libidinal urges are so great that the superego representation of the church cannot retain them any longer. In order to establish some semblance of homeostasis, these teenagers decide to deny the power of the church. Agnosticism, atheism, and irreligiosity in general become rampant ideologies during this phase of adolescence. As a reaction formation to the prohibitive influence of the superego pressures, the denied sexual impulses become even more intensely activated. The sexuality and the forbiddenness become merged into one phenomenon, namely the libidinization of the forbidden. The guilt ensuing is often projected onto other objects by the release of aggression onto the church or to scapegoats of other religious or cultural identities.

The tempo of change from a very religious to a very irreligious attitude may vary greatly, depending upon many personality and cultural factors. Often the high school period can be a very religious one and college the opposite, but this shift may occur earlier. There are often cases when the early adolescence is irreligious and for various reasons the late adolescence is very observant. The true religious identity based upon spiritual values satisfying to that individual often does not take final form until adult life.

home identity

Most of the behavior of the adolescent which has been described in the previous pages has been centered on what his or her performance is outside the home. Let us turn back to the home setting. Emphasis was placed upon the emancipation or freedom from the parental scene in the behavior in the orbit of sexuality and the social, school or occupational, and religious setting. This emancipation may reflect itself in direct face-to-face rebellion with one or both parents, but there remains in spite of this surge of independence, a small residual of the little boy or girl who needs to keep a foot inside of the parental home. This big-little polarity may well be a reflection of the conflict which exists in the minds of the parents as to whether they want to see their children approaching their majority. Such a confusion may reflect itself in the admonition at one moment, "You are too big to be so helpless," followed by the opposite admonition, "You are too little to take such liberties!" When the parents themselves become reconciled to the changed sexual and social positions of their offspring, then there is a concomitant easing of the confusion of the teenagers.

Adolescent boys are handled differently from adolescent girls. Whereas mothers are more likely to have a fairly free attitude toward their daughters, fathers are more likely to be strict. With the boys there is less concern with the movements outside the home by either parent than there is with girls. Girls are encouraged to be affectionate with both parents, e.g., kissing them both goodnight. Boys no longer kiss their fathers; they may still kiss their mothers goodnight. Parents may permit a girl to sleep at another girl's house, but will be very careful about what time she comes home when she is out with a boy. Kinsey claims that this encourages homosexual activities and makes normal heterosexuality appear forbidden.

The teenage youngster may show an entirely different manner of behavior inside the home from that he exhibits outside. His performance may be more nearly adult when he is away from home and more nearly the child when he is at home. Still, when the parents are too insistent upon using the youngsters to carry out their own particular aims or goals without considering enough the aims or goals of their offspring, clashes are likely to occur. On the other hand, the teenagers may labor a point just for the sheer gratification of winning. A youngster fought with his parents for the privilege of smoking. When it was granted, he chose not to. "I just wanted to see if I could." A conversation overheard in an ice cream parlor between two teenage girls is as follows: "That dress I bought is much too old for me." "Yes it is, but you sure nagged your mother long enough to let you get it." "Yes, I know, but still she shouldn't have let me get it." This reflects both the desire for freedom and the need for some protective supervision. It also reflects, in this girl at least, a different level of communication between herself and her parents from the level she manifests with her friends.

The contrast between the home identity and the peer identity or social identity may be very marked. A youngster may feel very free and outgoing among his peers, but feels restricted, disciplined, and under wraps in his home situation. There may still remain all the memories of "children should be seen and not heard" or "mother knows best" plus the fact that the parents themselves may still be operating on the same basis that they did at earlier periods. Thus there may be a distinct lag in exhibiting the adolescent manifestations in the home setting when they have already been established in other spheres of operation. Other cases show just the opposite trend. Because of the inability to move freely in the group situation, the home identity becomes a freer and more relaxed area in which to express one's feelings. Such teenagers may appear very rebellious in the home when there are frustrations in the outside world, but maintain a brave front in the social situation. In part it may appear that the duality of a home identity and a social identity is a reflection of the action of the parents themselves. Parents by example put on "company manners" when there are visitors in the home. Children are warned not to discuss "family secrets" with outsiders, or the parent may be jovial, friendly, and generous to his friends or business associates and then become grouchy, ill-tempered, and noncommunicative with his family. There is little

Fig. 2.

Figs. 2 and 3.—These diagrams are approximations of the libidinal and hostile forces that are brought to bear in the individual toward or against the parents. Figure 2 is the representation of the psychosexual development of the male and figure 3 is the female.

The first figures represent the ambivalent attitudes to the external objects displayed during the latter part of infancy. The arrowheads represent positive feeling and the reversed arrows represent negative feeling. The child loves and hates the persons who are responsible for his care. Roughly speaking, we can say that the cathexis is positive when the needs are gratified and it is hostile and negative when the demands are frustrated.

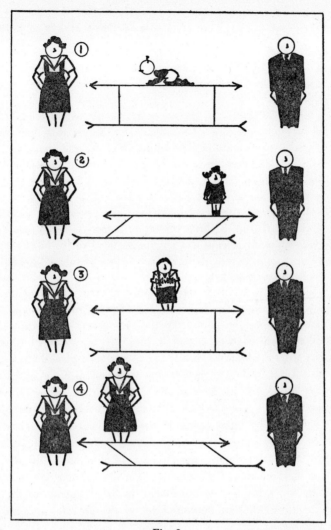

Fig. 3.

The second set of figures shows a shift of the ambivalence in the Oedipal phase. The boy shows a greater degree of affinity for his mother and a concentration of hostility to the father. The girl shows greater affinity for the father and greater hostility to the mother.

The third set of figures shows the latency period. In this phase there seems to be a lessening of importance of the parents. There is less hostility but also less libidinal attachment.

The fourth set of figures represents the identification with the parent of the same sex. The hostile arrows indicate the emancipation from the incestuous objects that takes place during adolescence.

wonder then that the teenage youngsters have learned to operate on different levels. This is not a new experience at adolescence; it is an outgrowth of the two worlds in which the child revolved in the early Oedipal years.

Stress has been placed on the concept that the social identity is a reflection of the masteries of libidinal excitations that had arisen in the original parent-child relationships. We can add the point here that during adolescence, though to a much lesser degree, the home disposition of the teenager is largely contingent upon his or her successes in the sexual and social orbits. Failure to accomplish anticipated gratifications causes many teenagers to blame their parents for their frustrations. One girl was bitterly resentful of her father because she resembled him facially, hence was not successful with the boys.

When things go smoothly, there is a subsidence of turmoil toward late adolescence. After establishing, to some extent, a foothold in the sexual, social, and particularly the occupational areas, the home identity takes on new meaning. The identification with the parent of the same sex, which has been the goal from the very start, now becomes an accomplished fact. Figures 2 and 3 illustrate the shift of libidinal forces first from the ambivalent attitude of late infancy and the toddler period to the Oedipal age, then to the detached position in latency, and finally to the isosexual parental identification. It is this final acceptance of the parent which permits a friendly interchange of feeling on a nearly equal basis. If the adolescent has received the support he needed during the trying period of the sexual maturation, the ego is enabled to attain the strength of adulthood through this process of identification. Unfortunately, not always does this occur so completely, as we will see in more detail in the discussion of the subject of the crystallization or consolidation of the total ego identity during this period.

the amalgamation of the ego identity

Reference was made earlier in the text to the concept of integration. This process, it will be recalled, consisted of the uniting of various motivations into a single unit or whole. For attainment of an identity, or more specifically for the organism to function as a whole or integrated unit it is necessary to reconcile each of the identities described in the previous pages into some sort of compatible common denominator. It follows that if there were completely conflict-free identities in each of the orbits, all the ego masteries would unite to form a single set of autonomous conflict-free ego traits.

It can be left to the theorists to speculate as to what takes place in the brain during this process of integration. There may be some explanation along metapsychological lines, but there is evidence to indicate that integration of function can be explainable on purely mechanical or physiological bases. The cyberneticists, Wiener and others, explain such phenomena on the operating principle of the electronic computing machine. A recent book by Ashby [92] should prove of interest to the theorists. His book, *Design for a Brain* contains a description along mechanical and mathematical lines of the processes of control of action and function. He describes a system which affects internal controls of the organisms by coordinating the multiple stimuli which reach the brain. The stimuli that we have reference to here are those which govern the action of adolescents in each of the spheres of influence in which they operate. In Erikson's words the process of ego synthesis is an attempt "to make one battle and one strategy out of a bewildering number of skirmishes."

The ego identity that emerges from the successful mastery of the problems of adolescence gives the individual a "character" or uniqueness that bears a resemblance to the ultimate adult pattern of being. Within the self the young man or young lady has the feeling of being very much a part of the surrounding society, yet with a right to have an identity or "self" all his or her own. This is the true self or "anima" of Jung [93].

As a part of the nonconflictual ego attitude which takes into consideration the biological drives towards the establishment of a reciprocal heterosexual affinity, there emerge the ego traits of "charm" and "romance". These traits not only take into consideration the fact of "falling in love" or overevaluating a person of the opposite sex who is to be considered as a potential mate, but involve the recognition of the need to be fascinating and interesting to the other person.

Although the adolescent period has been described as a new phase of growth for the individual, there has been in some ways a repetition of early patterning. The latency period was described as a repetition of the infancy and training and indoctrination periods applied to the group. By the same token, we can say that adolescence is a repetition of the Oedipal phase applied to the group. Jones [94] particularly calls attention to the recapitulation of the libidinal cycle of early childhood during adolescence. Our point of emphasis is that the cycle repeats itself but with wider orbits of operation. It will be shown later that the early adult years or late adolescence recapitulates a sort of latency period when the turmoil subsides and the individual figuratively "catches his breath" before entering full maturity.

The one main difference between the integrative processes in the Oedipal phase from the integrative processes in the adolescent phase is that of pure motivation (or instinct) in contrast to that of motivation plus orbits of identity. In other words, the conflict of the Oedipal age child is one of confusion of instinctual motivations whereas in adolescence there is in addition, or exclusively, the confusion or conflict of identities. This means that both biological and cultural success must be attained.

Before discussing the conflictual adaptations or maladaptations that occur, let us turn to the tabulation of the identities as they appear in a specific case. The man in question is a fairly well integrated individual except for poor selectivity in the choice of a mate. (See chart on p. 157.)

late adolescence

Let us return now to normal or average adolescence. As the various identities become integrated into a workable unit, the organism seems to come to terms with his or her own body and with the many facets of outside reality. With this emergence of an identity there supervenes a sense of calm. It is as though the organism is collecting its forces for the problems that lie ahead. In this respect there seems to be a slight difference in the sexes. The boys stop their wild devil-may-care attitudes, especially if they find an interest in a particular girl. They lose interest in their hot-rods and jalopies and would rather borrow the family car for that special date. The thought processes of the girls vary with the success or failure they have with the boys. If there is cause to worry as to whether they are headed for matrimony, they may become irritable, restless, or despairing. However, if the girl has an kindly offered to allow the author to use parts of his life history for this presentation. He spent his early years in a small rural community as the fifth of six children. His mother was a rather timid person, fifteen years younger than his father, who was a tyrannical, strict, religious, and exacting person. His latency and adolescent development is listed as follows:

Age	Occupational Identity	Social Identity and Home Identity	Sexual Identity	Religious Identity
8	Became interested in things rather than people.	Had to take care of a baby sister. Was obliged to be with her constantly. He did his duties as sister's caretaker grudgingly, because of having been intimidated by father.	As a boy captive was forced to take a role which he felt very degrading, namely, taking care of his sister. Although he entertained his sister by doing girlish things like sewing, etc., he felt that this was not for him except that he took pride in doing a good mechanical job.	Compelled to go to Sunday School and Church. Father had been prominent in the Methodist Church. More impressed with teachers and minister rather than any diety.
	Was fond of toys which had an element of motion.			
	At first began to roll spools, then fashioned them into miniature vehicles. Played with little wagons and a small iron train.	Felt fairly close to mother. In school did what he could to avoid disapproval.	Fantasy world was only one of engaging in masculine pursuits.	First impression was that of "the Devil". Was fearful of burning in Hell. Had heard stories of having fallen in the fireplace as a baby. Wore scars on forehead.
	Learned how to whittle. Made a wooden train.	Outside the home neighbors began to notice his inventive genius. He was adulated for the trains that he whittled. Was particularly admired for making a cider press, engines and a wooden dancing doll.	No particular sexual curiosity. Accustomed to observing mating of barnyard animals.	
		Developed stature in the group because of his superior mechanical ability.	Hero worship of older boys who told fantastic tales of adventure.	
		Whittled with other youngsters. Made bows and arrows and slingshots.		
		Became proficient in games and athletics.		
		Was teased a good deal for being fat. Became a good fighter to avoid being picked on.		
		Became very popular in the group. Had a close "buddy" relationship with four or five boys. "I would fight for them, they would fight for me."		

Age	Occupational Identity	Social Identity and Home Identity	Sexual Identity	Religious Identity
10	Wanted skates, but had no use for them in the country. Enjoyed toys with lifesize transportation, scooter, wagon, velocipede. Rode his brother's bicycle.	Became involved in a "scandal" because of interchange of notes with a girl in class. Girl's father threatened him with jail. Lost social status. Was ostracized by group except for close buddies who remained loyal. Returned to old hobby of whittling. Social status improved when he was invited to play baseball because they needed a pitcher. Maintained a fairly isolated position. Some male companionship, hunting, swimming. Wanted to break away from family.	A girl showed interest in him. Was kidded by boys, but nothing "registered". Girl four years older who had sexual experience sent him "love notes". Was teased by brothers. Answered the notes by means of a secret code. More of a game than real sexual interest. Was aware of sexual activities by boys, including activities with animals. Had been told by mother of the wonders of sexual pleasures. Imitated older brother.	Concept of God came later. God could be appeased, but was always angry. Never learned quite how to appreciate Him.
12	Became interested in adult transportation. Spent a great deal of time watching trains. He learned all he could about airplanes and boats, but concentrated on land travel by mechanical means. Saw few cars, but was fascinated by them. Became interested in telegraphy. Became acquainted with and admired the telegraph operator at the local railroad station.			Jesus was not a very important figure. Never attained stature of a full diety. More like a messenger. Was never taught much about the Virgin Mary. She merely was the Mother of Jesus, but had had no power whatever.
13			Masturbation became a steady interest. More of a localized pleasure rather than any association with	

the actual act of intercourse.

Age	Occupational	Social	Sexual	Religious
14	Read books on transportation and railroading.			
15	Left home, went to Normal School where he was given a chance to work his way through school.	Encouraged by male school teacher. Away to school. Decided never to return home until he could return as "conquering hero".	While away from home, he was taken to a prostitute by an older boy. Thereafter used women only to gratify sexual needs. Did not have any real regard for females. Was convinced that basically he hated women.	After leaving home, he attended church regularly for four months. Became friendly with non-church-going people and quit going. Still influenced a great deal by old "hellfire" teachings, but no formal attendance.
16	He learned Morse code by diligent self-study.		Fell in "love" through the mail with an old school mate.	
17	Secured job as station agent and telegraph operator. Was inspired to travel by "boomer operators". Quit job. Secured work as "news butcher" on railroad. Also worked in grocery business. Became a "sharp operator" even though he felt "out of character".			
18	Went back as station agent. Had continuous line of promotions. Sought adventure. Later moved into traffic department where knowledge of sales and transportation supplemented each other.		Became involved with a divorcee. Passively drifted into marriage.	After marriage, returned to church. Because of doubts regarding anything "definite" from ministers, regarding anything with which to go across the "huge abyss" of life—afraid of the black marks which would keep him from the pearly gates. In search for "getting away from the devil". Began to formulate ideas of life and hereafter. Finally turned to a metaphysical philosophy.
20			Wife left him.	

ample supply of eligible young men who are paying her attention, a sense of well being and self-assurance is likely to emanate. Even before the actual selection or finding of a mate, assuming that all other situations had been adequately mastered and integrated, the older adolescents of both sexes seem to slow down in their desperate efforts to "play the field." It is this slow-down which has been likened by Wittels [95] to a second latency period.

As to the exact point at which we can say adolescence ends and maturity begins, there is no point of complete agreement. There is an imperceptible merging from one phase into the other. If we judge by physical manifestations, we arrive at one conclusion; if we judge by social or cultural standards, we arrive at another. For example, if we consider choice of mate as the dividing line, we will vary from the child bride to the aged bachelor as the borderline. Termination of physical growth, such as closure of the epiphyses, may be a convenient point, but this is not coordinated with the thought processes as far as is known.

The thinking processes and ego growth of the terminal phase of later adolescence and those of the young adult show many overlapping features. It may suit our purposes better to discuss the subject from the point of view of the young adult male and female with some references back to the residuals of the late adolescent period.

ego failure in adolescence

As pointed out in the previous paragraphs, the adolescent period is one in which the individual finds it necessary to coordinate many factors of ego growth. It is no surprise to find that not all adolescents are fortunate enough to be able to make the necessary integration. This places the adolescent period as a time of great emotional crisis. It is almost axiomatic that the crisis of adolescence is not one of great moment if all the other previous emotional crises have been adequately weathered. It is a sad paradox of the human mind that when there have been failures in the past, there is not established any immunity to subsequent failure, but rather there develops a suscepti-bility or vulnerability to new failures. Although it may be considered a fairly safe rule that if there is extreme psychopathology in the realm of one identity or ego boundary, there is likely to be disturbance in other areas, this is not always the case. Furthermore, even if there are disturbances in more than one area, the types of disturbance may not be in harmony with each other and may even be in decided disharmony. It goes without saying that all of these occurrences are contingent upon the current events in the life of the individual. The fortuitous happenings in one area can lead to a specific mastery there whereas traumatic happenings can lead to specific disturbances which do not affect the other areas. Still, we have seen how happenings in one zone can also influence the organism in all the orbits of operation. The disturbances of ego integration can be divided arbitrarily into three categories:

1. Total distortion of integration leading to peculiarities of characterological development.

2. Maintenance of isolated roles or identities with changeable patterns of behavior in different settings.

3. Varying degrees of ego disintegration or total collapse of adaptation.

Each of these categories will be discussed in some detail. Whereas the normal, well adjusted adolescent has united his identities like the strands of a cable, the cases we are now discussing entail a great deal of internal juggling to effect a unified self. This unification or integration is brought to bear by the organism in order to avoid tension. As such, the reparative integrative faculty serves as a defense mechanism against painful emotions. These emotions can arise from the conflicts of motivation within the sphere of one area, but more particularly during the adolescent period the painful reactions occur when the youngsters attempt to correlate one set of adaptations or identity with other areas of identity. Disastrous results may occur when there is confusion or conflict of identities, but the organism in its adaptive capacity, particularly in individuals who are prone to deny tension for various reasons, sacrifices some aspect of its identity in order to make the best possible adjustment which will meet its innermost needs in all areas. Thus what ordinarily may appear as symptoms or ego alien reactions become incorporated into the ego organization in an ego syntonic fashion. These ego syntonic adaptations produce total character abnormalities such as homosexuality, criminality, prostitution, or other psychopathic behavior, or specific characterological disorders such as pseudo-feeble-mindedness, inadequacy, or hoboism. The identity which harmonizes the various conflictual areas, although presumably satisfying to the individual as the best possible adaptation that person can make, still leaves within the organism the imageries of the painful emotions as ingredients of the distorted total identity.

The foregoing points can best be illustrated by citing a case. The person who was selected for the purpose of illustrating the distortion of integration during adolescence was a woman who came into analysis at the age of thirty-six. Her main problem was one of homosexuality. She had been married and divorced. There were two children from this marriage. The overt participation in sexual affairs with women as a major interest did not occur until several years after her marriage. Her husband had previously been critical, domineering, and demanding. She was convinced that she would never have reverted to homosexuality if her husband had been the kind, considerate, and affectionate man that she had considered him to be at the time of her marriage. At the outset of her analysis she was pessimistic that anything could be done for her homosexuality. She was mainly concerned about the emotional turmoil she had gotten into as a result of the complications resulting from her various "affairs". The homosexuality she now considered part of herself because she recalled that in her adolescence she had an affair of this sort to which she attached little significance because it seemed like a very natural form of behavior for her.

After working through some of her thinly veiled defences, it was revealed that she had a very masochistic makeup with a tremendous need for affection, but she always managed to get herself into situations where she was rejected or abused. Her greatest source of comfort was to be with a group of homosexuals of both sexes where she felt accepted and at ease. Among "squares" or "straight" people she felt uncomfortable and out of place. She considered them "stuffy". She could never spend an evening at home alone for fear she was missing something. All of this changed in the course of the analysis, but this is not our story. The integration of her homosexual identity during adolescence is the point for which this case is being presented.

A little background information will be offered first. As far as she was able to remember, the first six years of her life were quite happy. In fact, it was very difficult to elicit many memories of her early years. What did come back were pleasant recollections of adoring, kindly parents. She described herself as having been happy, carefree, and playful. She had many friends of both sexes. She recalled having been fascinated by the sight of boys urinating. She vaguely recalled hearing her parents say that they had chosen a name for her before she was born which could have been used for either a boy or a girl. Her father played a small role in her early life, partly because he was away from home for a long period of time during World War I. Her relationship to her mother was quite friendly, but she did not recall freely very much other than playing with her friends outside the home. She did not play with dolls; in fact, she did not recall having had a toy of any kind.

When the patient was six years old, her mother became pregnant. The patient was informed of this fact. She became excited over the prospect of having a baby brother. She prayed constantly that the baby be a boy. When the baby was born, it turned out to be a girl. This was a terrific let-down to her, to which she reacted with a feeling of strong resentment to her sister. When her sister was about one year old, the mother developed tuberculosis and was taken away to a sanatorium. Her absence caused a complete disruption of the household. Aunt B. took over the care of the patient and her sister. This aunt was the father's brother's wife, also the mother's blood aunt. She gave both children excellent physical care, even though there was a period when the patient had to sleep on a billiard table because of crowding. It was then that it was discovered that she had a mild form of childhood tuberculosis. The aunt took extreme precautions that she should stay at home and have bed rest. For about three years, from age seven to ten, she was not allowed out of the house. She spent a good deal of her time with her nose pressed against the window watching other children play games in which she was not permitted to participate. Furthermore, her aunt told her to call her "Mother" and never to mention either of her parents again. Her uncle, now "Daddy", was a weak, ineffectual man. She was not permitted to see her real father. Her new mother was solicitous of the patient's health but demanded strict obedience. There were no overt displays of affection. The patient's reaction to all this was an outward submissiveness but inwardly a seething defiant attitude which often broke through the surface in acts of mischief.

When she was permitted to go to school, she quickly made friends and found a good deal of comfort and pleasure outside of the home. The onset of her menses was uneventful. She made intense friendships with a few girls and was generally popular. Her diary indicated intense feelings for both boys and girls. Her adoptive mother permitted her to sleep at other girls' homes. Her biggest disappointment came when she was not pledged to a high school sorority because she was Jewish. This had never been a problem before. At about this time she also had a crush on a boy who seemed more attentive to her girl friend. When it became evident that her girl friend was chosen in preference to her by the boy, the patient promptly turned all of her affections to the girl friend. She seduced the girl friend into acts of mutual masturbation. After a while, the girl friend tired of this but the patient did not. She felt worse about this than about the boy friend. This pattern of failure with the male, then turning to the female was the one which was repeated when her husband turned out to be the cruel, rejecting person that he was.

A great deal can be said about the integrative quality of the homosexuality of the foregoing case. When she was frustrated by the group, she intensified her libidinal affinity with a heterosexual object. It represented a defence by progression. When this failed, she regressed to a mother affinity, but this also had the quality of a masculine identification by replacing the boy friend whom the patient now unconsciously hated. Her hostility to her more successful girl friend was now converted to sexual aggression. All of these feelings were reflections of the distorted Oedipal picture which had developed in relation to her hated aunt, her longings for her real mother, and her inability to reach her real father. Homosexuality was her best method of adaptation in the face of frustraneous experience.

Let us now turn to the second group of adolescents who have failed to make a wholesome integration of their orbits of identity, namely the ones who maintain isolated identities that operate differently in their respective settings. The phenomenon of isolation is a defense mechanism which is particularly associated with the type of individual who retains residuals of the ruminative type of thinking. In the earlier stages of development, isolation is used to master the confusion of motivations. In those instances there may be an isolation or loss of connection in memory between emotions and events or persons, or loss of the connection between instinctual drives and the external objects. The most common isolation that is seen is the separation of the phenomena of love and sex in the spiritual and carnal aspects of sexuality. In at least one instance in my experience it appeared that the defense of isolation represented a carrying out of the wish to isolate the parents from each other. Certainly in cases of separation and divorce, where the child forms a relationship with each parent in a different setting, the isolation of ego identities becomes a necessity which is encouraged by the existing situation.

In short, we can say that the process of isolating the orbits of identity is an outgrowth of learnings and repression. The youngster has learned to keep apart things which ordinarily should be together. Just as in the mechanism of isolation in general, as stated by Fenichel, there can be an interpolation of spatial or temporal intervals between the two realms that the individual finds it necessary to keep separate. Thus, assuming the identity, in the home, of a little boy or girl can become quite compatible with acting like a pseudo-sophisticate in a social setting. The home identity is bound to a past pattern and the social adaptation or school performance can be bound to new levels of performance.

A short sketch of a man in therapy may illustrate this point. He was a very much overprotected and over-restricted child. There was nothing that he asked for which was not granted, but he was also prevented from engaging in any hazardous activity. When he would resist going to bed, an older sister rubbed his stomach and touched his genitals. He was kept inordinately neat. Once an older man joshed him by saying there was a spot on his face. This made him cry. His mother had to stay with him in school for a long period of time, or else he would run home.

In college he had a good time. He never failed a course because he crammed at the last minute. When he made up his mind to get his degree, he successfully covered a tremendous amount of work in the last part of his final quarter.

He became a bond salesman and was a success, but he never really seemed happy. He remained dependent upon his mother and was terrified of his father. Around his parents he felt and acted like a little, helpless boy, but when he made up his mind to sell bonds, he was a charming, energetic, poised, dynamic person. At home he was a devoted husband and father to his two children. When he became bored or unable to work, he would play with mechanical gambling devices or go to a massage parlor where he experienced passive sexual stimulation. In the course of his therapy his total identity improved. One factor was difficult to dislodge. He found it difficult to make new contacts with prospective clients because, it turned out, he could not stand "getting the brush-off", but when he had a prospect he was a master at manipulating him to close a deal. He solved his problem by taking into his office a man who was superior at making contacts. He would then follow the leads and would uniformly make the sale. This method also gave him the chance to think up new plans which utilized a latent creative talent that stood him in good stead financially.

The phenomenon of isolating his spheres of performance began during his adolescence when he attained some success in athletics and in group acceptance with his contemporaries of both sexes. Thus he found new external objects to whom he reacted in manners more commensurate with his age by virtue of his sexual maturation and by identification with his peers. However, the home patterning remained essentially the same. Other areas were influenced to some extent by these patternings, but there was unmistakable isolation. In his own words, "In diffrent situations I act and feel like different people."

Now let us turn to the discussion of the more serious forms of failure to affect an ego integration in the adolescent period. When the various identities are so incompatible with each other that not only is it impossible for the organism to harmonize them into a unit but to act in one area will do violence to another, a disorganization of the total adjustment takes place. It is for this reason that the schizophrenic breakdowns of adolescence are so common. The term "dementia precox" refers particularly to the syndome of the breakdown of youth.

The disintegrative process that takes place when the confusion of identities is great leads the teenager to react as though he has no identity whatever. He may be plagued with questions within himself like, "Who am I?", "Where do I belong?", or he may become so detached that he is not even able to raise these questions. The loss of identity or the feeling of depersonalization may be a carrying out in action and thought of the greatest fears of loss of self or loss of part of the self as in the castration threat. This confusion of identities or conflict of identifications has been described by Erikson as "role diffusion". His ideas in this respect represent a major contribution to the understanding of human behavior. What he refers to as role diffusion includes the doubts that the adolescent has about his own sexuality and his social position. As the youngster feels driven back to the incestuous external objects for whom he also has many old unresolved conflicts and cannot adjust to his new objects because of new conflicts, he is left "hanging in the air."

The alarm signals or threats which alert these individuals arise from many sources. Extreme social anxiety and castration threats from superego influence upon the sexual drives operate not only to prevent the organization of a mature identity, but to motivate the organism to seek refuge in older patterns of performance. As the mature identity of the adolescent period consists of establishing reciprocal affinities with heterosexual contemporaries as external objects, there is the complete drawing away from such activity. In fact, the prospect of establishing an intimate relationship with somebody of the opposite sex looms as a threat in its own right. This is because such a relationship is invested with the secondary perceptual imageries of the Oedipal period.

If there is evidence of complete disintegration or decompensation of the integrative function of the ego, there occurs the same type of emotional experience that existed in the Oedipal confusions that set in motion a regressive action. The progress action, which is the other type of defensive maneuver used by the child in the Oedipal period, does not lend itself so readily for planning "when things will be better" because the full brunt of reality has now descended in full force. The most that can be expected at the adolescent stage is the accomplishment of some form of "restitution" or mending of the broken fences. When the disintegrative process is minor, there may still be some hope because youth and its promise for a world of the future may still act to hold the ego together.

As in the motivational conflicts of the Oedipal period, the identity conflicts in adolescence precipitate the regressive forms of secondary perceptual thinking, namely, the archaic, ruminative, and sadomasochistic. A thoroughly disorganized adolescent has almost invariably experienced a phase of archaic or autistic regression earlier in life, stemming from Oedipal plus pre-Oedipal confusions. This does not particularly refer to those childhood schizophrenics who probably developed their disorganization in early infancy, as in the permanent "awayness" or libidinal detachment described in the chapter on infancy. A certain amount of this type of reaction may have occurred and may have remained as an encapsulated or lacunar facet of the personality. Under the stress of the disorganization process that takes place in these cases when the adolescent pressure becomes too great to handle, the entire thinking processes may become overwhelmed by the archaic forms of imagery. Added to the infantile thinking forms is the imagery of the physiological manifestations of the sexual function. Translating the thinking processes into action, the youngsters may withdraw from people and evidence all sorts of affective reactions from complete apathy to overwhelming anxiety. There is also a return to the sense of timelessness in archaic thinking probably because the infant has no sense of time other than the perceptual present.

The ruminative type of regressive reaction leads the adolescent back to the level of the stage of indecisiveness of the bowel training period. As is characteristic of this type of thinking, there may be disturbances in each of the developmental areas, e.g., bowel and bladder, speech, locomotion, and time. The time factor is the most troublesome in the disorganization of the individual. As this ties in with the relation to reality, a disturbance of time sense really disrupts the individual completely.

In the ruminative process the past is treated as though it were the present, or more disturbingly as the inevitable future. The defensive aspect of the disruption of time sense may represent the motivation to make time stand still in a magical way. In addition, any of the secondary autonomies of the anal period may be represented, e.g., compliance-defiance, loquaciousness-taciturnity (stuttering), hypermotility-hypomotility (locomotion syndromes), etc. Because the ruminative thinking at this phase of development already includes strong genital excitation, the imageries may be colored by genital imageries and actions. Compulsive masturbation or its complete denial and the symbolic doing and undoing form the framework for the obsessive-compulsive pattern.

At a less pathological level, the disorganization of the individual whose thinking processes are colored by sadomasochistic imageries produces a variety of clinical syndromes in the adolescent. The hysterias, somatization reactions, and the pseudoaggression or failure patterns are cases which fall into this category. It is beyond the scope of this presentation to go into detail in each of the clinical categories. It will suit our purposes merely to make these references. Our primary purpose here is to illustrate the general principle of disintegration as a manifestation of the failure to attain ego growth.

A vital point, which can be reiterated at this time, is the fact that the language of the individual is first biological, then translated into social terms, and finally back to biological terms. To elaborate further, every social action or interpersonal relationship has within it the libidinal or anatomical representation in an internal imagery. Some observers like Sullivan [84], Fromm-Reichmann [96], Horney [97], and many others may stress the interchange between the organism and the external object, but we cannot escape the concept of the basic motivations that arise from the excitations of the organs. The question as to whether one believes or does not believe in the libido theory is a specious one, as all factors must be considered in the approach to the understanding of human thought. All the primary motivations are essentially libidinal but do not always appear as physiological expression. They are translatable into social terms. Conversely, social situations or conflicts dealing with disturbances in interpersonal relations are translatable into anatomical and physiological terms.

With this thought in mind, let us discuss another case which shows evidence of early disintegration at the Oedipal level and a second phase of disintegration in late adolescence. In neither instance was there a complete break with reality, so that the factors that made for the stressful situations are fairly well delineated.

The case is that of a woman in her thirties who sought treatment because of her feelings of complete disintegration. She had distorted ideas that she was worthless, that her husband merely tolerated her out of charity, and that nobody wanted to help her; nor could she accept help when it was offered. In addition, she was irritable and complained of fatigue and numerous somatic difficulties. In the course of therapy it was learned that she became thoroughly disorganized at the age of seventeen following a ruptured romance with a boy. She said that she married her husband at eighteen while she was still in a daze, almost detached from reality.

Her early history indicated that her mother was an anxious woman, very pleasant for long periods of time but then becoming a frantic, hostile, and rejecting person. Her father was given to ridiculing her about everything, including things about which the patient was very serious. Below the age of three years, the patient had been placed on special diets for various forms of allergy. It was constantly necessary to curtail her eating habits. The patient interpreted the mother's concern over her as indicating she was bad or that there were bad things in her. She could not tell people how she felt. She had been told that she was tied to her bed so that she would not scratch herself or wander about the house at night, which she was prone to do. Most of her time was spent in swinging and daydreaming. At about six she was sleepless for many nights because she feared that the house would burn down. For a short while in her latency period she was a tomboy. Although she found playmates, she felt that she was different from other people. She thought she was bad and stupid. She went to camps and had a good time each time she went. She felt distant from her family.

In college she became affiliated with some activities and dated with the boys. One boy in particular was in love with her and pressed his attentions upon her. In the meanwhile, she felt that she was in love with another boy, who was of a different religion. She had many conflicts in her own mind because of the feelings of some members of her family. The boy ran into obstacles with his family, and the relationship was severed abruptly. At this point, the patient went into a sharp decline and was obliged to quit college.

Whereas this patient had found her greatest autonomy in her early adolescence around newly discovered social and sexual identities, she was not able to integrate these in her late adolescence. The incompatability of her religious identity with that of her boy friend and the ultimate frustration and collapse of her romance caused her to disintegrate completely and return to an archaic form of autistic performance. Her imagery, though sexually colored, became similar to that of the time she was struggling with her Oedipal situation and her oral frustrations.

To return now to the subject of integration rather than disintegration, there are many adaptations that the adolescent can make to satisfy some of the conflictual areas. Just as in the previous stages of development, during adolescence the adaptive quality of the ego organizes some of the distorted motivations or identities on the basis of secondary autonomy. Some identities overshadow the others in the establishment of fixed traits of an adaptive or defensive nature; hence one can develop foibles or idiosyncrasies with colorings characteristic of a particular orbit of operation.

For example, the conflictual portion of the ego adaptive reactions particularly concerned with the sexual identity may lead to the trait of brashness or brazenness or its opposite, prissiness or primness. On the social level, there may develop such traits as arrogance, insolence, high-handedness, and rebelliousness, vs. unobtrusiveness and subserviency. These two types stand in marked opposition to each other, the latter group serving as "yes-men", "stooges", or "hangers-on" to the blustering youths. The aggressive types of defensive ego reaction may show marked daredevilness or rashness of action; whereas the submissive types may show cowardice as a fixed character trait.

All adolescents have the faculty for daydreaming, but some attempt to dramatize or put into action some elements of their fantasy; whereas others adhere to strict secret fantasy. The faculty for extreme preoccupation with such imaginings leads to the exaggeration of this propensity in the form of a special ability exhibited by many adolescents, termed eidetic imagery. Fenichel designates individuals with this trait as having "perception fixations". Eidetic imagery or very clear or intense visual imagery is usually not a fixed trait but is lost after adolescence. It probably represents the use of the internal perceptual process as a type of defensive maneuver.

Whereas the adolescent period is one of flux and crisis, most young people are well able to weather the storm. Successful mastery of this period involves the integration of the libidinal drives and the environmental pressures into a unit or identity characteristic for each individual. As such, it prepares the individual for a positive way of life in the ensuing years.

| marriage · work · ego
| of the young adult ·   THE ADULT YEARS
| the mature adult ·
| adult conflict

The period of comparative calm that occurs at the close of the adolescent period, which was described as being similar to the calm of the late latency or prepubertal period, has a dynamic quality of its own. The forces which operated to produce the resolution of the Oedipal situation, namely repression and maturation, continue to exert their influence at this stage of ego growth. Several important dynamic processes related to repression and maturation seem to be operating at this time. Each of these certainly has an influence upon the others, and may be the motivating force which produces the others, but which is primary and which are secondary may be subject to differences of opinion. These are the observable phenomena: (1) an intensification of the superego; (2) an easing of pressure for sexual gratification; (3) a beginning of an appreciation for the values presented by the parents; (4) a focusing of interest on a single object choice.

The intensification of the superego may arise from the internalization of the ego ideal and from the guilt feelings resulting from the uncontrolled impulses which may have been released during the adolescent period. Accompanying this internal self-discipline may be a wave of morality and religious affirmation. By the repression of the sexual impulses, or as a result of it, the libidinal energies are driven to the selection of a single comparatively desexualized or superego charged object choice. In any case, there is a settling down of the individual into a less boisterous, more organized, more patient person who shows an interest in the adult world. The line of communication between the young adult and the parents and other adults is more nearly on a level of parity. Actually, this parity may in part be an acceptance and integration of the cultural standards of the parents without the necessity for the continual struggle. This equalization process occurs in part from an easing of the parental restrictions as the youngster attains his or her majority, but more especially does this occur when the young adults themselves seem more responsible and trustworthy.

The easing of the pressure for sexual gratification on the part of the males is obtained partly by having actual experience. The knowledge that he has partaken in this realm of human experience gives the young man stature with himself and among his friends. This obviously is a purely cultural determinant and may not necessarily be a universal reaction. The young adult female, however, if she still has not had full sexual experience, still prizes her virginity. The well adjusted young woman who has just passed her adolescence is strongly motivated toward marriage. The sexual or more specifically the matrimonial pressure is lessened at this time because if she is attractive and poised she will have had one or more proposals for marriage. This raises the girl's self-esteem in the same manner that the young man's is raised by sexual conquest.

As the libidinal pressures become less overwhelming and the internal controls become more effective, the appreciation of the standards of the parents as external objects becomes more understandable. Not only are the major considerations of parental lessons removed from the areas of conflict, but through the processes of identification become part of the individuals themselves. The cultural values or standards of the family become the standards for themselves. A good example of this point is illustrated in the novel, *The Late George Apley* by Marquand, wherein a young man attempts to break with his Bostonian background and marry outside of his accepted social sphere, only to return and fully accept as his own the staid Bostonian values of his father. Many persons tell of having appreciated the slogans and philosophies of their parents for the first time when they reached their late adolescence or early adult years. We shall discuss this more fully when we talk of the highest form of conceptual thinking, namely, the sense of values.

There are two other sobering effects upon the maturing process, which usher the youth or maiden from adolescence into adulthood. First is the actual object choice or falling in love with a marriageable partner and second is the awareness and mastery of the frustrations of the real life experiences in this period.

Let us consider the latter first. One or two frustrated romances in late adolescence is a usual rule. Either the young man and young woman did not get together because the desire for the affinity was not mutual or there were other intervening circumstances such as quarrels, family intervention, or loss of interest of one of the parties, etc. This could lead to serious emotional disturbances until the libidinal cathexis is sharply withdrawn. But with a high enough level of self-esteem, the individual in question can bounce back and let the experience serve as a challenge for a more satisfactory relationship later. Other frustrations may come when friends or room mates attain success in their love relationships and they are left behind. This, too, can be accepted as a challenge or defeat depending upon the ego organization of the person. The real frustrations serve the organism in the same manner sometimes as the artificially imposed discomforts of the initiation rites. Just as the young man was subjected to the humiliation and pain of the fraternity initiation before he could find himself in the society of men, the real life situations can act in similar ways.

A young man in analysis reported that the thing that finally made him feel like a man was the amputation of a foot while in college. This is an extreme case but it illustrates the point. He accepted the loss of his limb as punishment for all of his previously guilt-laden impulses. This young man was replete with slogans from his father, e.g., "You've got to pay for what you get," "You never get anything for nothing."

Now let us turn to the subject of the selection of a mate and the establishment of a permanent reciprocal affinity. We have already discussed to some extent the motivations for marriage of both sexes. The desire for the attainment of a sexual union and the desire to bring forth children become a mutual interest for both sexes. As pointed out earlier, the male is primarily interested in the coital aspect of the relationship, the female in the procreative. The actual mechanics of both of the phenomena are completely held in abeyance during the initial period of meeting and "falling in love."

Although the concept of falling in love or loving in general is one which is so vital to the processes of human living, psychoanalysts have not offered adequate explanations thus far for its occurrence. Take, for example, the statement made by Silverberg: "Until we can agree upon a definition of love, and until we can be certain that what we attempt to define is not merely an ideal but rather a capacity actually demonstrable in a large number of persons, I feel we do well to omit the capacity for this difficult-to-define something from the list of criteria of mental health, though possibly something of the kind belongs there."

Freud had many things to say on this subject which were largely descriptive. A few of his statements follow: "The highest form of development of which object-libido is capable is seen in the state of being in love, when the subject seems to yield up his whole personality in favor of object cathexis." "The state of being in love consists in a flowering-over of ego libido to the object. This state has the power to remove repressions and to restore perversions. It exalts the sexual object to the position of a sexual ideal. . . . Whatever fulfills this condition of love becomes idealized." On attraction between the sexes, he wrote: "When the object becomes a source of pleasurable feelings, a motor tendency is set up which strives to bring the object near to and incorporate it into the ego; we then speak of the 'attraction' exercised by the pleasure-giving object, and say that we 'love' that object."

Freud hints in some places that being in love is some sort of illness, a fact which we are certain he did not really mean. Take for example his following statement: "It (complete object-love) displays the marked sexual overestimation which is derived from the original narcissism of the child, now transferred to the sexual object. This sexual overestimation is the origin of the peculiar state of being in love, a state suggestive of a neurotic compulsion, which is thus traceable to an impoverishment of the ego in respect of libido in favor of the love-object."

The subject of falling in love or being in love and the one of object-choice or selection of a mate, although inseparate phenomena, for purposes of description should be considered separately. The actual state of being in love has many distinct qualities. Although the genital excitations remain the source of the driving energy, there are generalized features about the phenomenon that are quite apart from the actual stimulation and relief of the local areas. It is as though being in love is almost an end in itself. Freud's statement regarding overestimation or overevaluation of the object is a crucial point. But there are others, perhaps derivatives of the first, namely the acceptance of the wishes of the other person as being more important than one's own and the willingness to relinquish all other libidinal ties to family or others for the sake of the loved object. These are still only descriptive to a degree and do not fully describe the phenomenology. Even to apply metapsychological terminology such as the merging of the ego with the ego of the object does not fully satisfy the facts, even though this is a truism.

There is only one phenomenon in human behavior which seems to resemble that of being in love or falling in love, and that is the ecstasy or pleasant elevation of emotional spirit associated with the original response of establishing an emotional union with mother. This was described in the chapter on infancy as a pleasurable channel of communication with mother on a primary perceptual basis. It is the main ingredient of the religious experience and to a lesser degree the esthetic experience. Perhaps it is also the same as the "oceanic feeling" described by Freud [98].

The actual emotion of loving in the sense that is being discussed here is the one where this kind of feeling exists in the presence of a particular object and in the obsessionally acquired imagery of that individual. It is a clinical fact that this type of feeling, or the ability to fall in love, is predicated upon the prototype experience of the infant-mother ecstatic gratification. It is also axiomatic that the individual must have had a similar experience of communication or acceptance by the group. As stated earlier, the group of peers in the latency period is a symbolic duplicate of the mother. Thus, for the person to be able to enjoy freely the experience of valuing, or especially overevaluating, a person, he or she must have had both the gratifying experience with mother and the gratifying experience with the group. The outgrowths of the gratification as autonomous ego traits were described as trust and faith at the infant level and as loyalty on the group level. It always contains the elements of the feeling of belonging and the wish to preserve the love object. Loving and feelings of tenderness to specific objects require these basic learnings. Szurek [99] in his article "Learning to Love" emphasizes a similar point of view.

Although there are essential differences between male and female thinking, the ability to love and the basic feeling of security are learned from the mother with both sexes. The object then possesses in some aspects of the relationship, a quality of being a mother. In this connection, Blitzsten [100] pointed out that in psychoanalysis the psychoanalyst is always a symbol of the mother during a portion of every analysis. Thus, the protective parent is generally the mother and conversely the disciplinary parent for both sexes, as pointed out by H. Deutsch, is generally the father. To return to the religious experience, which was referred to as the union with mother, there may be some question as to the paternal identity of the Deity and the subject of phallic worship. This feeling of worship of the father or the phallus when studied further has its source in the symbolic relationships and memories of mother and the breast. The mother figure, or Mother Church, can also secondarily become the symbolic father. We have at points in our presentation referred to mother, in addition to this, as the symbolism of Heaven, Mother Nature, and the past in time, and to father as Hell, the Devil, the bogey man, and Father Time or the future. The ecstatic experience has a timelessness but also a quality of the denial of all evil. Evil may be symbolic of badness, originally bad mother but later bad father. There is nothing "bad" or "wrong" in the love relationship, however. The poets and songwriters equate "love," "mother," and "heaven." As loving leads to greater intimacies, nothing seems wrong both as to the qualities or deficiencies of the other person or what transpires in the relationship. This does not mean that to be in love means that one has not had resentments or hostilities in the course of his or her development, but it does mean that at the moment of loving these resentments are absent. As such it reactivates the unambivalent or preambivalent relationship of the early mother-child union.

The state of loving or falling in love, as described in the previous paragraphs, suggests a submissiveness to the partner and a participation in a magical union with the highly valued object. If this state of affairs were prolonged in this one-sided way, it would indeed be pathological as it would indicate a strong need for this state as a regression or repetition compulsion for earlier frustrations. The normal state of loving or remaining in love requires a similar inoculation of overevaluation or overestimation by the loved object. Otherwise the libidinal overestimation is withdrawn because this state of submission would be in decided conflict with the individual's autonomy or self-esteem. When the overevaluation is mutual then the reciprocal affinity becomes a self-perpetuating relationship.

The question of object-choice is the next one to be considered at this point. First, there is the matter of the attraction to the opposite sex. This has already been discussed as the outgrowth of the motivations arising from the excitations of the genital apparatus which lead to the desire to penetrate or to be penetrated. The male-female affinity which derived its theme from the Oedipal situation has led to the concept that "opposites attract." We can say categorically that this is as far as the concept goes; i.e., only as to respective male and female identities. There is another just as important concept, namely, "What do we have in common?" Freud pointed out how the narcissism or appreciation of one's self, or more specifically one's own body image, is an important factor in the selection of a mate. Certainly this is true in the animal kingdom where mate selectivity regarding species and colorings runs fairly true to form. If one were to observe large groups of people and were to look at the physical makeup and facial contours of the couples, one would find striking similarities in appearance. The idea that married couples get to look alike is a mistaken notion. The truth is that they often look alike at the time of their marriage. Easy confirmation of this concept can be obtained by observing the pictures of couples to be married in the society pages of the newspaper. This physical identity is but one small factor. The other elements that go to make up an identity seek similar parallels in the identity of the mate. Thus even an unstable makeup of a person may lead that individual to find another with a similar emotional makeup. It is a common whim among psychiatrists that "one neurotic will marry another neurotic." Colby [101] mentioned the natural matching of defense mechanisms in the male and female which occurs is an attempt to establish a harmonious marital syndrome. Other factors beside that of the finding of one's own identity in the other person are those of finding in the object elements of what one was formerly (a regressive binding) or what one would like to be (a progressive binding). In the latter instance the person's own ego ideal can serve as the pattern which is fulfilled in the identity of the mate. On the id motivational level in the female in particular, the desire for a penis or a masculine identity can be satisfied in the maleness of the mate.

Another factor in the object-choice is tied up with the Oedipal situation itself. Resemblances to the incestuous objects either in physical appearance or in the advanced age of the love object are familiar to all observers. The object-choice may bear many unconscious resemblances to the infantile or Oedipal external objects. These resemblances may not always be salutory as they may even represent the defects or habit traits which are least desirable or which may have given the individual a great deal of trouble in his lifetime. The new attachment may carry enough of the libidinal ties to the original incestuous object to help the individual bridge the gap of relinquishment of the original parent figure. On a defiance or reaction-formation basis, this object-choice can reach extreme proportions of oppositeness from the incestuous object. For example, selection of a widely divergent race, e.g., White-Negro, White-Oriental, or different economic, ethnic, or religious affiliations may represent this denial of attachment to the incestuous objects. Similarly, selecting a much younger person may be a similar denial of the incestuous object and may at the same time represent a perpetuation of the early youth attachments. As to the object-choice on the homosexual level, this is the arch denial of incestuous object-selection. The dynamics of such cases may be quite complicated as pointed out in previous pages. There is present to a marked degree the narcissism or love of the carbon copy of the self, but more important is the question of the sexual identity. The "feminine position" represents a submissive attitude to the feared and hated male as a means of obtaining ascendency and control over him. This phenomenon is fairly normal in the female but decidedly abnormal in the male. The "male position" is the subjugation of the female as a victory over other males or as a means of subduing the female. The ecstatic experience of the successful operation of this act is experienced by these people as "love" or "falling in love," but this type of loving which occurs in homosexuals is so completely involved with defense mechanisms and repressed hostilities that it has an entirely different character from heterosexual love. Furthermore, homosexual loving, besides being "counterfeit" (Bergler), has all the social pressures and condemnations of an intolerant society. Whereas normal heterosexual love, especially when it is adequately reciprocated, leads to the proposal and acceptance of the institution of marriage. Just in passing, we might say that marriage is still a highly respected phenomenon in our culture.

Let us now turn our attention to the thinking processes of the young couple in love who are moving toward a decision that the union should be perpetuated by marriage. This decision is one which in our culture is primarily made by the young people themselves rather than one which has been made in advance by the parents. Nevertheless, a certain amount of parent-participation still takes place, not always to the pleasure of the young people. The participation is generally looked upon as parental interference and may be dealt with in the manner of the general emancipation at adolescence or by confusion of loyalties.

Let us be mindful of the fact that there are many cultural factors which encourage and discourage the emancipatory processes and discourage obedience to parental wishes. The mechanical age, the urbanization of the population, transportation, the movies, and television all combine to furnish many ideas including those about marriage which tend to undermine the exclusive authority of parents in our culture. Furthermore, the tenacious quality of the state of "romantic love" brooks few obstacles from any source, including parents. A more important consideration than mere parental disapproval is the economic factor. Even in the emotional state of bilateral romantic love, there is still the reality concept of making a living. In fact, this element of the occupational goal, or at least the promise of some work success, acts as a great determining factor in the establishment of sufficient self-esteem to allow the ego to move in the direction of this new growth experience.

Dependency needs in either sex or the needs of those in whom there is a strong motivation to get away from a troubled home situation are other driving forces, but these clearly fall into the conflictual or adaptive reaction patterns and do not form the basis for the true reciprocal affinity which occurs with well adjusted autonomous young adults.

Up to the point of the betrothal or engagement there is a strong sense of ascendency with ivory-tower fantasies, mutually shared, of the relationship itself. Within the structure of this period of courtship or romancing, there may arise grave doubts as to the sincerity or intentions of one or the other of the parties. These doubts lead to varying degrees of anxiety or anticipatory excitement especially provoked when the opposite member may seem to exhibit a diminished ardor. Prior to the binding of the troth and sometimes shortly thereafter, there may exist other doubts in the minds of both parties. There may be doubts of the fact of marriage itself as well as those of choice of the mate. "Can this be really true?" "Am I doing the right thing?" "Will he be able to make a living?" "What am I getting into?" "Will I miss my freedom?" These doubts represent a lag in the maturation. It is as if the person is taking one last look at childhood and adolescence.

The consummation of the engagement by the purchase of a diamond ring by the young man for the young lady or to a lesser degree the "pinning" ritual, giving the girl his fraternity pin (a pre-engagement ceremony, e.g. "engaged to be engaged") represent symbolically the awarding of the phallus to the female. The girl's display of the pin or engagement ring is clearly a substitute for the phallus which she does not have in actuality but now does have in effigy. With the exhibition of this token there is accorded the young lady a tremendous spurt in her self-esteem. For the young man, the feeling that he is capable of affording this amount of gratification to the object that he esteems in like manner serves as a boost to his self-esteem.

The engagement period shows many changes in the individuals in question, depending of course on the many circumstances of the life situation itself. In some people the fact of the engagement motivates them to erase all doubts as to the wisdom of their choice of mate. Even to the point of rationalizing away slight defects that may have been noted, the parties in question now are convinced that each has found the "one and only" in the other. However, there are many realities as to marriage plans and readjustments and realignments of family relationships. For the engaged people a big problem is the one of premarital sexual intercourse. In the course of courtship, the biological forces have been operating to bring the couple into situations of increasing intimacy. There is never any turning back after new levels of sexual intimacies have been enjoyed. Even though most engaged couples agree in principle that actual complete intercourse should be reserved for after the wedding ceremony, a large percentage do not wait for the official event. According to a survey by Wallin and Burgess [102], 47 to 49 per cent of young women engaged in premarital intercourse. This figure is in sharp contrast to a study of the 1890 era which showed an incidence of female premarital intercourse of 7 to 13 per cent. While we are reporting figures, we might add that these same authors showed an increase in the percentage of marriages in the general population over the same period from 59 to 74 per cent for males and from 69 to 81 per cent for females. The figures for unmarried women and unmarried men as released by the U. S. Census Bureau are very different, as they include widows and divorcees as "unmarried." These figures show a preponderance of unmarried females in the general population as compared to males. This will be discussed later as it is not part of the subject we are now discussing.

The engagement period is fraught with many perplexities and fumblings whether or not there has been actual intercourse. The ego ideals of each of the two partners is afforded an opportunity for comparison with those of the other. Even before this there is a testing period when the relative temperaments are revealed. The ego traits of dominance or submissiveness, impetuousness, procrastination, punctuality, tidiness, generosity, or others may be amenable to some adjustments by one or both principals if they are not extreme. What is most amenable to modification is the mutual establishment of the new ego ideal. It is worth mentioning at this point that some counsel and support from parents as to the realities of marriage is warranted. Successful marriages by both families furnish laboratory examples of such ideals, especially as the experiences in mastering the practical problems of living are discussed and shared. By merging the two ideals with what would be mutually beneficial to a successful marriage, a goal can be established which can become internalized into the superego. By virtue of the common interests and goals and by virtue of the high esteem that the two people have for each other, a set of standards for the union can easily be set at this time. The mistake is often made by one or both parties that these things are "taken for granted," only to find some disillusionment later. All other contractual relations have all sorts of specifications and stipulations, but marriages often wait for the ceremony to bring this about. In this respect, the emphasis of marriage as a duty or obligation of two people to each other seems to be changing to a concept of friendship and companionship. The ideal of each "respecting the other's wishes" cannot be carried to a point of license where the obligations of fidelity and trustworthiness are not suitably contained. These goals need clarification on a conceptual basis and need to be established as ego ideals during the engagement period.

marriage

The wedding ceremony is an event of highly emotional significance. There are many points in common with the initiation rites. It is actually the last real acceptance into the world of adults. All cultures, including so-called primitive tribes, make much of the marriage ceremony. The major element in the ceremony is the public sanction to engage in sexual union. With this permission goes the promise to remain faithful and to afford mutual protection and adoration. From the social point of view this is centered largely around the female. Thus the wedding ceremony is largely a bride-centered function.

Inasmuch as the father "gives the bride away," he relinquishes his incestuous demands upon the daughter and gives her permission to form a liaison with her new love-object. This is such a sad situation that often the bride weeps, as do many sympathetic females in the audience. Other affects related to doubts, shame, and guilt are allayed or dissipated in the reverential atmosphere of the religious or judicial service. The ring ceremony is clearly symbolic of the act of penetration, although it is performed in reverse.

A most noteworthy feature of the wedding ceremony, and one which makes this occasion one of such great interest, is the emotional effect upon the guests who observe the function. For the successfully married people their own marriage vows are reiterated by identification with either the bride or groom. It is as though they were being married once again. For the unmarried females there is also an identification and a hope that some day this will be happening to them. For the males the wedding sometimes releases ideas about marriage that they had never permitted themselves to think about, particularly the concept that all this public sanction for sexual abandon could be true. At the termination of the ceremony, with the blessing of the minister and the good wishes of the parents and friends, there is a sudden almost orgiastic release of tension which signals the beginning of the festivities. The marriage celebration is a happy occasion with much hilarity and gaiety in all cultures. The bride generally removes the veil, which has a symbolism of its own, and joins the festivities. Sometimes in the course of the celebration, the bride and groom slip away on their honeymoon.

Let us get away from the specific details and discuss the subject of marriage in general. George Bernard Shaw [103] made the statement that the institution of marriage is a success because it is a place "where there is the maximum of temptation and the maximum of opportunity." Sociologists, however, take a much more pessimistic point of view. The fact that one out of every four marriages ends in divorce lends some credence to the concept that in our culture there is a high measure of instability in the institution of marriage, but still there are the three marriages out of four which do not end in divorce. Certainly some of these are successful. Questionnaires which have been given married couples as to whether they considered themselves completely contented have given results varying from 5 per cent to 15 per cent with the majority of studies closer to the smaller figure. This fact and the general knowledge of the large number of discontented people that everyone knows about have led numerous investigators to devise methods for the prediction of the success or failure of marriages. Inasmuch as our emphasis at this point is upon normal ego growth, let us concentrate on the relatively small number of individuals who are "divinely happy".

Inasmuch as the institution of marriage has changed from a compulsory love-honor-obey to a voluntary self-imposed relationship and from a parental selection to a self-selection of object-choice, there are chances for both greater successes and greater failures. Success of a marriage relationship depends upon the establishment and adherence to the joint ego ideal established at the time of the courtship. This means that all the reality factors and the instinctual drives have been adequately dealt with on an autonomous ego level. As such, it presupposes a well functioning ego in each of the partners. The romantic love of the engaged couple is slowly replaced by a newer and more realistic reciprocal affinity termed "conjugal love." Duvall and Hill [104] point out that conjugal love appears in the companionable phase of the engagement and develops greatly during the early months of marriage.

When the realities of married life become apparent to the young couple, there is often an early phase of let-down or disillusionment. This is particularly true in young people from small families who have never observed the operation of establishment of a home by brothers and sisters. Add to this the desire to "go it alone" without parental help or supervision and there is understandable confusion and anxiety in the minds of many young married people. There is little doubt that in nearly all marriages the expectation that the union will last a lifetime and will bring forth children is present. When children are planned and hoped for, the chances for success of a marriage are greater. This point has been statistically validated by Wallin and Burgess. They point out that persons with higher marital success scores tend to have a stronger desire for children, whether they have them or not, than those with lower marital success scores.

Marriage entails the assumption by each of the partners of a new role or identity. The role of the "married woman" assumes a quality of ego integration that can be both relaxed and replete with confidence and self-esteem. For the married man there is similarly a feeling of pride, a giving up of the "chase" and diversion of energy into new channels. These two roles of husband and wife augment each other through the mutual appreciation of each other's roles as home-maker and provider respectively.

For a marriage to be a success the two parties involved must not consider themselves as solo performers each playing his own selection, but rather as a harmonious duet. It does not mean that the two people must act as one, but rather as separate individuals with each making his or her contribution. Just as in music, there are moments of complete fusion and there are others in which the counterpoint of each personality lends to the enrichment of the theme. With this there should emerge a measure of ego growth which is higher than that which had been attained individually.

It is interesting to note what the sociologists say about marriage. Psychiatrists are concerned with individual cases and sometimes lose sight of the over-all picture. La Piere for example [105] not only describes marriage and the family system as being in complete decay, but seems to advocate the concept that the institution is not worth saving. He says that clergymen and novelists are the only ones who preserve the spiritual ideal of the family. "Such idealization," says he, "is more probably a reflection of public nostalgia for the 'good old days' than of any deep conviction that the old family system is essential to human welfare."

Although modern invention has to some extent freed women from some of the arduous tasks of the home and women to a large extent have proved they can be self-supporting if they choose to be, it is indeed open to question whether such a statement as "women have long since escaped from the home" is entirely true. Nor does the experience of most students of human behavior condone La Piere's statement that "the institution of the family exists today mainly as ideological fragments and outmoded social sentiments." He considers modern marriage as a purely experimental relationship. He stresses, as do other sociologists, the "companionship" aspect of marriage, a phenomenon which is presumably brand new and has never existed before. He is also quite cynical about this, as he says that it may by sheer luck be secured through a marital relationship.

This type of sociological teaching, although purely "realistic" from the point of view of the statistics, makes no more sense than it does to advocate crime because there is such a high rate of crime in this country. Certainly there is something wrong with both, just as there is with homosexuality or schizophrenia. Decay or deterioriation in any form is hardly progress in any sense.

There is no question about the fact that there are many changes in our society and in family life in particular which are both the results of influences in the culture and at the same time causes for new difficulties or aberrations of adjustment of the individuals within the social structure. On the sociological level, these present the same picture that the vicious cycle of emotional disease presents to the individual, e.g., he is sick because he is nervous and he is nervous because he is sick. It would appear then that we are dealing, according to Fromm [106], with one "sick society" and the sick society affects people. Certainly there are indications that this is so, but the question arises as to whether there has ever been a time or place in history where the social structure was entirely "healthy". We can only describe what exists, with all of its defects, and attempt to make our adjustments and hope that with these adjustments the total picture can change. Thus healthier people can be in a better position to shape a healthier society.

Although it is beyond the scope of this book even to attempt to make widespread observations of the social scene, a few salient facts seem to find expression from working with individuals who present personal problems. One point which stands out in sharp contrast to other cultures and even to our own culture at a previous time in history is the change in the relative position of maleness and femaleness. In Japan or Egypt, for example, wives may not eat with their husbands and must walk a few paces behind their husbands when going down the street. Wives are trained to serve the best interests of the man. In our society there is presumably an open "battle of the sexes" where the females have striven for "equality" or perhaps even a position of dominance. Bergler refers to the basic contempt that females have for males in his allusion to the "myth of the he-man". It seems that males almost consciously give the female a place in the sun because of the guilt involved in all of the males' advantages. Formerly man dominated woman through physical strength. He hunted game and dragged logs to the fire and felt that it was his due to be in the position of dominance. Today, with a push-button economy, women do not need the male display of strength nor do they fear it as much.

However, here too we run into all sorts of paradox. Males jealously guard their alleged position of social supremacy and revel in the chance to have a woman serve their needs, and at the same time they resent the idea that they must be indebted to the woman for this service and thereby put themselves in a position of dependency. Certainly this is a reflection of the dominance-submissiveness struggle that exists in many people and reflects itself in the male-female struggle. The implications of the so-called masculinization of women and its attendant effeminization of man have a great deal to do with the concept of a successful marriage, but more important than this alone is the influence that such changed relationships have upon the rearing and indoctrination of children. Certainly there may be some very successful marriages between two people who may suitably adjust their respective ego traits and ego ideals to each other as a team but who would not be in the position to afford the necessary elements for the proper care of their offspring.

Let us examine one or two other items that seem to have a bearing on this subject, for example, the cultural attitude toward alcohol. Drinking, to some extent, has become very much a part of current Americana. Presumably to have a few drinks in a social situation inhibits the highest level of ego activity and superego functioning so that social anxiety is more adequately controlled. Because of the guilt from the drinking itself or from the release of repressed instinctual forces, the person who drinks feels himself accused and defends himself (or herself) against this by accusing the would-be accusers. Thus to the social drinker, the non-drinker is a "stuffed shirt", a "wet blanket", or a "deadhead". As such, there may be leveled at him the threat to his adult status (or masculinity) and he may be influenced to join the crowd.

Loosening of the reciprocal affinities through the casual flirtations and infidelities of the drinking party is encouraged by the loosening of some of the inhibition of expression. A well established marriage, for example, may be strained when one or the other parties is accused of being dominated by the other. "Gosh, you are stuffy! Relax!" "She leads you around by the nose!" "How can you stand that husband of yours?" "Who wears the pants in your family?" Then there is the competition in the economic scene. The keeping-up-with-the-Jonses tradition is such an important motivation. If the family car is more than two years old, or if one is seen in the same dress more than one season, or if the other ladies have better fur coats, tension and friction may result. These things are all too familiar.

The effects of both World Wars, the Prohibition era, and the current world tension have all had their hand in influencing the society in which we live. Volumes have been written on this subject by social psychologists and others. Still there are many things that occur before our eyes which we either refuse to see or feel helpless to deal with. Certainly the Kefauver report points out many things. Yet comparatively few people know its contents. We will speak more of this later.

As to the looseness of the marriage ties themselves, men who need to travel as part of their jobs or women who feel it important that they have careers of their own, make for a family situation that is not conducive to a permanent intense degree of conjugal love. It seems that the situation in which the man is the breadwinner and the woman is the homemaker and takes a great deal of pride of accomplishment in the successes enjoyed by the husband, furnishes the happiest solution to emotional adjustment in our culture. A well adjusted male does not object to and even enjoys, the support he receives from his wife, and her self-esteem is high when she feels she is needed and valued.

A successful marriage is one in which there is an enrichment of the ego organization of each partner. Out of the relation there grows a mutual respect for each other's role, especially when the established "ground rules" have been no hardship to either partner. These ground rules or combined ego ideals may have taken a few years to work out, especially when they had not been worked out in advance. This occurs particularly when issues had never been anticipated or when crises of various sorts made this mutual reshuffling of principles necessary. The instinctual pressures of being the only child or the favored one operate in both sexes. Furthermore, all the old jealousies and rivalries of the Oedipal situation seem to maintain the intactness of the marital situation both by the elimination of all competitors and by the elevation of self-esteem afforded the mate whose affections are so closely guarded.

Aside from the mere "obedience" of the ground rules set up by the partners of the conjugal relationship, there is an internal quality of superego or ego ideal control which helps people maintain a stable marriage. Often in the early years of marriage there may occur some regressive behavior such as the indiscriminate or less discriminate love-making with a chance object. The remorse reactions that occur after-ward, such as the consideration of the feeling of unfairness to the mate who has placed all faith and confidence in the other, can make the casual relationship an entirely sordid and unclean affair.

Disturbances in the original Oedipal situation produce disturbances in the marital relationship. To discuss all the permutations and combi-nations of the reactions of husband to wife and vice versa would cover the whole field of psychopathology. Suffice it to say at this time that the marital relationship has within it the capacity to bring out not only the best in people, but also the worst. One wonders why young people who are romantically in love later fail to establish the conjugal love relationship. The answer can usually be found in the fact that the partner assumes a role in the mind of the individual in which he or she is no longer a non-incestuous object but instead a symbolic repre-sentation of the parent. This works a particular hardship when the parent figure has been critical, frightening, or unfriendly so that the free interchange of libido becomes seriously impaired. There may be not only a withholding of affection in the form of frigidity or impotence but evidence of overt hostility in the form of irritability, infidelity, or other breaches of the ground rules.

Unfortunately, there are many marriages in which failure to main-tain the reciprocal affinity produces the reverse picture. There may exist what appears to be a postmarriage rebound phenomenon. Whereas the premarital or daily marital relationships were associated with a good deal of overestimation and rationalization about the fine choice he or she had made, when the cycle is reversed, the same energies are applied in producing a set of rationalizations in the direction of devaluation. Whereas formerly one could see no faults in the other, when this process sets in, one fails to see any virtues in the other. Whether easy divorce laws would tend to encourage the devaluation rationalization processes one hesitates to say, but when such a phenomenon does take place there has been a great deal of hostility already engendered which may be very hard to reverse or keep in bounds. The conceptualizations arising from the rationalization process are defensive maneuvers against emotional tension of childhood in-stinctual conflict or the conflict of ideals or values, which is more characteristic of the adult thinking processes.

work

Let us turn once again to the subject of man and his work. The adult years see the crystallization of the ideal in choice of vocation as well as choice of mate. It is the fortunate man who is capable of carrying to fruition the occupational identity which was established in his earlier years. Equally important is the value accrued to the individual himself in his ability to maintain a motivation for sustained and useful work, even if the eventual goal is not the same as that for which he prepared himself.

The ego gratification that comes from man's work is not only in the expression of a skill or talent but rather it is one of purpose or direction. The motivation to work, in other words, becomes intimately bound with what one may be working for. These gratifications can be of a purely narcissistic nature such as the admiration of one's own handiwork or of an altruistic nature such as provision of the wherewithal for the care of one's family.

Let us first consider work from the angle of the basic instincts and from the ego traits which emerge at early levels of organization of the individual. As mentioned earlier, Bartemeier mentioned work as having its roots in eating. Then absorbing work or education as a process of ingestion follows. It is not surprising then that the conflictual ego trait of greed may tie up with the hunger for knowledge or the motivation to "swallow the world." The anal aspects of work, e.g., creative and the urethral (phallic) competitive components, with their associated ambition, pride, and displays, are all factors which enter into the work situation. One consideration, however, which is particularly worthy of mention regarding work is the matter of the job or position itself. Because of the fact that the place of employment is the agency for gratifying the narcissistic needs of the individual, it is not difficult to see how a dependency situation is established. As such, the job to these people becomes the symbolic equivalent of the protective mother.

As Ginsburg points out, there are distinct ego values placed upon the concept of hard work. These become watchwords and slogans which both rationalize the action and motivate the individual for greater action. The social and economic advantages that arise from the recognition of good work enhance the concept of the value of work. The autonomy, self-esteem, and assertiveness factors which particularly accrue from the feeling of accomplishment through one's own effort are noteworthy. As to the concept of the "self-made man", there are other ego growth factors, particularly the fact that that individual may feel that he by-passed his father in attaining his goal. We can see that work acts not only as a device for the direct gratification of the impulses, but also as a means of sublimating some of these impulses. Not only through this sublimation but because of some of the other factors mentioned, the activity of useful work serves as a defense mechanism against anxiety and depression. As such, one can say that work is a useful device for the integrative functions of the ego.

Because of the ego integrative value of work, many individuals utilize the work situation to keep their hold on reality when there are disturbing situations in other areas. On the other hand, there are other persons whose disintegration is first manifested by an inability to carry out the work situation. Sometimes this creates added problems in that the guilt for not being a provider may fortify the illness. The inhibition of working often turns out to be an inhibition of aggressiveness or assertiveness. The imagery of destructiveness either to the fellow workers, to the boss, or to the work itself may lead to fantastic conflicts in the face of confusion in other areas. Fenichel in this connection mentions that often work inhibition represents the superego type of inhibition. He also points out, as do others, that conflicts regarding work merely represent the general attitude toward "duty", hence call forth the conflicts regarding authority. Compliance-defiance, rebellion-obedience are the polarities of attitudes towards work. In such a situation work as such or the job in particular can be symbolic of the authoritative parent. More specifically, the boss, foreman, or employer can represent the punishing father (or bad mother) as a transference figure from early childhood conflicts. The reaction type of working situation where the desire to quit is compensated for by an over-determined motivation to work, may be revealing of the mocking type of compliance. The late Judge Edelbert Gary [107], the famous steel magnate, some years ago said, "I work hard because all my life I have struggled against my natural tendency to be lazy." In relation to the matter of work success, there is one ego quality which seems to be one of major importance in the American scene. It is the matter of having a "pleasing personality" or an ability to "get along with people." This is an outgrowth of the trait of "charm" which was mentioned in the chapter on adolescence. In many other parts of the world it has been and probably still is more nearly the truth that there is a direct relationship between the ability, skill, and creativeness of the individual and the recognition he receives. There is the one notable exception, of course, which is the matter of racial or religious prejudice, but with these factors neutralized, an outstanding person is one of outstanding abilities or one who has made major contributions. The boy "most likely to succeed" in our culture is not the one who has the highest marks in school. There are other intangibles which are measured by extracurricular activities and the social identity. These are important factors in the matter of success in the industrial and professional worlds. Personnel managers and business executives are alert to the potentialities of the people whom they hire or offer promotions as much for their effectiveness in getting along with their co-workers or their customers as they are for their technical skills. It is a unique phenomenon in our culture that very frequently the physicians with large practices are ones with a "bedside manner" and not necessarily the ones whose names appear in the medical literature. This phenomenon is such an important ingredient of success that books like Carnegie's *How to Win Friends and Influence People* are best sellers.

ego of the young adult

This section will be devoted to a discussion of the ego development of the individual prior to the peak of maturity. In this precursor stage, represented by the young adult, we shall consider the integration of ego in two spheres of operation, namely, the establishment of a home and the realization of an occupational goal. Parenthood, which is the sequence of these aspects of ego function, becomes the focal point around which is crystallized the gratification of home and the motivation toward job success. Out of the concepts of matrimony, parenthood, and job realization, emerge a series of ego traits. These are the ability to establish conjugal love, which is a permanent reciprocal affinity, a feeling of confidence, self-reliance, and industriousness, and the willingness to bring forth children and to assume the responsibility for their care. Here we re-emphasize an important point. The forementioned ego traits receive their original impetus from instinctual motivations, but they are finally formed from the learning or cognitive functions of the individual. Thus we see the importance of salutary life experiences, wholesome identifications, and healthy outlook on the development of ego traits.

In the young adult, the reciprocal affinity, which we have seen develop from adolescence, becomes an autonomous ego trait. This means that two young adults are now ready to maintain matrimony because they are able to fulfill the basic requirements of marriage such as sexual love, mutual tolerance, respect, and common goals and a preparedness to be parents. The desire to have children, from the point of view of the individual, is made of several ingredients. Perhaps the strongest motivation is narcissistic. The wish to perpetuate one's self is very strong. There is also the desire to recreate the image of the love object the desire to produce in one object the representation of the union. Other ego traits, which arose in previous stages of development, such as creativity, pride, and self-esteem, are now again operative in the development of the role of parent.

It is of interest here to differentiate the concept of parenthood in the male and in the female. In the male unconscious, the ability to become a father means that he has not been castrated. The child is living proof of his potency. Here we see how the ego traits of self-esteem and pride are realized. For this the father bestows upon the child his love and his willingness to protect and provide. In the female, the operation of the unconscious is more complicated. Here we deal with two sets of fantasies. One concerns the imagery of the interior of the body and the other is the outgrowth of the wish for a penis. During pregnancy the woman feels full. Even extremely neurotic and sometimes psychotic women have the sense of well being. Gestation counteracts the feeling of emptiness which has its oral origins. At the birth of the child, the stable woman has a feeling of accomplishment and gratification. The neurotic woman, on the other hand, may feel that she has lost something and suddenly finds herself in competition with her child, who is now a separate object. The feeling of fullness may also be correlated with penis envy. The fantasy which developed during the Oedipal period, that of the wish for a penis, first from the mother and then from the father, followed by the compromise for the wish for a baby from the father, now reaches its unconscious fulfillment. The feeling of fullness in the unconscious is related to the fantasy of having the penis within one's self. This may be the reason some neurotic women react to the birth of the child as if it were a form of castration. In the normal woman, where the imageries are not so intense, there is a strong cultural impact on the attitude toward pregnancy. In a civilization where the emphasis is on a high birth rate, pregnancy is very fashionable and a woman has stylish pride in her distorted figure. In our culture a woman is often impatient with her pregnancy and anxiously awaits the return of her slim figure and her ability to resume an active social or occupational life.

Now we shall return to the ego traits of confidence, self-reliance, and industriousness. These too are discussed from the male and female points of view. The young adult male begins to assume the responsibility for independent maintenance and for the support of his dependents. In our culture, the full assumption of financial burden may be delayed by prolonged educational training or military service. In many instances, where families are unable to help, marriage among young adults is postponed. However, with good maturation, the ego traits exist. The feeling of self-reliance and confidence is reflected in all the activity of the young adult. This invites the trust and reliance of others upon the individual who, gaining recognition and encouragement, responds with added increments of ego growth.

The ego traits of the autonomous young adult female will be considered from two points of view, namely, the management of home and children and the management of her career. In spite of all the cultural emancipation of women, urbanization, and the availability of mechanical and commercial substitutes for functions formerly performed in the home, the concept of home remains strong in most young women. The actual realization of the home may come later but the wish is present at this stage of development. In recent years, the importance of home-making has been recognized. Courses in homemaking are now included in the curricula of many schools and colleges. This trend encourages the natural feminine role and prepares young women to accept the position of homemaker as a positive goal. The ego traits of industry and creativity are afforded great opportunity for expression in the home. The young woman who feels that her home reflects good taste and that her table deserves praise receives a high measure of gratification. Becoming a homemaker is the goal realization of the organizational thinking of the little girl. However, if the work identity of the female adolescent is away from the home, the role of housewife may present difficulties. However, it is remarkable that in spite of this, when the ego organization of husband and wife are well integrated, the wife's interest can shift to meet the circumstances of maintaining a home. The importance of the home even to the point of its libidinization will be discussed in the next section.

In our culture, the young woman, either by personal choice or force of circumstance, may turn to a career. Where no conflict exists, the young woman expresses her ego traits of industriousness, confidence and reliance in about the same manner as does the young adult male. Although some young women seem to integrate home and career, especially if there are no children, others present difficulties. Women with strong masculine identification or those who have invested much in preparing for a career and resent the loss of this identity, e.g., the actress, the doctor, may do so poorly as homemakers that it may be wise for them to remain in their chosen careers. Obligation to remain in the home may create serious emotional difficulties in these women.

Let us now turn our attention to the young adults who did not develop autonomy but who are in conflict because of disturbances carried over from previous stages of development. There are young men and women of marriageable age who find reasons for postponing marriage or continually proclaim that they cannot find the "right" person. These people, because of their own foibles and idiosyncracies, are really unattractive to other people. In addition, their own attitudes are such as to sabotage any opportunity. Such phenomena as latent or actual homosexuality and sadomasochism, which represent unsolved conflicts from the Oedipal period, militate against the formation of a normal conjugal relationship.

The situation that is most familiar to the psychoanalyst is the one in which a reciprocal affinity which might lead to marriage is sabotaged by one of the partners by virtue of his or her disturbed thinking processes. It seems that when a person has been rejected in childhood, the pattern of being unloved and unwanted remains as a fate or destiny in future human relations. It is a clinical fact that such an individual manages to engineer his life situations so that he is rejected by the partner. If the rejection does not occur, then the individual takes an active role in rejecting the prospective mate. In other words, this type of person needs to reject or be rejected. It is as though the rejection theme operates in such a way that it must be present either in a passive or active way. This is, of course, due to the overprinting or montage of the childhood pattern onto the new reality to make it fit or resemble the old pattern. Such behavior is motivated by the repetition compulsion in which the person is impelled to make the present resemble the past. Although the repetition compulsion is usually destructive, it can sometimes offer a prospect for the establishment of a relationship. The following case is an example of such a solution:

The analysand was a disturbed young woman with great feelings of inferiority. Actually the inferiority was not based on reality, because she was attractive, intelligent, and well educated. She had had several opportunities to marry attractive and eligible young men. In each instance she retreated into panic or found some reason to reject the male. After a period of therapy, she met a suitable young man who wished to marry her. Having gained insight into her previous behavior patterns, she guarded against destroying the relationship. She harbored many imaginary faults but did not express them to him. Because of her own feeling of inferiority, it was necessary that he be less than he actually was so she could be his equal. In this way it was permissible for her to love him. In addition, another factor operated toward cementing this relationship. In many respects his family was a duplicate of hers. Her father was an alcoholic, much to the shame of the family. She felt contaminated by the actions of the father so that, as a little girl, she felt "dirty and from the wrong side of the tracks." The prospective father-in-law was eccentric and quite paranoid. The family were shamed by him and tried to ignore his actions as much as possible. This was reminiscent of her family pattern and gave her a sense of familiarity. She admitted that had her fiance's father been an outstanding gentleman, she would have been so uncomfortable and frightened that she would have probably run away from the situation. As it was, she fitted into the family and made preparations for marriage upon the completion of her analysis.

If people with serious neurotic conflicts marry for any reason, be it social or economic, the marriage often fails. The divorce rate is very high among this group. Here, too, serious breakdowns, suicides, and even homicide occur. Perhaps it would be better if these people were not to marry. They may make satisfactory adjustments in their occupational life but are dismal failures in the marriage situation. The home in particular seems to be the area in which all the childhood ego adaptations or maladaptations seem to repeat themselves. Hence, the neurotic ego conflicts find their greatest play when disturbed people marry. The phenomenon of repetition compulsion induces the individual to re-enact the old situations. The wife may try to make the husband resemble her father by his actions. The husband may try to force his wife into the patterns of his mother. Often the neurotic in-laws exert their unhealthy influence to further complicate the marriage. Sometimes two people with mild neurotic ego reactions can make satisfactory adjustments to each other. This is accomplished by each accepting the other's eccentricities and respecting each other's qualities. Others with the autonomous trait of "sportsmanship" feel that they will make the "best of the bargain" and adjust accordingly. Religious principles and super-ego factors operate to make a successful integration of the marriage situation.

A certain number of young adults, by virtue of hidden inferiorities or as a defense against actual frustration, assume a false front of sophistication. This blasé, worldly-wise attitude is an adaptation or a cover-up for disillusionment in the life situation. It contains elements of exhibitionism as well as aggressive ego traits. The ego trait of conceit is closely related to pseudosophistication. These young people seem to have an exaggerated opinion of themselves, especially after they have had their first taste of goal attainment. The young person in the business world may become quite obnoxious with his feelings of indispensability. As a result of this attitude, the young man or woman may overextend himself or herself. This overextension may involve the assumption of responsibilities beyond the ability to handle them. There is also the young man or woman who never gets going. These are the ones who, in spite of hope, mark time indefinitely. The young man may not like his job but because of fear or because of family responsibilities he stays in a "rut". The lack of venture on the part of these young people is bound up with basic personality traits. Dependency, inadequacy, and cowardice render a person unwilling to venture too far toward goal attainment. He is likely to be satisfied with a small measure of goal realization because of his fear of losing what he already has.

The ego adaptive trait of conceit described previously can show its opposite in the young man or woman who is thoroughly unsophisticated or naive as to the real problems of marriage and the occupational world. As many young men and women have not had to make a living for themselves while they were in school, they do not have realistic pictures of what to expect. Women are more fortunate in this respect as they can maintain a high degree of naiveté in the married state. Men who are thus immature or inadequate in their makeups may do perfectly well in a marriage where they can maintain their dependency needs but where their self-esteem is not threatened. To assume fatherhood, however, is another story. This new level of identity will seriously threaten the adaptive processes which were able to integrate work and marriage into a working unit but which cannot withstand further alteration.

There are some young adults who have reached this age without having established an efficacious start toward goal realization. They are the ones who constantly complain that misfortune always comes their way or that it is someone else's fault that they are not progressing. Such a trait, successlessness or inefficaciousness, stems from the masochistic picture or inadequacies of the previous age periods. It will be recalled that masochism was described as "libidinization of guilt". This surely is an oversimplification, but it must be remembered that whatever form it takes, masochism is an ego function. Although the ego trait here described is an adaptation to the life situation, its early roots were established as far back as the infancy period. Berliner was first to point this out. Menaker [108] both confirms and extends this view. The feelings of worthlessness and self-devaluation, which are part of the chronic inadequacies, originated at the oral level of development. The traits perpetuate a bond between the self and the punishing or depriving external object. Fortification of the original deprivation was obtained from the feeling of having been in the background with siblings and with peers in the group situation. Now as a young adult the pattern of ineffectiveness or defeatism is established.

the mature adult

From the point of view of physical maturation, the adult age not only represents the full development and functioning of all the organs including the generative apparatus but also presents a good deal of evidence of degenerative processes already under way. We pointed out in the section on childhood that the well functioning child is one who has been fortunate in integrating or setting into a working unit all the motivations that are operating upon him at that time. These motivations, it will be recalled, stem from the primary motivations or tropisms arising from the basic instincts and the secondary motivations or tropisms arising from the superego. In the adolescent, the integrative function involves the coordination of the various identities or spheres of operation involved in the growth process. In the mature adult there is also need for establishing a suitable adjustment through the process of integration. The ability to integrate and furthermore the ability to recognize the forces that need to be integrated constitutes a part of the concept of maturity. Specific areas are involved, in which the adult mature individual is obliged to operate, which call for ego attitudes that are unique for this age period. Things that may have appeared important to the youngster do not have this same importance in the grown man or woman. In other words, there develops a changed emphasis upon one's needs and as a result there is a change in one's values. To go a bit further, there emerges in the growth of the ego a type of organizational thinking which is based upon the highest levels of abstraction. This will be referred to as a sense of values. To say that a person has a balanced sense of values, is to say essentially that we are dealing with a mature, well integrated person. Here we come into further difficulty because there are many variations on the theme of what one considers a "value" to be. Certainly one person's values may not be exactly the same as another's. What we are trying to find here in our discussion is the concept of the ability to establish this sense rather than the nature of the values themselves. Philosophers, for thousands of years, have engaged in the discussion of this very subject. For example, there are fixed and transient values, values to the self and values to others, immediate and ultimate values, real values vs. assumed values, etc. Let us first arrive at an arbitrary definition of what we are referring to. Ginsburg offers the following definition: "A value is a criterion which helps us to distinguish between alternatives and affords us a base for recognizing ourselves in relation to the rest of the world." Concerning autonomous ego traits, Rapaport says, "The hierarchy of values belongs in part to the conflict-free spheres. While values are derived from social value hierarchies, their selection and development have their own genetic history in the individual. They are synthetic achievements of and play a role in mastering anxiety. They may or may not be such as to gain social rewards or to be in harmony with the interests of society."

We can see that what we mean by values contains elements of highly conceptualized forms of thinking. It represents a culmination of thought at the highest levels of abstract thinking which serves the organism in an adaptive capacity.

Having defined values, let us see how they apply to the main orbits of operation in the mature adult: (1) the home life and the concept of parenthood; (2) the occupational life; (3) the social and recreational life. Each of these will be discussed to some degree. Actually it is almost unnecessary to go into great detail. Many excellent books have been written on this very subject. From the point of view of the general theme of this presentation, however, some of the forces which operate upon the organism in the current scene will be mentioned.

In the home life of successfully married couples, each person brings to the marriage elements of salutary ego organization or character traits. In other words, marriage, among mature adults, is an enriching experience because each partner gains many things from the union. This includes mutual acceptance, tolerance for each other's ideas, and a fusion of some areas of interest. This fusion of interests can be the greatest bulwark for the solidarity of the marriage since it includes the sexual, religious, and social identities.

Method or frequency of the sexual act is not the complete barometer of the success of a marriage. It is true that mutual orgasm at regular intervals contributes to a satisfactory integration of two individuals. However, considerable tenderness and affection beyond the bedroom situation marks a mature conjugal relationship. It must be remembered that even mature individuals can have differing sets of values regarding the sex act. Granted that there may be individual differences on bio-logical grounds, previous inhibitions and guilt factors dating from the Oedipal period affect one's values in regard to sexual matters. Sexual compatability can be on various levels of sexual interest.

Religious identities offer no problem in marriage when they are similar or nearly so in character. Here we must recognize the difference between belief and ethnic groupings. For example, the actual religious beliefs and basic philosophies of two groups may be very similar, but there may be wide differences in the social and ethnic affiliations. Where there are no differences, there are no problems. Some differences can be reconciled or integrated into a working arrangement. Religious differ-ences ordinarily do not pose a serious problem where only the two people are involved. Pressures from various sources, especially the in-laws, and the need to establish a religious identity for the children can create serious areas of friction.

Social and esthetic interests of a similar nature do much to cement the marital state. Similar tastes in music, theatre, friends, community activities, etc. maintain the channels of communication between husband and wife. The capacity to obtain pleasure together serves to fortify the libidinal ties.

The concept of parenthood has been discussed in the previous section. We know that parenthood represents the culmination of the procreative function of the organism. As the ego identities of husband and wife become integrated into a teamwork relationship that is mutually satisfying to both, the advent of a child does little to alter this balance. However, this balanced relationship is sometimes based upon secondary autonomy, hence it bears with it all the original conflict situations from previous levels of existence. This will be discussed in detail in the section on conflict situations. As our emphasis at this point is on the healthy or normal integration of ego values, let us concentrate on the effect of the child on the married team. In the already well-integrated couple, the addition of a child acts in an integrative way. The very fact that the child must be integrated suggests that intrinsic challenges must be mastered. As pointed out earlier, any anxiety-provoking situation can act as a challenge or a threat. The healthy parents master the frustrations of disturbed sleep, illness, baby-sitters, loss of freedom, and the general disruption of established routines. The intense instinctual satisfaction of parenthood overshadows all inconveniences. The interests of parents shift with the advent of a child. This point is illustrated by the following brief report:

> The father was an architect and the mother an interior decorator. This couple, though happily married, spent most of their lives in their respective careers. The father was more anxious to have the child. The mother had misgivings and hesitations. Actually she had little interest in the management of her own home. After the birth of a baby she left her business and devoted herself completely to her home and her child, with ardor and enthusiasm. This pleased the husband very much. He ceased to tarry at his work unnecessarily and rushed home early every evening. The center of interest for both parents became the home.

Elevation of self-esteem goes with parental pride. The value of the child is reflected upon the parents. Their own worth is increased for having brought forth this prized object. This feeling can reach a point of exhibitionism or display. The child affords the parent an opportunity for reliving some of the pleasurable experiences of his or her own childhood. On the integrated level this parental pride can create an atmosphere in the home in which the child feels wanted and loved. This permits the child to integrate his own sense of belonging and to develop the autonomous ego traits which will permit him to become a good parent.

The ideal home situation is one in which there is an adequate balance between the needs and interests of the parents and the needs and interests of the children. This means that all activities and decisions in the home are part of the general conference method or, in a measure, the democratic process. Still, as in all democracies, the parents or one parent in particular, preferably the father, must assume the responsibility for good leadership. This leadership entails the ability to give affection and praise and to register objections when necessary. This implies "home rules" that have been mutually agreed upon and which call for disciplinary action when broken. No attempt will be made at this point to delineate specific methods of handling individual problems. Certainly the effects of poor handling have already become manifest in the discussion of ego development in the childhood years.

The less than ideal home situations show a type of attempted integration in one of two directions: (1) the parent-centered home; (2) the child-centered home.

In the parent-centered home there is very little regard for the children. All decisions are made and handed down from above. There may be either extreme discipline or extreme neglect. The disregard for the children may be based on a fundamental rejecting attitude toward children in the first place. Some selfish people do not feel that having children should in any way interfere with their lives. This attitude often prevails in the highest level of our society. When people are brought up by maids and governesses, it is a most natural thing to turn their children over to hired help.

Fathers are of necessity out of the home a great deal. But when mothers, too, insist upon a career, the children are often left without parents. It is striking how this type of parent often permits or even urges the child to call both parents by their first names. Such children unfortunately never associate "mother" or "father" with any really pleasant external object. It is as though they never had a father or mother.

There is the story told about the child whose parents were both psychiatrists. When asked what he wanted to be when he grew up, he replied, "A patient!"

I do not advocate as a strict policy that the work identity of the career woman must necessarily exclude her from having a family. There are some women who manage to do both well, but it certainly requires a good deal of management to have the time available for a career and a home. There are instances when mothers are so frustrated at giving up their careers that they vent their rage at the unwanted child. In such instances it may be better to have a career, at least for part of the time, than to give it up entirely.

At the opposite extreme from the parent-centered home is the child-centered one. Here we see another part of our current scene. In the last few decades there has been a great deal of emphasis on "doing the right thing by our children." First it was the era of behaviorism and the conditioned reflex; later it was the "do not frustrate the child" era. In either case it was centered around the concept, "What is best for the child?" The concern about the best way to bring up a child is based partly upon the small size of the average family and the thorough inexperience of the young parents with babies and children. Or perhaps it is, as Erikson says, a product of the mechanization of our culture in which we look for push-buttons on the wrong and right way of dealing with the problem.

Where the interests and demands of the children supersede or exclude the interest of the parents, strain or disruption of the family scene is invited. Some years ago a case in point came to the author's attention. A fifteen year old boy became so unruly and undisciplined, his demands so outrageous, that his over-indulging mother finally consulted a psychiatrist. The mother granted this boy his every wish and permitted him any extravagance. The boy disdained the father and told him to leave the house. The mother did not let the husband discipline the boy and induced the husband to live at his club from time to time. When the son threatened to leave home or commit suicide unless the mother obtained a divorce, she sought help. The case ended very simply when the mother was assured that the son would neither commit suicide nor leave home were she to take a firm stand. She was particularly impressed when it was suggested that were she to die in the process of appeasing the son, father and son would become friends at her funeral. As a result, the mother told the boy that his father meant much to her, that she would not permit him to break up her home. She offered to help the boy pack his belongings if he still felt like leaving. The boy was very surprised. He did not leave and things worked out very well for the family.

Although the two extremes of home situation, namely parent-centered and child-centered, seem extremely pathological, they are being described here under the section of the mature adult. The reason is that there is a measure of flexibility in this regard in our culture within the framework of what we consider "normal" people. These people are not suffering in any way and perhaps bring up different kinds of children with different values. This exaggerated case may well be an exception, but it is presented here purely by way of illustration. What is more important is the ability to make changes when they are indicated. Fixed forms of behavior that do not respond to a logical approach put one in the class of the neurotic ego reaction type. Hence we can point up one factor in the mature adult as in any other age level—the ability to reintegrate values into a more adaptable form of thinking and action suitable to the maintenance of a comfortable situation for all concerned. Specifically in regard to the home situation, it means an ability to discharge the obligations to the family to the satisfaction of self and all concerned.

The sense of values in the working life of the individual has already been alluded to. From the maturity angle a man must have arrived at what he considers his life's work. This may have entailed many compromises along the way, including the lowering of his sights in terms of the realities of the economy in which we live. Furthermore, the mature individual is one who is able to capitalize on opportunities when they present themselves. This may involve the ability to appreciate calculated risks and not be amazed when things do not work out well. In short, it is the ability to grasp the next higher rung on the ladder and the ability to bound back and begin climbing again if the foot slips.

The mature adult is one who is able to submit voluntarily to all sorts of unpleasant situations in his work in order to remain steadfast in his goal. For the sake of the pay check and the knowledge that he is performing a useful service to his family, mature men (or women, if necessary) are capable of withstanding long hours of hardship and boredom. Whether they do or not is another matter. Here, there may be other values as set by trade unions, but the capacity to work is there. The concept, "man must work", is part of the superego. "Man must work so many hours per week" is still another superego force. As Lantos points out [109] work derives its energy from libidinal and aggressive sources and is under the influence of the superego which, in this respect, is no longer destructive to the self but acts in a constructive self-disciplinary manner.

Work goals as a criterion of maturity are not determined by money alone. There are many contented people receiving great gratification and small remuneration from their work. There are people capable of working a lifetime for the purpose of making some contribution to mankind. Another criterion of maturity in the work situation is the ability to take success gracefully and to continue to extend one's self in the work situation. Many men and women have the happy faculty of diverting time and energy to gratifying hobbies as a means of counteracting the boredom of too much leisure or a dull job.

One cannot conclude that it is mature or "manly" for a man to forbid his wife to work. Certainly it appears more acceptable, in our culture, for the man to feel that he is the main or even the sole provider. Still, circumstances may be such that both husband and wife must work or want to work. However, whether a woman is gainfully employed or devotes herself to the tasks of homemaking and mother- hood, the same autonomous ego traits of "enterprise", "perseverance", and "industry" apply. The wife who is in possession of these mature ego traits augments these same traits in the husband. Thus his success is her success. Husband and wife functioning as a team derive mutual gratification from both their joint and respective roles.

Up to this point emphasis has been placed upon the interpersonal relationships in the home. However, mature adults are capable of relat- ing, and willing to relate, themselves to people outside of the home on a social and recreational level. The relationship to these external objects in the mature individual is not invested with strong libidinal cathexis. Nor do these external objects arouse intense irrational hostile reactions. The mature couple recognizes the social group as an enriching experience but in no way uses it as a substitute for the important values of the home. The mature husband and wife behave in the social situation in a manner acceptable to both and based upon long established ground rules.

The next item in the codification of ego traits in the mature individual is "poise". Actually the word means balance. In psychological terms, poise implies a well balanced person. The individual with poise is one who is able to control or release the expression of his instinctual motivation in terms of the reality principle. It is as though the organism has within it a set of gyroscopes or governors which keep the individual at an even keel. It is an inward calm or "peace of mind" which comes with mastery and control of life's problems. The processes which have brought this about come from all the learnings acquired in the growth process. These learnings, as pointed out earlier, are essentially inhibitory in nature. When the needs of the organism attain a measure of fulfill- ment, the excitations can become less demanding; hence, in a sense, they become inhibited. Furthermore, the mature person can select those demands that can be gratified, those than can be postponed, and those that require modification or repudiation. An individual with poise can adjust to new situations. A native chieftain could be bewildered by city traffic, but would soon adapt to the new situation if he chose to. Poise involves the merging or integration of the values of the individual in all settings, in the home, at work, and in the social scene. Polatin and Philtine [110] said it quite well: "We maintain our balance by achieving a reasonable compromise between the pressures within ourselves and the pressures of society, between what we want and what we get, between our aspirations and our limitations, whether the latter arise from economic circumstances or from our own deficiencies."

The ability of the individual to exercise good judgment, tact, and decorum is a measure of his sense of values. It is suggested that the sense of value, in and of itself, becomes an autonomous ego trait.

As a further extension of the concept of a sense of values, we may say that the mature adult is able to discriminate between levels of values in a sort of scale or hierarchy of value systems. Thus he is able to exert a power of selectivity about things which require action. Let us give a few examples.

1. There are some situations which may not be comfortable but about which he can do nothing. He is able to recognize the fact that to worry himself about such matters is an utter waste of energy; hence he directs his forces elsewhere.

2. There are some matters which are of such minor value that to expend energy to make corrections would not be worth the effort.

3. There are multiple situations which require attention. He is able to select the situation which is most important and give it priority over the situations of a more trivial nature.

4. There are situations that require his complete attention. He is able to exclude all other matters that interfere and work out a plan which will call for some definite decision, and he acts accordingly.

A sense of values permits an individual to select from his environment basic principles by which he lives. Before a selected value can be integrated into the ego structure, several stages take place. These stages proceed in orderly sequence. It first begins with an awareness or apperception of the idealized version of what would be of most value in a given situation. The next step requires a genuine interest and acceptance of that particular concept or group of concepts which may constitute a new frame of reference. This is followed by a stage of concentration and attention. This point has been stressed particularly by Burrow [*111*] and his followers. The final stage is one of application. This whole sequence is clearly observed in psychoanalysis. An interpretation or concept is offered the patient. He goes through these four stages before a new and less destructive set of values are established. The mature adult, unlike the patient in analysis, is not too influenced by the overprinting of childhood values and can accept new values readily. The patient, on the other hand, must first develop insight and understanding into old patterns before he is able to choose new values. If a person is unable to accept and integrate new values, psychoanalysis is indicated. The sequence of integrating a new value is as follows:

Awareness

↓

Interest

↓

Attention

↓

Application

There are other items of autonomous ego growth in the mature individual which can be subsumed under the designation of sense of values as honesty, fidelity, and integrity. These traits are almost self-explanatory. However, if we look closely we can differentiate shades of meaning. For example, honesty is a purely relative matter. It may be expedient or "good business" to be honest in the commercial world, but this is not bound necessarily with superego motivations as true honesty indicates. But here, too, honesty can be so exaggerated as to appear as a neurotic compulsion. Fidelity is based upon adherence to the principle of mutual loyalty. Even though sexual interest may wander outside of the home, the sense of values serves to dictate that it is not worth the effort nor fair to the mate.

Integrity is that state in which the individual functions as a total unimpaired unit. The mature person possessing, as he does, this autonomous ego trait is not subject to the pressures of corrupting influence or practice. He abides by his obligations and fulfills his contracts.

To have reached maturity a person must have developed all the autonomous ego traits described in this section. He is then an integrated person in possession of a discriminate sense of values. With these traits he has developed a nice balance of emotional reactions to his life situations. He is thus on his way toward the peak of attainment which is within the limits of his capacity.

adult conflict

Individuals who have been suffering from neurotic disturbances in childhood do not generally overcome their difficulties in the adult period. In fact, their childhood troubles are reflected in all the areas in which they operate. The home with the problems of marriage and parenthood is the barometer of the adult adjustment. Many investigators are of the opinion that sexual difficulties or "incompatabilities" are the cause of neurotic conflict between married people. It is much more likely that the sexual difficulty is the result of the internal neurotic problems rather than the primary cause for disruption of the conjugal relationship. It is true that when the sexual problems arise, the gap is widened, and estrangement or loosening of the libidinal ties becomes manifest.

Let us examine the symptoms of sexual impotence in the male and frigidity in women. We have already mentioned the repetition compulsion in regard to sabotaging human relations in a previous section of this chapter. The neurotic pattern of unconsciously courting rejection or of actively rejecting the mate may occur many years after marriage. The precipitating cause for this attitude may come from many sources, e.g., business or professional worries, disagreements about the handling of the children, or interference by the in-laws. The covert emotional reaction may be hostility to the mate and as a result unconsciously effects a state of withholding libidinal communication with the spouse.

On the other hand, the neurotic pattern may be accompanied by a large measure of anxiety or fear reactions which stem directly from the secondary perceptual thinking of the Oedipal period. After a period of marriage the mate who was formerly the nonincestuous external object becomes "family"; hence he or she takes on the character in the unconscious of the original incestuous object in the manner of a "transference" reaction. In this way the marriage relationship operates under the principles of incest taboo. All the forbiddennesses and the naughti-ness of sexuality affect the marriage relationship to the degree of making sex in the home an unwelcome occurrence. As these processes are not in the range of consciousness in the individual, the explanation in the minds of many people when these things occur is to think that they have "fallen out of love" with their partners. To review some of the repressed imageries that occur in the minds of many people who are suffering from impotence or frigidity, let us consider the following:

1. The actual fear of castration by the father represented in the super-ego as a strong internalized secondary motivation for suppressing the genital impulses.

2. The fear and hatred of the mother who had curtailed the libidinal activities in the child and who had withheld her affections and care, thus making it impossible to offer affection to the mother-representative.

3. The fear of being swallowed by the mate as a projection of the person's own wish to swallow the external object in his hunger for love.

Often all three of these fantasies occur in the same individual. Each type of thinking process contains elements of these fantasies from the childhood scene but can be fortified by actual occurrences in the life situation. There are many instances where the neurotic individual may be having difficulty with his boss and feels intimidated, insecure, and frightened about his job. This stimulates his earlier castrative thoughts and he reacts with impotence with his wife. The same can apply to the direct relationship of husband and wife. If one or the other becomes overly critical, domineering, or argumentative, then the marital partner reacts with the old patterns that had occurred in childhood. In short, the individual becomes a child again and the mate becomes a critical parent. In the face of such intimidation or stirrings of resentment there is hardly room for sexual freedom. These persons are already sensitive individuals and bear with them the stigmata of the vulnerability from the Oedipal phase or even the basic vulnerability from the infantile phase. A wife or husband who presents to his or her mate a picture of being a critical, authoritative, or punishing person can duplicate in effect the training and indocrination period of the toddler. All the original reactions and secondary autonomies can be brought to bear. Subtle defiance can exist in the form of absence of sexual desire in the home and potency or infidelity outside the home. The third point, regarding the fear of being swallowed, represents a regression to archaic thinking forms. It occurs in persons who have residuals of intense infantile fears. It goes without saying that many of the instances of impotence and frigidity, which are so intimately bound with old neurotic patterns, result in broken marriages. However, if these people were fully aware of the true nature of their problems as having stemmed from childhood and not from the real change in the object relationship of the marriage team, many otherwise doomed marriages could be salvaged.

Let us look at the other extreme of sexual interest or responsiveness, namely, the excessive demand for sexual gratification. Nymphomania and satyriasis are terms which have been applied respectively to the female and male counterparts of this phenomenon. These are neurotic manifestations and represent the sexual expression of the secondary autonomous traits of greed and insatiability, which had their roots in early oral deprivations. Just as overeating or bulimia represents the hypertrophy of instinctual expression as a defense or reparative mastery of the original deprivation by the use of instinct against the frustration of instinct, the same can apply to the expression of the sexual impulses. The sexual organs, either male or female, in such instances become the symbolic expressions of the unconscious dynamic motivations for the persistent hunger or oral greed.

The lack of responsiveness sexually by one of the partners in the marriage team may be just as devastating to the marital relationship as the excessive demand of one of the partners. In either case the dissatisfaction may be present in the person with the sexual problem as well as with the other partner. Unfortunately, many marriages are broken by the evident "incompatability" when the problems are not basically concerned with the sexuality but merely express themselves in that way. For example, there are cases where the individual exhibits relative impotence or frigidity which may manifest itself in either loss of interest or inability to have a coital orgasm. This engenders feelings of inadequacy within one's self or dissatisfaction with the partner. Because of these inadequacies, infidelities may be condoned in their partners or may stimulate their own imaginations to attempt experimenting with extramarital relations.

It may be noted that I do not make any distinction between the susceptibility of males and females to react by their sexual expression to various emotional stimuli. Whereas Kinsey makes the statement that male sexuality is "psychological" and female sexuality is "physiological", if anything, the opposite is true. By male standards many females feel inadequate in their sexual responsiveness, but they show a higher degree of specificity and selective responsiveness. Those individuals, both male and female, who presumably are of the opinion that they are experiencing sexual "freedom" when they are capable of all sorts of sexual experiences may be highly neurotic persons who use sexuality as a defense mechanism. Often they represent persons who by reaction formation are denying severely repressed Oedipal conflicts. By the Kinsey standards, however, they would be considered highly "efficient" as sexual partners. From the psychiatrist's point of view, the persons who find recourse to expressions of exaggerated sexuality may be expressing various types of ego reaction, e.g., the wish to dominate or to deny a deep-seated submissiveness or passivity, or over-compensations for grave doubts as to their masculine or feminine identities.

On a less neurotic level there can be conflicts in the marital situation that are not so deeply rooted in neurotic patterning as the foregoing, but represent a confusion or conflict of values. For example, a husband who seems to value his golf game more than his wife and children can sometimes create animosity that could have been avoided. If the wife retaliates by flirting with the husband's best friend, then the stage is set for trouble. On the social scene, one of the partners may find values in some friends or activities, such as cards or concerts, while the other belittles or remains antagonistic. Perhaps these things seem a bit banal or superficial but they may represent deep fundamental differences which cause relationships to disintegrate. What may be of more concern in the consideration of the failures of ego growth in the fully developed adult is the conflict of values within the person himself. The values that accrue from a change in environment, such as moving from a rural to an urban community, or from one country to another or from one work situation to another, may present conflicts because of the need to acquire new values and to relinquish old ones. A motivation to accept a new philosophy of life is obligatory when a change of economic status occurs in either direction. The change of attitude as a result of loss of economic status is, of course, the more difficult to integrate.

Mention has already been made of the religious question. Conflicts regarding religious values do occur particularly in the matter of the bringing up of children. These conflicts can occur in persons who may have agreed completely with their mates along certain lines about matters of worship or lack of it early in marriage, but who regret having made such commitments later on. Even though they may carry out their original plans, they may harbor resentments when their old religious adaptations make themselves known. Proddings by the grandparents or situations in the social scene may further add to the confusion of religious values within the minds of some adults.

Conflict situations may arise in the case of childless couples. When it becomes a matter of great importance to one parent to have a child and of no importance to the other, cause for tension can be engendered. Of course, if both partners want children and are unable to have them, it becomes a matter which requires a reintegration of values by both husband and wife. Most couples are able to make fairly good adjustments to this situation, but occasionally the resentments and disappointments are sufficient to strain the relationship. More frequently, however, the fact of being childless may furnish an excuse for the dissolution of a marriage when other more pertinent factors have been in operation.

The manner in which the children are being brought up often creates another area of adult conflict. For example, the father may think that the mother is too indulgent. The mother may feel that the father is being too harsh. Each parent reflects his own bringing up in the evaluation of the proper methods of rearing children. A couple I know got along very well even though the husband was very untidy and a chronic procrastinator. When their first child was a few years old, the father became very hostile. He exercised severe discipline because the child evidenced untidiness and procrastination. The mother resented the father's attitude and protected the child even though she too found these traits unattractive. The father's hostile and rejecting attitude so angered the wife that she became totally frigid to him sexually. The marital relationship became so strained that the wife came into therapy in an effort to effect some solution for her problems.

Some people so exaggerate some of the normal values that they cease to become healthy values and become pathological. Take for example the value of owning a home. In some instances women have libidinized the home to such a degree that it transcends the importance of the people within it. The physical structure of the house and its contents symbolize the person's own body and are invested with all the narcissistic elements that exist within the individual. The gratification of the house becomes an end in itself. The house, in such an instance, is not enjoyed by the family; hence does not constitute a home. Some women not only pressure their husbands in the overevaluation of their homes, but also press them beyond their earning capacities by extravagant tastes in clothes, furs, and jewels. These women are not realistic in their sense of proportion and frequently suffer great frustration. These inordinate demands or spurious values, when fixed and unmodifiable, have their beginnings in early oral fixations. Other distorted values, which have their origins in the foibles or idiosyncracies that constitute the secondary autonomous ego traits, such as extravagance, stinginess, juvenile exhibitionism, contribute to adult conflict. Husbands may reveal their hostilities to their wives, who show such unattractive traits, by direct or subtle means. Wives can show their resentment in like manner. This can be a source of constant irritation.

Another aspect of conflict in the physiologically mature person is in the realm of his occupation and the values attached to the work situation. In many instances man receives small value or gratification from his work. As a result of mass production methods and precise division of labor, the average worker never experiences a feeling of personal accomplishment. The assembly line methods do little to encourage a man to become a skilled craftsman. As the result of the little satisfaction that a man receives from the work situation per se, the energy of his competitive ego traits is directed mainly toward the economic aspects of his work. The pay check, not the product of his labor, is invested with strong libidinal motivations. As a result of the emotionalization of the pay check, distorted values are established. As the sociologists point out, it is this distorted value system which breeds unwholesome competitiveness and separates man from man or may even set man against man. This competitive or even hostile attitude exists in order to gain every economic advantage or prestige value that it is possible to obtain from work. Many men live with constant fear in their work situation. Anonymity, with its absence of human value and cordiality and the intense pressures for increased production and sales, keeps the individual in a constant state of tension. Fromm points out that from the point of view of human values man has become a commodity. Although man's chief interest is in selling himself, it is unfortunate that he is not convinced of the value of his product. This places him in an inadequate position, constantly insecure and never content. As a result, a person either compensates with less pretentious behavior or resigns himself to disillusionment or mediocrity.

On the other hand, some people sacrifice economic security for work gratification. This sacrifice may lead to conflict in the domestic situation. Whereas the individual may be engaged in work activity that satisfies his personal interests and self esteem, it is quite possible that his family will resent the lack of economic advantages. In order to avoid such conflict, some men give up their prime interest as a source of livelihood and enter more lucrative fields. If this shift of activity brings satisfaction, albeit on a new set of values, no problems ensue. If, however, the man is discontented in this change of work identity, forces of disintegration may operate. Restitution may occur if he displaces his original work gratifications onto an avocation or secondary work interest.

It is a well accepted concept that work is a great stabilizer. Freud stated that work is directed to reality. When there are, in a person's life, situations of great emotional stress, the work may act as a rescue phenomenon. Many factors operate in a combined way to prevent the person from ego disintegration.

When a person loses his work, be it gainful or otherwise, the disintegration process begins. On the ego level he loses one important aspect of his identity. On the unconscious instinctual level he is rendered sub-masculine under the principles of the castration complex. On the reality level, unemployment creates many problems, economic and social. These further lower his self esteem. Such defeats can start the individual on a downward spiral.

As a result of various conflict situations at the adult age level, the individual either makes major environmental changes or readjusts his value system, or he disintegrates into some form of physical or mental illness. The physical disintegrative processes engendered by emotional stress can produce hypertension, coronary disease, peptic ulcer, etc. On the more overt emotional level, the disintegrative processes are evidenced by depressions, phobias, conversion reactions, and other forms of mental illness. At this age level, there are many people who attempt to solve or avoid their problems by the use of alcohol. Reference is made here to the use of alcohol as a medicine in an attempt to allay anxieties arising from conflict. Alcoholism is mentioned as a part of the disintegrative process and a thorough discussion of all its ramifications is beyond the scope of this work.

Let us now apply the perceptual and conceptual thinking theme to the conflict of values and show how it is related to the integrative and disintegrative processes. It was pointed out earlier that "being adult" implies the acquisition of a well organized, nonconflictual sense of values. This acquisition is based upon high levels of concept formation and represents the uppermost level of ego integration of the mature adult. In terms of brain physiology it is represented by the stored memories of masteries of all the life processes in a region of the brain. (The exact area is thought to be the cortex in the tempero-parietal region.) This cortical brain function, wherein value systems are conceptualized, acts as an inhibitor and regulator of all the other functions of the organism. Nevertheless, perhaps because it is the most recently acquired level of integration, it is also the first and most easily lost. Thus when there are irreconcilable conflicts in the value systems, there is an invitation to the disintegrative processes. As in conflicts of other levels, there is a loss of the most recently acquired adjustment and the emergence of more infantile forms of cerebration. The degree of disintegration depends upon the other previously established areas of ego autonomy. When it is impossible to reconcile two or more intensely ingrained value systems, a complete breakdown into psychotic or neurotic thinking forms may result. The mechanism of such disintegration appears to operate in a manner of the release of primitive reaction forms which had been adequately governed or controlled by the inhibitory effects of the ego organization. As a release phenomenon, of existing archaic patterns, the emergence of a psychotic picture can be nearly the same when the disintegration results from psychological causes as from brain tumor, toxic states, senile atrophy, or the use of cortisone or ACTH. Thus the highest integrative function is most vulnerable psychologically and physiologically. The result of the disintegrative process at the value level does not differ from the conflicts of motivation and the conflicts of identity which were described earlier. As in the other conflicts, the negative tropisms or secondary motivations stem from superego and ego ideal concepts which color the value systems.

Just as there are secondary integrations when there are conflicts of identity in the adolescent, the same process applies to the reparative mastery of the conflict of values in the adult. The phenomenon of isolation may act as a defense mechanism to encapsulate value systems into logic-tight compartments. Such individuals may have one set of values in one setting and another set of values in another.

The secondary autonomies which result from the adaptation to the conflicts of this age period and which constitute readjustments of the value system, will be mentioned. Aberrant behavior such as infidelity or promiscuity can become fixed personality traits. When a degree of instability already exists and life's problems become complicated, these individuals rationalize their behavior on an altered sense of values.

Although it appears that emphasis has been placed on reactions to the life situation itself as a cause for adult conflict, let us not lose sight of the fact that many conflict situations are brought about from the pre-existing levels of ego organization. For example, the secondary ego traits of doggedness or ruthlessness have their origins in sadism or the libidinization of hostility. The submissive traits stem from masochism. For example we can cite the individual who goes through his adult years wavering from one job to another or from one marriage to another and never settles upon a satisfactory life plan. The term "irresoluteness" has been applied to this type of person.

To summarize the ego growth of the adult, we can say that there are many life situations that call for adaptation and reintegration of the hierarchy of values. Out of these integrations there emerges a philosophy of life unique to each individual which is sometimes in keeping with the needs of his home life, his work life, and his social life, but sometimes is a mere compromise for survival on a defensive-adaptive basis in one or all of these areas. What we can consider as real maturity involves the efficient organization and integration of experience with all of the problems that are inherent in all the areas in which man operates.

the menopause · life
begins at forty · con-
flicts in middle years ·
secondary autonomy in
middle age

CHAPTER EIGHT

THE MIDDLE YEARS

W e are now approaching the middle years or the beginning of the decline of the organism. The term climacteric is applied to a critical period in the life of the individual in which a great change is taking place. Specifically, it is most apparent in the female as the menopause. There are many psychological as well as physiological factors which must be considered in the study of the ego development of this age period. It will be shown that there are many problems at this time of life. But what is important is the acknowledgment of the fact that these years are the most useful for the benefit of society at large.

In many species the physiological end of the procreative period marks the end of the usefulness of the organism. All life thereafter is burdensome to the progeny. This is not so among the human species. I am in partial agreement with the recent contribution of Lentin and Courtney [112] regarding the life cycle of the human organism. It is their feeling that by and large there is a gradual progression of useful function of the organism from birth to death and not merely from birth to the climacteric or the period of involution. There has always been rampant the notion that man is useful only as long as he is capable of reproduction or at least able to perform the sexual act. All the quests for the Fountain of Youth, the monkey gland operations, and the current use of gonadotropic substances are expressions of the attempt to prolong the usefulness of the organism with sexuality as the main barometric focus. This need not be so, because the middle years can be the ones where both men and women reach their highest point of dignity and effectiveness, not only to themselves but to their families and to their community.

the menopause

It is in the female where the more dramatic events occur regarding the termination of the procreative function. With the cessation of menstruation, there is the tangible evidence that reproduction is no longer possible. This change has distinct physiological repercussions upon the organism. Most gynecologists and endocrinologists are convinced that the lowering of the estrogenic levels in the body causes distinct reactions in the organism especially those that are mediated through the sympathetic nervous system. They are thoroughly convinced that emotional instability, irritability, depression, hyperesthesias, vertigo, and other symptoms are definitely attributable to the lowering of estrogen content of the body. Certainly the "hot flashes" of the menopause are relieved by injections of estrogens as are many of the other symptoms. But there are many reactions which are not helped by supplying the missing endocrines because they are purely psychological. Certainly when there are pronounced symptoms, both estrogen and androgen therapy should be attempted but not prolonged indefinitely when the symptoms are not relieved. The behavior of the menopausal woman is often indicative of previous emotional conflicts which were only brought to the surface by the endocrine imbalance. As such, it represents another critical period in the lifetime of the individual. Our remarks will be mainly about women at this point because the climacteric as evidenced by the menopause is not characteristic of the male. Although there is presumably a male climacteric as well, there is little evidence to show that it is of a pronounced physiological nature.

As to the decline in sexuality, there is nothing to indicate that the female sex life is altered in any way by the menopause. In fact, by virtue of the absence of the fear of pregnancy, many women begin to enjoy coitus for the first time in their lives. Kinsey reports that responsiveness of females sexually continues at a uniform level throughout the major portion of their lifetime once their peak has been reached at about the age of twenty-seven or twenty-eight. Males, on the other hand, show a gradual decline to a nearly vanishing point around the age of sixty. Some exceptional males continue an active sex life much longer than this age figure. This makes for a strange set of circumstances in many middle-aged couples where the female is willing and desirous and the male is disinterested and embarrassed.

The menopause or change of life is often a very mild affair in healthy, stable women. This is not so in the case of the tense, disturbed females who have probably had an unhappy life up to this point. The concept that the menopause is such a critical period is so well known that many women develop anxiety at the prospect of the approaching menopause and either react because they had expected to or remain alert for symptoms that never arrive.

Turning now to the psychological aspects of the menopause, let us first look at it from the point of view of the sense of values. There has been up to this point in the lifetime of the individual, a strong emphasis upon growth and improvement. With the loss of reproductive function there must be a readjustment of a set of values that is in keeping with the slowing down and cessation of part of the vital body processes. Lentin and Courtney, referring to the growth process as "evolvescence" and the decline as "senescence," make the following statement: "The individual perceives his own metamorphosis from evolvescence to senescence. He fights the change because our society has placed all its values in evolvescence and has not voiced or even recognized the more subtle values in senescence."

We shall speak more fully about the ego changes and growth increments that occur during this age period, but let us first make mention of the fact that in the case of unstable people there is not only a conflict situation in regard to the sense of values, but there is a step backward toward the adolescent period where there is a conflict of identities. It is where the new role of not being considered young any longer is in conflict with the youthful identity, that troublesome tensions arise. The menopausal or involutional period resembles the adolescent period as being the time when serious breakdowns in adjustment may occur. Whether the upsurge of endocrine substances in adolescence and the downsurge of endocrine substances in the menopause bear any relationship to physiological reactions or whether both are purely psychological reactions to the endocrine changes, one cannot say with any degree of definiteness. Benedek [113], who studied these cases psychoanalytically, believes that the endocrine role is not to be discounted. She states that when the endocrine balance is low, there is diminution of the ego's integrative strength.

Menopausal age sometimes is a signal for feeling better. Such an instance is the case of the woman who had a hysterectomy at the age of twenty-seven. She became quite depressed and unhappy because of the loss of her procreative powers. This she felt in spite of the fact that she was already the mother of two attractive, healthy children. She maintained a rather sullen, moody disposition for a period of eighteen years. At the age of forty-five, she quite suddenly began to feel better. She consciously accepted this age as the normal one in which she would have had her natural menopause. As a consequence, she no longer felt the feeling of loss. At the earlier age she was not emotionally ready to accept the menopause as she was able to at the time that it would have normally occurred.

life begins at forty

The catch phrase introduced by Pitkin [114] as a consolation to people who have passed their fourth decade has a measure of validity that is not to be ignored. In our culture the emphasis is placed upon the importance and glory of youth. There are historical, social, and economic reasons for this. However, let us not lose sight of the pressures put on youth to establish a family and business or profession, so that it is not until the decline begins to set in that most people are able to enjoy the fruits of their efforts. Unfortunately, there are people who still need to struggle long after they should relax. This may be due either to the exigencies of their economic situation or to traits in their own ego organization. Let us first turn our attention to the healthy and successful men and women.

While the younger generation is still striving for emancipation and independence, the men and women in the middle years have already attained this stature. These middle years are ones of power, influence, and authority. These years are also the ones in which a person takes on a new identity. It is that of becoming a grandparent. This identity is very different from the one of becoming a parent. Grandparenthood affords the pleasures of parenthood without its responsibilities. Most grandparents can enjoy indulging and overprotecting the grandchildren because the responsibility for the child's training and discipline is not theirs. In some instances this may be a salutary influence upon the children. The warm acceptance by the grandparents may compensate for the effects of the anxieties of the young parents, especially with the first-born. The grandparents receive narcissistic values from their investment of love in the grandchildren. The factors involved are: (1) the competitiveness with one's own children for the love of the grandchildren, and (2) an insurance policy that someone will love them in their old age. Although the young parents may have conflict about the overindulgence of the grandparents, the grandparents themselves generally are in no conflict. They thoroughly enjoy this identity.

In the work situation, the successful person has reached his peak in the fifties or thereabouts. If he is of stable character, he does not have any more axes to grind and eases his competitive pressure. It is at this point that the older man who feels secure in his own position extends a helping hand to the younger men who are climbing upward. He is able and willing to impart what he has learned from his own life experiences to the others who will eventually replace him.

Females in the middle years who have successfully raised their families, take on a gracious attitude to the younger generation and do not try to compete with them at their level. In both men and women the autonomous ego trait of "dignity" is applicable to the well managed and successful operation of their life plans. They are content with their achievements. This entails a feeling of "self-acceptance" which radiates from these people. It is a delight to be with such self-assured individuals because they are capable of putting others at ease and of inspiring confidence and trust.

It is at this period of life that a person's judgment reaches its highest functional capacity. Because of his own life experiences and those that he has observed in others and because of an appreciation of all the events of history that have transpired over the years, there is developed the ability to evaluate and discern the finer nuances of the environment. By this time the individual has had the opportunity of testing all the learnings and slogans of his predecessors and has available all the information regarding the outcome of various modes of action. It is at this point in life that the individual reserves the right to create the ethical and moral standards by which he lives and advises others to live. The energy which is directed toward social and cultural values is derived from the desexualization process and is diverted toward new types of ego integration.

During the middle years the autonomous nonconflictual individual turns his attention to the needs of society at large. As the needs of his job, business, and parenthood become less demanding and the sexual interests become less prominent, he is able to devote himself to community interests. By virtue of the ego traits of "tolerance" and "charity" the successful individual is able to return to society some of the blessings he has received. These are the men and women who should be the leaders in our society. Some find their ways into public office, particularly in times of stress. This turning of interest by the citizens in the middle years toward the interests of society acts as a safety valve against the younger generation, who demand as much from society as they can possibly obtain. Even though young people say that the old men make the wars for the young men to fight, there is no valid indication that this is of any personal gain to the older men. It is the older men who can see the over-all picture and that is as it should be. This does not apply to real old age or senility which will be discussed in the last chapter, but to the middle years, forty to sixty-five, or even later in many instances. It has been said that the older people distrust the younger people and feel that it is their duty to protect the younger ones from their own foolhardiness and thereby maintain their own positions as custodians of their respective cultures. As the older people feel that they have "been through the mill", they seek to assume positions of leadership for the maintenance of the common good, at least as they see it.

A few words can be said about "tolerance". By this we mean that the balanced personality at this period can be sympathetic or empathic to all people. He can be patient with dissident points of view and can exhibit tact and diplomacy with those who seek to foist their ideas upon him. He can be adroit in his handling of matters of importance and avoid gloating over the shortcomings of others.

Through the integration of all the experiences of a lifetime, including the ups and downs in all the spheres of operation, there is a tendency to be circumspect in all fields of endeavor. There is less likelihood of being too venturesome in all one's dealings. One begins to appreciate the watchwords of one's forebears and to exercise the traits of "caution" and "perspicacity".

As the years continue to roll on, the prospect of retiring becomes an important factor in the lives of most men. This prospect raises new issues. Many people look forward to the time when they will have a perpetual vacation, but remain in harness as long as it is possible to do so. There is always the feeling that the job is not quite finished, or that someone else may not do so well, or the fear of being no longer so important.

Well-adjusted individuals have long before this age period come into contact with the concept of death. The person who has a realistic attitude in this regard has already made provisions for his family by adequate insurance and a will. Realistically, the concept of death has been one which has been part of the experiential area. Usually one's parents have already passed on as have some of the other relatives and friends. An autonomous person comes to grips with the concept of his own death as something inevitable but one which he would still like to postpone. We have avoided talking about death in this manuscript as a positive instinctual drive. Freud postulated a death instinct as part of the normal process of life. Most psychoanalysts have been reluctant to accept this and have favored the idea that death is an outgrowth of the aggressive drives of the individual converted into an act of violence against the self. But death means something else too. It is the surcease from pain. It represents a return to mother, to Mother Earth, to Heaven. As such it is the complete relinquishment of pleasure and the complete relief of pain, hence the only true homeostasis. But in the well adjusted person there is no need to hasten the arrival of the Grim Reaper, nor should there be any particular fear of the inevitable.

conflicts in middle years

As stated previously, the conflicts around the menopause are often of a very serious nature. The imageries to which these women react include the concept of loss of self-esteem through loss of reproductive function, hence the picture is essentially that of the castration phenomenon (Jones [94] uses the term "aphanisis" or loss of sexuality as the term applicable to both sexes). Fessler [114] stresses the point that the female is especially content with her role as a woman because she is able to give birth to a child. This capacity is a compensation for her lack of a penis. Inasmuch as menstruation is a constant reminder of woman's child-bearing capacity, there is a loss of that feeling of completeness at the menopause. Where the person has already had other conflicts, the menopause appears as the last blow. This of course suggests that child-bearing potential is an ego integrative force which, when lost, permits the individual to disintegrate. Coupled with this is the imagery of getting old and losing one's physical attractiveness, producing a not too happy prospect for future adjustment. As long as the woman felt needed by the children, the ego was able to function. When this no longer prevails, many women go into a decline. Another factor which makes the woman less autonomous is the fact that she may not feel loved or needed by her husband. As he begins to show some signs of impotence, it may stimulate her imagination to the belief that he is being unfaithful to her. If such is really the truth, the conflict situation becomes even worse. Actually women past the menopause are often more intolerant of flirtations by their husbands than they had been before. This attitude is partly due to the older woman's lessened security and confidence in herself. If the marriage had failed earlier, she might still have been able to attract another husband or to find a job and support herself. At this point in life, however, both of these possibilities are lessened; it is not easy for an older woman to find a husband, nor is she particularly desirable in the employment market.

The neurotic woman who has been a burden to her husband and family finds herself even more useless at her menopause, and the feelings of guilt for a wasted life often accentuate the disintegrative process. Guilt feelings for actual sexual indiscretions or for having made a sham of the marriage may lead to self-accusations of a severe nature. Imageries of some form of punishment or affirmations of worthlessness may be part of the thought processes. Also fears of disease, such as cancer, or fears of insanity become part of the preoccupations in the breakdown situation.

Kroger and Freed [116] report a typical case of the menopausal conflict. This woman was depressed and suffered from insomnia, irritability, and "hot flashes". She had been brought up to look upon sex as something dirty. She had been frigid sexually all through her marriage but obliged her husband as she wanted to please him. She entertained fantasies of trying intercourse with other men as did some of her friends who enjoyed the act. She harbored hostile attitudes to her mother for having given her the negative attitude toward sex while at the same time she plagued herself for her extramarital fantasies. It was after she accepted her own sexuality that her symptoms abated.

So many women who have tried to repudiate their femininity, or more specifically their sexual femininity, throughout the ascendent years of their lives, suddenly face the prospect of losing their powers and go into a panic. It is as though they have suddenly discovered that they have never lived and must face the grim prospects of age without having enjoyed life to its fullest when they had the chance. They suddenly decide that they want to live their lives over again.

Males, at this stage of life, often seek their lost youth in extramarital relations. By virtue of the frustrations of the business world and by the tensions in the home, these men seek a "last fling". The adulation that they receive as "sugar daddies" from some young and attractive female seems to restore, temporarily, a flagging self-esteem. Guilt and remorse often supervene in such situations and create new areas of conflict.

The conflict situations in the business or professional world are often of a very serious nature at this age period. When a man has attained a position of some importance, he often finds himself at this age working and worrying harder than ever in order to keep his position secure. Furthermore, the man may be a victim of rivalrous and competitive situations. These rivalries are reminiscent of the old sibling rivalries in the family situation. This kind of rivalry stems usually from contemporaries. He is also meeting pressure from younger men who are quick to capitalize on his mistakes and anxious to oust him from his position. This situation is a reduplication of the Oedipal struggle for the dethronement of father. Even men in the highest positions are not removed from factional pressures. As a result of these pressures plus the demands of the job itself, some middle-aged men are obliged to work harder and harder under high tension. Coronary thrombosis or cerebral apoplexy may be the reward for his efforts. This has been termed "the tragedy of the successful man". It is a wise man who knows when to retire or when to accept a lesser position with less responsibility. Even when a man reaches the top in a certain field, particularly in the business world, he finds himself quite lonely. He feels himself too high to fraternize with his underlings. This is sometimes an outgrowth of an identification with the omnipotent figure that has been created in his image by his subordinates. Such an individual can often take on a tyrannical attitude, especially if his goal realization has become in effect the living image of his own tyrannical father. He may cast aside all he has learned about democratic principles and may obtain substitute libidinal gratification out of giving orders.

This attitude is often defensive against the threat of losing his status, but he capitalizes upon it, "pulling his rank" at every turn. The autocratic executive is often secure in his job because he makes money for the company and keeps any possible successor intimidated.

Sometimes the autocratic executive who rides roughshod over his subordinates is of a sadomasochistic character. I knew of such a man. He was the sort of person who had been whining all his life about the unfair way he had been treated. After he assumed a position of authority he forgot all about his struggles and made it much tougher for others than he had ever had it. To his subordinates he frankly stated, "I did it the hard way, so why should I make it easy for you?" He repeated actively the hurts he received or fantasied that he had received passively. As another executive reported, "It is my turn to cut a few throats now."

The motivation that keeps the man in his middle years so tenacious on the job, aside from the question of personal prestige, is the hope to leave a monument to his family. He often operates on the principle that his children will have it a little easier than he had it. Also there is the question of providing for the mate, after he has passed out of the picture. This brings us to the discussion of problems of the conflicts in regard to the death of the mate.

The problem of what the mate does after one or the other has passed on varies with the age period in which the tragedy occurs. There is also a difference in behavior between males and females. A comparatively young widow has a much better chance of remarrying than the female of comparable age who has never been married. This is due in some respects to the ease and confidence that the widow has in comparison to the neurotic old maid. Also it may be due to the fact that the widow is not as desperate as the unmarried woman. It seems that women can survive not remarrying better than men. Males show resistance to marriage in their early adult years, but after they have been married they often become quite dependent. They become accustomed to having their meals prepared for them and their laundry and cleaning taken care of and as a result feel quite lost when there is nobody to do it for them. Women, on the other hand, make no real change in their lives with the loss of their husbands, providing there is no great financial problem. They have always had to be quite independent in the matter of routine living. This state of affairs is frightening to both parties. To the man it is not too pleasing to think that the world will go on without him after he has gone. To the woman it is always a threat to think that someone else may take her place. It goes without saying that the more dependent the man is or the greater the loosening of the conjugal ties, the more likely it is that he will remarry. The same holds true for the woman, but her opportunities may not be as great.

Another conflict situation in the man or woman of middle years is the question of physical health. Because the human machine begins to show signs of wear and tear and the incidence of malignant disease begins to rise, the exaggerated interest in the body sometimes becomes manifest. The vigorous man who cannot accept the idea that he must slow up sometimes takes on distorted ideas of the change taking place in his body. There is a tendency to identify one's self with the illnesses of others in this age period. These preoccupations with physical health, often ill-founded in fact, are most pronounced in those individuals who are already anxiety-ridden and replete with guilt manifestations from conflictual situations of the past.

secondary autonomy in middle age

The autonomous ego traits have already been mentioned. They are listed as dignity, self-acceptance, tolerance, charity, and caution. The conflict situations described in the previous paragraphs give some clue as to the adaptive processes of the organism at this period. We are now referring to the defensive and secondary integrative processes and not to the disintegrative ones. The latter have already been alluded to in the breakdown situation wherein the organism regresses to previous instinctual pleasures, to complete surrender or despair, or to various degrees of anxiety or phobia. It is the reparative mastery of these disintegrative processes that we will now discuss.

In the matter of the motivation for youth, there are many people in the middle years who live in a world of desperate competition with young people. The women dye their hair, diet, and subject themselves to body massage and exercise and all manner of torture to maintain a youthful appearance. The men are no exception in this regard. Even though they do not lend such great support to the cosmetic industry, they try to show their youthful vigor in many ways. It seems that there is a strong cultural influence in our country for the preservation of youth. It has been suggested that the "glamorization" process is attributable to the movies. I have selected the term "sophomorism" as the secondary autonomous ego trait of the perpetual quest for youthfulness. It represents the high valuation or premium upon "appearing" young as though this made a person "be" young. It betokens a lifetime of things being not quite complete. Time, to these people, is an enemy. There is not only the fear of growing old and the rejection of this identity; there is the regressive element of "going back to when things were better." Time, however, does not stand still and the years begin to show. Sometimes there are strong defenses against the acceptance of aging and a most incongruous picture is produced. The children, in particular, are most embarrassed when one or both parents persists in looking or acting like adolescents instead of maintaining the dignity that would be more becoming to their years. Others may accept such foibles or idiosyncracies as being characteristic of that person but they seldom admire them because there is inherent in this trait the element of exhibitionism and more infantile needs. We must distinguish here a genuine progressive enthusiasm for new things shown by people of all ages, but which could be considered as characteristic of youth. This is not regression but perpetual progression. Sophomorism on the other hand, is not a genuine sparkle of enthusiasm but a spurious display of pseudo-youth on a purely defensive-adaptive basis.

At the opposite pole there is sometimes seen by virtue of reaction formation the individual who resigns himself or herself to old age before it is chronologically necessary to do so. This may be a form of regression into dependency where it is no longer necessary to keep up the struggle. It is a reflection of a lifetime of defeat. I have been unable to find a word which would cover this category of premature aging, so with a note of apology a new word is being offered. There is a rare medical condition known as "progeria", a degenerative disease of children in which they look like little old people. With this in mind, the word "progerism" is coined to describe the condition. Of course in the sense it is being discussed here it is purely psychological and not anatomical. Yet somehow when the motivation to be old takes hold of individuals they actually begin to look old. They neglect their postures, their clothing, and their grooming. There is contained in this trait an element of depression. This depression may be associated with the wish to be cared for and with it the buried wish to punish the world or the self for a frustrated life. There is another ego trait that may be closely allied with progerism and that is the one of "resignation". It is when all the starch and fight is gone after battling with life's problems. It speaks for poor mastery of prior conflicts and traumas, but there is here the additional element of loss of hope, because by the time they reach this stage of life they become aware that there is not enough time left to attain the desired goal in life.

As stated previously, many people at middle age believe that it is their duty to keep alive the tradition and instruments of our culture. Some exaggerate in their own minds the value of their own judgment in this respect or in all matters of decision. Just as the arteries begin to harden as the years go by, some people become extremely rigid in their thinking processes. This lack of flexibility makes such individuals very difficult to get along with in the business world and in the home situation. It is an adaptive-defensive reaction against the conflicts of that age period. It appears in the Table of Ego Organization as "rigidity".

There are some men who reach their middle years with a measure of success or a false idea of success and who fail to exhibit the dignity appropriate to their position. Such men are pompous, ostentatious, and boorish. They may exhibit varying degrees of the "stuffed-shirt" attitude. Such people are constantly in the process of boasting of past glories and accomplishments. They talk of the places they have visited and the important people they have known. They give the appearance of being self-satisfied with their own importance. Actually this trait contains a high measure of reaction formation against the inner conviction of the feeling of insignificance.

On the aggressive side, the ego trait of "ruthlessness" has already been mentioned. This ego characteristic may manifest itself in individuals who extend their feelings of importance far beyond the ordinary world of business or professional success. Such individuals use their powers not only to attain immediate gains, but to leave a mark upon society after they have gone. The creation of a monument, no matter how useful to society it may be, is often a compensation for the ruthless methods an individual has used in accumulating wealth. Such a monument is often a rationalization for other even more narcissistic motivations. It is a universal concept that man desires immortality. This desire is a reaction formation to the inevitability of death. It is because of this, no doubt, that man created the idea of the hereafter. Carried over into more realistic fields, many men try to construct a tangible hereafter by perpetuating themselves in deeds or gifts which bear their names. This might be construed as a noble purpose were it not for the fact that many of these men destroy more than they create in the building of their monuments. Such people find intolerable the thought that someday the world will go on without them or that they will no longer be able to wield their power. Hence, their monuments are often designed, not only for exhibitionism or display, but as a means of perpetuating the influence of their wishes over the lives of others. Just as some men will use their power to dominate or even hurt other people, they will attempt to continue this by reaching out of their graves in the heritages they leave behind.

On the submissive side there are many people in their middle years who become even more unctuous and pliant than they had been previously. They are the people who never had positions of leadership and have been content to be the Caspar Milquetoasts. As the middle years roll on they become more frightened of their jobs and become more ingratiating to their employers. They sometimes manage to keep their positions because of their willingness to do tedious or monotonous work in order to still continue on the work scene. At the same time they offer no threats to anyone.

In addition to the ego traits which have been mentioned in the preceding paragraphs of this chapter, all the other ego traits from the previous years may be manifest. The period of middle age shows a wide variety of manifestations as there are some evidences of tremendous growth and effectiveness, whereas there are other manifestations of regression and defeat. In all, the primary motivations from the infancy period onward are still manifest, but the accumulated learnings over the period of years makes for the differences in the ego structures. The successes and failures, the pleasures and pains, the surprises and accidents have all made themselves known and have influenced the person to be what he is. These factors have all been part of the ego identity of the man or woman in the middle years of life. The conflicts that occur seem, in part at least, to be based on a reluctance to face new identities or to relinquish the old ones when the capacities diminish.

social attitudes toward
the aged · the physical
problems · emotional
reactions and ego func-
tions

OLD AGE

As man begins to face the sunset of life, there are many adjustments that need to be made. These adjustments are in part related to the attitudes of society toward elderly people, in part to the physical health and strength of the individual and in part to the mental attitude and ego integration of that person. We cannot separate these factors entirely when we speak of a specific elderly person, because they all operate at once. For purposes of exposition, however, we shall discuss each of these separately.

The thinking processes of aged individuals have not been a matter of great interest to psychoanalysts because it is generally agreed that elderly people are not good candidates for analysis. Inasmuch as the infantile neurosis is the kernel of all human aberration, it has seemed a bit ridiculous to have a man of eighty discuss his toilet training as a child. Furthermore, there is a general feeling that old people are so inflexible that no amount of psychiatric treatment would affect their thinking in any way. It has been the lot of social workers, psychologists, and some nonanalytically trained psychiatrists to make observations and record the thinking processes and needs of elderly people. From the contributions of these workers, we have learned that even in old age, human behavior is modifiable.

social attitudes toward the aged

It has become necessary to think in terms of the social aspects of senility because of the increasing percentage of people who attain the position of advanced years in our current society. It is a well known fact that due to the decrease in the mortality rates from infectious diseases there is a corresponding increase in mortality from the degenerative diseases and old age.

In some countries, like Old China, the veneration of the aged was part of the cultural pattern. All the family decisions were made by the patriarch or matriarch. In this way, the oldest survivor was not only the head of his family but the head of his family's families. Being aged presented no threat but actually offered the individual a position of importance wherein his self-esteem was able to reach its highest point of attainment. On the other hand, some primitive groups found elderly people a distinct burden upon their economy. Because they were no longer of any use as warriors or hunters, they represented another drain upon the tribe's meager food supplies. Some tribes considered it the duty of the son to bury his aged father alive. It was also considered the duty of the father to submit to his own extinction.

Our culture shows vestiges of both of these extremes. There is both the tendency to "respect our elders" and to think of them as "useless burdens". Sometimes one, sometimes the other attitude prevails. Sometimes a person is in conflict because his feelings toward his parents are an admixture of both of these attitudes. It depends partly upon the meaning that the aged parent has had for the individual as an external object. Unfortunately, it often happens that sons-in-law and daughters-in-law feel neither obligation nor affection toward the aged parents. They resent the intrusion and the demands made upon them.

There are many reasons why a son or daughter may feel some justification for maintaining a rejecting attitude toward an elderly parent. These attitudes of resentment have been built up over the years. For example, a man had had a close relationship with his mother partly out of a need to protect her from the cruel and inconsiderate father. After the death of the mother, the son continued to feel little friendliness toward the father and resented the fact that he was obliged to take care of him. Certainly this hostility is understandable from a reality point of view, but is especially fortified in its emphasis as it fits so clearly into the Oedipal constellation. In other cases, the operation of the Oedipal forces are less rational. An example is that of the man or woman who harbors smoldering resentments because the surviving parent remarries. This attitude can continue even after the second spouse dies.

Other reasons for the rejecting attitude toward elderly people are that some of them show signs of untidiness and neglect of their personal hygiene. The intolerance of the children toward these parents is based upon the offspring's own ego traits, which stem from early indoctrination in the bowel training situation. Even in the absence of untidiness in old people, there is sometimes a rejection based on pure fantasy. Melanie Klein says that old people are not wanted because of the fantasies of the children that the longer one lives, the more one accumulates "bad things" within one's self, therefore old folks are "dirty" and "bad".

In contrast to the "bad things" accumulated by the old, there is also to be considered the concept of the accumulation of "good things" or "wisdom". Even some people who reject their own parents may have great respect for the wisdom of other old people. An appreciation of the sagacity and good judgment of old people carries with it attitudes of respect and deference. This enables the younger people to draw upon the stockpile of experience accumulated throughout the years by the old. When this situation exists, there is a great deal of deference shown to such individuals. When their faculties are still preserved, such men exercise great power when they are placed in important positions. Winston Churchill, Bernard Baruch, and Synghman Rhee are current examples, but history is replete with other such instances.

Sometimes the attitude toward elderly people is complicated by the secondary gains involved in inheritance. Even when children feel tenderness toward an elderly parent, there can be the egocentric wish for the death of the parent. In contrast is the situation in which a hostile offspring is obliged to act in a kind manner toward the aged parent in a desire for ultimate monetary gain. Many old people utilize this latter situation as a weapon of control over the heirs.

A basic factor influencing the social attitude toward the aged is the impoverishment of this no longer productive stratum of society. Although the aged pauper no longer need beg alms, he still feels the stigma of being a burden upon society. It was originally hoped that "old folks' homes" and "poorhouses" would be eliminated by Federal and State aid programs. Although such has not been the case, the character of these institutions has changed somewhat. They are now more like infirmaries and nursing homes caring for the physically ill and infirm aged. Despite this change, the fear of "going to the poorhouse" remains. There is a direct correlation between the mortality rates of the aged and their economic status. Poverty is not conducive to longevity.

There is also the strong conviction in the minds of many people that nearly all aged persons deteriorate and require institutional care. It is true that a fair percentage of patients in mental hospitals are aged persons, but compared to the large numbers of elderly people in the general population, the number actually committed is comparatively small. Yet despite this fact, there is the prevalent notion that old age and mental incompetency go together. This social attitude not only affects the regard that young people have for the aged, but serves as a source of anxiety to those who are approaching their three-score and ten.

In recent years there have been salutary cultural changes in the social attitude toward the aged. This change has not come directly from an alteration of the individual attitude, but has arisen in an extrinsic manner. Yet it has had its influence upon everyone's attitude toward elderly people. Society has become conscious of the problem of the aged. Many programs now operate in the direction of the avoidance of destitution among the old and for the understanding of their physical and psychological needs. Judging from the preceding paragraphs, we can see that the social status of the aged person in our society is certainly not at the top of the list. Even in situations where the aged person has managed to maintain the highest level of efficiency and self-support, there is a general feeling that his or her position is several notches lower in the social scale than the person in his or her middle years. This lowering of status is more marked where the individual has been an inadequate person all his life or has been weakened by the ravages of chronic illness.

the physical problems

Although there has been a great deal of study regarding the phenomenon of the aging process, there are as yet very few answers. From the point of view of body metabolism, there are always growth and destructive changes going on. The growth or anabolic changes lag during the process of aging while the deteriorative or catabolic processes assume an ascendency. This alteration of metabolic balance has been attributed variously to the influence of the endocrines, to nutritional changes, to the enzymes, or to specific changes in certain tissues such as the reticuloendothelial system. The sexual hormones have been incriminated particularly because of the concurrence of the loss of sexual function and the aging process.

Experimental work with laboratory animals is being conducted. Short-lived and rapidly multiplying animals like the rotifers are being studied for the purpose of determining the biological aspects of aging. One fact stands out. When growth stops, aging sets in. Although only physical aging is mentioned at this point, it will be shown that the same basic formula applies to psychological aging. A fact worthy of emphasis is that the aging process does not involve all systems of the human body simultaneously, nor at the same pace. This means that not all old people age in the same manner nor at the same rate. Thus people of the same chronological age may present marked variations of senescence. Among the aged we see those who present problems of physical health and those who retain a state of vigor and good health far into advanced years.

Students of geriatrics call attention to a difference between what is referred to as the "degenerative diseases" and the aging process. Kountz [117], for example, states that actual aging of man has never been carried to an end point, i.e., no one has ever lived long enough to have died of true old age. Nevertheless, the susceptibility of aged persons to illness and the gradual loss of strength, speed, and precision are well established facts. It is true that there is a varying tempo of these losses in different individuals. Also there is a wide range of effectiveness of different aged persons of the same chronological age. This latter is due in part to the differences between people in general. Superior people excel in old age as they did in youth. Mediocrity in youth does not improve with aging.

Aging cannot be discussed as a single physical fact because even the physical process itself has many facets. Each degenerative disease, circulatory, auditory, visual, etc., produces a different set of problems involving psychological aspects and calls for a different program of care. There are other factors that influence the physical health of the aged. These have to do with personal neglect and malnutrition. However, what is of particular interest to us is the involvement of the brain on a physical basis.

There are two types of cerebral change in advancing years, namely, arteriosclerotic and senile atrophy. Both of these changes can appear in the same individual. It is beyond the scope of this presentation to go into detail in regard to the clinical description of these two types. Suffice it to say that there are organic changes which are accompanied by real loss of function, both sensory and motor, and with it varying degrees of disturbance in the thinking processes. A most noteworthy feature, especially of the senile cortical degeneration, is the loss of memory especially and characteristically the loss of recent memory. Strangely, the elderly people become aware of this memory loss. A recent interview with a one hundred and seven year old Civil War Veteran revealed a man quite alert in many respects, but he told his interviewer that his memory was bad. Said he, "By tomorrow I'll forget that I talked to you today."

It is only natural that with the loss of strength and health and with disturbances in memory, many elderly people are not able to earn their own livelihood and require actual physical care. In this respect they become invalids. These are the people who become burdens either to their families or to the community.

Ziffron [118] makes the interesting point that medical science has done very little to alter the death rate of elderly people. In other words, if a person reaches eighty today, he will not have a better chance of surviving longer than he had many years ago. The speciality of geriatrics is now engaged in altering this condition both for the prolongation of life and for the purpose of rendering comfortable the remaining years for aged persons.

There is good reason to believe, yet there are no statistics available to prove it, that a proper mental attitude has a great deal to do with longevity. How this is related to the organic aspects of deterioration and debilitation is hard to say. Nutrition and physical neglect has already been alluded to. Whether improper motivations for survival can have any direct connection with the catabolic or destructive processes in the body one cannot say with certainty. However, this idea is being offered merely as a matter for speculation and is one which is widely supported.

emotional reactions and ego functions

Because of the wide distribution of the variables affecting old people, there is a great deal of difference between particular individuals who have lived their full quota of years. As a matter of fact, the correlations of similar types of aged persons is not on the basis of years but rather is based upon the other factors, particularly the organic change and the emotional adjustment. We have already touched briefly upon the organic factors; now let us consider emotional adjustment.

It is a fact that there is a strong relationship between the social attitudes toward aged persons and their personality reactions. This is particularly true when the aged suffers from the physical effects of his or her age and must turn to the environment for some measure of care in order to survive. On the other hand, the elderly people who are alert, vigorous, and in possession of their economic resources can rise above the social attitudes and not only live their lives as they see fit, but can also be in the position of influencing the lives of others.

Of the persons whose personalities are not contingent upon the social attitudes, we see the old age period as one which is in a direct line of continuity with their previous ego organization. There are many people who have prepared themselves psychologically for the advent of their declining years. This preparation may have taken the form of developing new interests, skills, and recreations. If they have been fortunate in accumulating a share of wordly goods, such old people maintain their dignity and self-esteem and can even rise to heights beyond those attained in their younger days. There is absent, however, the great burning drive for preparation for the future. It is all now and not tomorrow. But there is also present the wish to make some contribution to the welfare of the younger people and toward the improvement of society at large. There are a few investigators like Lentin and Courtney [112] who have idealized old age as the period in life when the broadest social interests are expressed. They consider old age as the period of life when intuition and judgment are highest and when the reservoir of retrospective experience serves as the highest level of evaluation. They also subscribe wholeheartedly to the theory that the organic deterioration of senility is purely a result of the breakdown of psychic defenses with a consequent impairment of physical resistance. We have all seen elderly people who are possessors of strong motivations to live and enjoy life. If I am obliged to select a word which would best describe the ego mastery of old age, I would suggest "serenity". This serenity may manifest itself in the quiet acceptance of favors and care from the children who are now returning some of the affection they so freely received. There is another type of serenity or inner peace which is of a more active nature. This is the serenity that comes from the feelings of independence and self-reliance. These people are able to draw from the reservoir of accumulated successes.

In a recent study by Dunbar and Dunbar [119] of a large number of centenarians, some interesting facts emerged. Their findings show a high correlation between longevity and a particular type of ego structure. These superannuated individuals did not reach this age because of tender loving care by their children. Most of them refused to live with their children. They not only chose to be independent but more often they helped support descendents rather than be supported by them. Another fact of great interest was revealed in their sexual histories. Many had an active sex life until very late ages, with a good number still potent beyond the age of one hundred. Another point of interest is the fact that the real oldsters were people who were good-humored and cheerful persons most of their lives and remained that way. As to whether hard work or a life of ease following retirement correlates with longevity, the odds favor hard work. The Dunbars failed to find a single centenarian who had retired to do nothing.

It seems that the main element in the successful ego organization of old people is the continued maintenance of work activity in something which the person enjoys and takes pride. Having and maintaining cordial contact with a large family also seems to be conducive to a deceleration of the aging process. There are very few really old people who have not married or have had no children. Mention was made previously about the biological concept that when growth stops, aging sets in. This seems to be particularly true regarding mental growth. There are so very many instances of men who retire and develop such a sense of uselessness and boredom that they go into a decline and die. On the other hand, many people combat this tendency toward decline by maintaining lively interests in some sort of work. Women are better off in this respect if they are still in their own homes. When they are guests in their children's homes, however, unless they feel that they have some duties or responsibilities to discharge, they feel useless and superfluous.

As to the work identity of aged persons, there seems to be a preponderance of long lived people who have been generally self-employed. Farmers are particularly long lived. There is much to be said for the relaxed and independent attitude associated with a successful business or profession in contrast to the strain of working for somebody else in the industrial world. We have already pointed out some of the pressures that are brought to bear in industry. Comparatively few people who have lived for a long period of time in their early and middle adulthood under the pressure of industry reach very old age except the owners or highly placed executives whose fortunes are assured.

In our culture, few old people reach serenity, which is the highest point of maturation. A less fortunate aspect of old age is a feeling of uselessness. This feeling is a reflection of the attitude of young people toward the aged, who have grown old in this culture and have absorbed the maxims of the superfluity of old age as part of their own super-ego structure; hence they almost feel guilty in many ways for still being present on the social scene. As such, many old people are ready to accept rejecting attitudes from the environment and assume an apologetic attitude about themselves. This self-derogatory attitude, plus the waning strength and vitality that comes with aging, sets the stage for the return of the individual to the basic narcissistic level of primary motivation characteristic of the infancy period. Before this return takes place, there is a recapitulation of the growth process in a reverse direction aided and abetted by the frustrations which are encountered at this stage of life.

There seems to be a distinct correlation between the degree of disintegration that takes place in aged persons and the state of ego disorganization that had occurred at the earlier stages of the life cycle. In other words, a neurotic individual is likely to give way to complete infantilism when he or she has the added stimulus of old age. The conflicts of living which had always been difficult, become insurmountable and force the elderly person to regress to the dependency position.

The problems and conflicts of the elderly have been admirably described by Simon [120], Lawton [121], and Bowman [122]. The foremost problem of the aged is the grim spectre of approaching death. To many elderly people this is a cause for anxiety or at least grave concern. Such individuals are averse to talking about death, become panicky when their contemporaries successively pass away, and live in perpetual dread of the development of physical disease. The anxiety itself may not be manifest, but there may be evidenced a great concern over minor symptoms and bodily complaints. Defensively there may be a tendency to cover up the death anxiety by the process of denial. These people talk and act as though they are going to live forever.

Every death of a friend or relative is looked upon as another indication of their own immortality. There are others who deny their anxiety by acting as though they are ready for death and would welcome the end. This may be a truthful statement where there is physical disease and the end is inevitable. One elderly gentleman said to me, "I have lived long enough; I have seen and done everything, and I am ready to go."

Perhaps even worse than death itself is the fear of invalidism or chronic debilitating illness. The imagery of being rendered helpless, dependent, impoverished, and useless reactivates the old castration anxiety. As such, it encourages the state of regression so that the elderly person assumes the role of the child and the offspring assumes the role of a parent. When the old actually reach the point of being dependent, they are no longer in a position to obtain gratification out of the things they were formerly able to enjoy. This leads to a constant state of frustration and unhappiness. To integrate this situation and make the necessary adjustments are not easy tasks for old people. In the first place, the ability to adjust to frustrating situations is not as easy for the elderly as it is for the young, because of the lack of resiliency of the thought processes. In the second place there is lacking the one element of "hope". The latter implies that perhaps sometime in the future things will be better. For the old there cannot be too much future, as time is beginning to run out.

Students of gerontology are averse to considering the human machine as one which ordinarily runs down by the same laws of attrition that apply to mechanical devices. There is one property of the living organism which separates the living from the lifeless and that is the ability to regenerate itself by virtue of the natural qualities of repair and reconstruction. It is admitted that the rate of efficiency for reconstitution is slowed down in the aging process. However, in the face of adequate motivations and physical requirements there is present a good measure of restitution and growth in spite of the general tendency toward debilitation.

The loss of mental acuity is considered part of the aging process. Carried to an extreme degree the concept of "dotage" or intellectual impairment by age is one which is exaggerated to a great extent. Actually any general lessening of alertness to new learnings may be more than compensated for by the prudent system of evaluation that has been garnered by the experiences of life. There is a tendency among old people to simplify life. Their conceptual thinking becomes less abstract and more concrete. Every life situation touches off recollections of old experiences which they are actually willing to impart to others in the form of anecdotes. The repetitious character of this propensity prompted the statement by Disraeli, quoted by Freud in his "Wit and Its Relation to the Unconscious" [123], to the effect that old persons are apt to fall into "anecdotage."

From the social point of view, old age often presents a picture of loneliness. Inasmuch as the average American home is based upon parents and unmarried children living together, it is the rule for elderly people to find themselves bereft of family when they need them most. This condition is intensified by the loss of friends by death or invalidism. The feeling of loneliness may not be so great if both husband and wife reach their old age period together. The loneliness supervenes after the spouse dies. Long before this, many old folks have had to abandon their former homes because of the need to conserve funds and because of the physical inability to maintain their homes. This means moving to new and unfamiliar surroundings and away from their old friends. For the woman, the death of her husband means economic readjustment and changed living conditions; for the man it means the loss of a homemaker; for both, there is the loss of a companion and helper. All the interpersonal relationships become diminished by virtue of the loss of other relatives and friends. Added to this is the inflexibility and lack of readiness to make and accept new or younger replacements.

The importance of a well sustained conjugal love relationship in the perpetuation of the motivation to live on and on is illustrated by the following situation. It is the story of an aged couple who had been happily married for seventy-eight years. At the age of ninety-six, the male partner developed a minor illness which led to pneumonia and a quiet death. His wife was only mildly saddened. She did not allow the numerous offspring to mourn. Instead, she insisted that "Papa" had had a happy and full life and it was time for him to go.

When plans were being made for her, she told the children and grandchildren not to bother because she would be dead in six months. Physicians failed to find anything physically wrong with her. She insisted, however, that "half of a person cannot live." Almost six months to the day, at the age of ninety-seven, she just failed to get up for breakfast one morning.

The problem of an elderly parent living with a child is often very complex. By the reversal of roles from being a parent to the child to being a child to one's own child, there is a shift of identities. This shift may afford the child an opportunity for unconsciously avenging himself for the wrongs, actual or fancied, that he received from the parent. It is as though old scores are settled when the patriarch finally becomes completely and effectively dethroned. Toward an autocratic matriarch the same may apply. More often than not, however, the children seek at all costs not to take in an elderly parent who has been a rejecting person and is likely to be a troublemaker in the home. If and when such a person is taken into the home of the child, the loss of status may be very difficult for the oldster to handle. By virtue of his own sense of guilt and the inability to exercise his former status, he has no choice but to be grateful for the home he is receiving. Many do so grudgingly and remain perpetually maladjusted and discontented.

To some people, old age itself is a trauma and produces a conflict situation. This has a tendency to reduce elderly people to positions of dependency. Consequently one finds personality reactions that are characteristic of the childhood and infancy periods. The emotional reactions are sometimes as intense as they were at those early periods of life. Childlike fears, rage reactions, and self-pity may be manifest. There may also be expressed feelings of depression, boredom, apathy, and withdrawal. In many instances these reactions can be quickly reversed by affording comfort, protection, and genuine affection and interest. The old are quick to respond to such pleasant perceptual gratifications in the same manner as the baby. The more regression that has occurred, the more the thinking processes of the old resemble those of primary perception. Thus we can almost assert that life begins on a perceptual level and ends the same way, at least for some people.

Even though there is a decided lack of flexibility in elderly people, the process of integration and adaptation is still capable of taking place. Thus all the defense mechanisms of the ego still continue to operate in many individuals in an attempt to make some sort of adaptation. Here we have again the bi-polarity which has appeared at every age level, namely, an aggressive adaptation or a submissive one. On the aggressive side we have the cranky, cantankerous, irritable old people who fly off the handle at the slightest provocation. They try to dominate every situation, make excessive demands, find fault with everything and are easily provoked into fits of anger. For these persons, the adjective "irascibility" was chosen to place in the Table of Ego Organization. Individuals who fall into this category have probably always used belligerence or dominating tactics to master their own sense of inadequacy. At old age they ward off their fears of death, loneliness, or sense of helplessness by this aggressive ego trait.

At the opposite pole there are the individuals whose best adaptation is to give way to the infirmities of their age. They are oversensitive to the hostile attitudes of people to the aged and are eternally suspicious of the intentions of those about them. They suspect the best intentions of their children as being insincere and performed out of unwilling obligation. In extreme degrees this suspiciousness could border on the paranoid.

Other elderly people give up the fight for existence and despair of ever enjoying life any more. These are the people who have been neglected or rejected by their families and have not been motivated to live by their own resources. There are many elderly people, especially men, who either die shortly after retirement or become seriously saddened by their own loss of effectiveness. The loneliness, depression, and sense of futility pervades the personality. These people are not easy to live with as they emanate an atmosphere of gloom. When the other spouse is still alive, the despair of the one reflects itself upon the other. This is especially true of the man. When he despairs of his existence, it makes the wife feel old even though she is far from ready to give way to the concept of age. Conversely, if the wife shows evidence of submission to the ravages of time before the husband, he is likely either to take a protective role or assume a cocky attitude that he is the better preserved and in possession of greater strength and vitality.

The despair and irritability that elderly people sometimes exhibit may lead to serious difficulties between the husband and wife. Often these spouses are not the original ones to whom they had been married; hence they have comparatively little hesitation about breaking up the relation. Thus we see a surprisingly high incidence of divorce or separation in elderly people. Another resultant of the despair and discouragement of the aged is the frequency of thoughts of suicide. There are many more old people who threaten suicide than actually commit it. However, enough actually carry this out to warrant mentioning at this point.

This feeling of despair may be a fixed ego trait in old age, but can also appear as a reaction which is quite reversible. Take the case of Mr. D. At the age of seventy-six he had had a series of operations from which he rallied slowly. He felt that he had very little time to live. He decided to just relax and let time run out. Before the illness he had been an energtic man, supporting himself and his second wife by growing vegetables and raising some chickens. After his operation he thought he could work no more. When a youngster made a remark about his age, he defiantly dragged himself literally along the ground out to his garden and did his planting and weeding. Although he seemed to get along with gradual recovery of his vitality, he still felt that his days were about over. He had lost contact with his family, except his own son and daughter-in-law. All his brothers and sisters were older than he. He thought he was the last survivor. His son was travelling in the area of Mr. D's former home and chanced to look up other D's in the telephone book and discovered to his surprise that his father had many living brothers and sisters. One brother, aged eighty-four, was still active in business; another, age eighty-nine, was still thriving; and a sister, ninety-one, was just beginning to feel a bit old. Mr. D. said to himself, "I'm the youngest and I thought I was old!" He did a little jig and went about his chores with renewed vigor. As the baby of his family, he had no right to act old. A year later, at seventy-seven, he did his work with more spirit and vigor than most young people.

Old age has often been credited with having an effect of "mellowing" some people. The implication here is that the aging process improves a human being in the same manner as the aging of a Stradivarius or wine. There are many people whose temperaments were such that they seemed chronically angry and hard to please. They are the ones who maintained infantile rage patterns whenever they were crossed or whenever circumstances did not suit their fancy. They may have intimidated their children and their subordinates. At old age, however, they seem to lose their fire and become quite calm and tractable. The mechanism here is usually a combination of many factors. For one thing, they realize that they do not exercise the power that they formerly did. For another, they become aware of the fact that there is nothing to gain by their aggressive attitudes and much to lose. Furthermore, they feel that time is running out and there is no sense in wasting their energies on having their own wills prevail. This is especially true when they see that they are not so indispensable as they thought, as the younger people have shown how very well they can carry on. It often comes as a delightful surprise to the children to find their parents no longer frightening and insistent that they are always right. This affords the children an opportunity of mending a few fences and setting to rights their own hostilities to their parents. In this way they are better prepared for the passing of the old folks.

The sexual problems of the aged cannot be completely dismissed. One is wont to look upon elderly people as though sexual matters no longer exist for them. For the most part this is true. However, the assumption that they are not motivated by both the sexual impulses and the memory patterns of sexuality is erroneous. The lack of consideration for the sexual aspects of the aged is due in part to the wish that is present in most individuals to desexualize their parents. This is certainly true about grandparents. But the fact remains that not all elderly people are devoid of sexual interest. The story was told about an old man who stood outside a church as a young couple who had just been married emerged amid a shower of rice and confetti. He looked on and said, "Do people still think of those foolish things?" This story was either fabricated by a young person or was spoken by a cynic.

Male sexuality, in regard to potency in intercourse, generally wanes to a vanishing point after the age of sixty. This is not universally true, as was pointed out earlier. Even some centenarians still have an active sex life. The newspapers often report men in the late eighties and in the nineties who have become fathers. These cases are well authenticated. But there are other sexual activities besides actual intercourse. Sexually tinged conversation and childish manifestations of sexual activity are sometimes exhibited. Masturbation is revived in many instances as a form of sexual gratification. The molesting of little children by aged persons is more than a matter of casual frequency. These activities are not without the usual feelings of guilt. In fact the guilt for former sexual activities is sometimes revived. An eighty-two year old man once travelled a long distance to see me. He had heard that his grandson was being treated for a nervous disorder. The purpose of his visit was to determine whether the masturbation he had engaged in as a youth might have caused some abnormality that was transmitted downward. The old gentleman had evidently carried his guilt and shame with him for a lifetime.

Although female sexuality does not show the same decline as the male, the opportunity for sexual gratification by elderly women is at a low point. Women who have been frigid all their lives welcome the loss of potency by their husbands and present no problems. But women who have had a happy sexual life remain interested in sexuality for many years. Some elderly women show a freedom in talking about sexual matters that they never exhibited in their earlier years.

Memories of old romances and recapitulation of the life they have had with their spouses constitute a large part of the wool-gathering fantasies of the old folks. They often feel that only they had the feelings which they experienced. They think too, that the young are always headed for ruin by their actions and do not appreciate real tenderness as they had known in their days. When the elderly man saw the young couple looking at the stars, he said, "You should have seen the stars when I was young!"

As we come to the end of our story of the growth of the ego, let us engage ourselves in the issue of the decline of ego function in old age. Much progress is being made in the understanding of the needs of elderly people. The beginnings of the psychological approach to aged persons were probably made by professional workers in the homes for the aged. Recreational and group work activities which were designed to occupy the interest and attention of the oldsters showed remarkable results in the emotional frame of mind as well as the physical well-being of these people. These lessons have spread to the establishment of centers for the aged persons where skilled group work and recreational activities are engaged in. This movement is spreading to many cities throughout the country. A detailed account of such a program has been prepared by Kubie and Landau [124].

Individual attention, when not afforded by families, can prove of benefit when it is obtained from professional sources. The frustrations of the aged lead to the feeling of isolation and the regression to the position of "second childhood". Elderly people in this childish state are subject to the same susceptibilities for gratification or threat as the very young child. The feeling of vulnerability and sensitivity may prevail as when the threats were severe. By the same token, they are capable of responding to pleasant perceptions from the outside world. As children respond to tenderness and loving care, so do the aged persons. When dealt with properly, aged persons who have built up a shell of isolation can find renewed interest in life if they are afforded the opportunity of using some of their neglected skills, such as in art work, crafts, or dramatics. When encouraged to do so, they can also become active participants in discussion groups or public forums. Some aged people can not only find gratification out of the reactivation of some of their old interests, but they can develop a new and meaningful pattern of living by finding new interests and potentialities that they did not know existed within themselves.

The individuals who have made preparations for their old age by the development of hobbies or other interests are much better off than those who drift into old age thoroughly unprepared. This lack of preparation comes from the belief that one is not going to live to old age or from its opposite, that he or she will never really grow old. Both of these views are unrealistic. These people may find themselves in a situation of complete isolation and boredom. It is not conducive to good emotional health to get up every morning with absolutely nothing to do and no place to go. In contrast, the zest for living comes when there is a project or activity waiting.

With old age we have come to the end of the development of the ego. We have tried to emphasize the concept of growth from the infant to the aged. The thinking processes that accompany each of the phases of biological maturation have been described. The earliest stages of ego formation were shown to have originated in the phenomenon of perception and later to have become a product of conceptualization. A fairly consistent sequence of ego growth on the basis of direct mastery of inborn instinctual pressures in terms of a reasonable reality has been offered. The reader is invited to follow vertically the items listed as ego traits in the column labeled "mature ego" in the Table of Ego Organization. The fortunate individuals who fall into this column are the ones who have been or are enjoying life to its fullest degree. They are the healthy persons who help to make a healthy society. Conversely, there are many people in our society who may not be suffering from severe symptoms, but who may possess habits or traits of character which are considered to be peculiarities, eccentricities or idiosyncrasies. These traits appear in the column labeled "The Neurotic Ego." These persons have established learnings from their life processes in which there had been varying degrees of trauma, conflict, grief, and pain. They have had to master their life situations on the basis of reparative mastery and secondary integration. As in all things that are broken and repaired, the secondary autonomy that ensues contains the elements of the original injury. These are the persons who are most likely to disintegrate when the stresses are great. Persons with a mature ego, however, can withstand greater life stresses. They are also the persons who manage their lives in such a way as to avoid the pitfalls. By integrating the thought processes with the phases of ego growth of the individual, we have attempted to present a synthesis of human behavior.

BIBLIOGRAPHY

1. Freud, Sigmund: Collected Papers, London, Institute of Psychoanalysis and Hogarth Press, 1924, vols. 1–4.
   ——: Civilization and its Discontents, New York, Cape and Smith, 1930.
   ——: New Introductory Lectures on Psychoanalysis, London, Hogarth Press, 1937.
   ——: Collected Papers, London, Institute of Psychoanalysis and Hogarth Press, 1950, vol. 5.
2. Rapaport, David: Emotions and Memory, New York, International Universities Press, 1950.
3. Colby, Kenneth: Energy and instinct in psychoanalysis. Paper read before the San Francisco Psychoanalytic Society, Jan. 14, 1952.
4. Mackay, Roland P.: Memory as a biological function. Am. J. Psychiat. *109*: 721–728, 1953.
5. Vigotsky, L.: Thought in schizophrenia. Arch. Neurol. & Psychiat. *31*:1063–1077, 1934.
6. Kasanin, J. S. (ed.): Language and Thought in Schizophrenia, Berkeley and Los Angeles, University of California Press, 1944.
7. Piaget, Jean: The Language and Thought of the Child, New York, Harcourt, Brace, 1926.
8. Cameron, Norman: in, Kasanin, J. S. (ed.): Language and Thought in Schizophrenia, Berkeley and Los Angeles, University of California Press, 1944.
9. Goldstein, Kurt: in, Kasanin, J. S. (ed.): Language and Thought in Schizophrenia, Berkeley and Los Angeles, University of California Press, 1944.
10. Erikson, Erik: Childhood and Society. New York: W. W. Norton, 1950.
11. Hartmann, H., Kris, E., and Loewenstein, R. M.: Comments on the formation of psychic structure, in: The Psychoanalytic Study of the Child, New York, International Universities Press, 1946, vol. 2.
    ——: Comments on the psychoanalytic theory of instinctual drives. Psychoanalyt. Quart. *17*:368–388, 1948.
12. Federn, Paul: Ego Psychology and the Psychoses, New York, Basic Books, 1952.
13. Allport, Gordon: Nature of Personality, New York, Addison-Wesley, 1950.
14. Hendricks, Ives: Instinct and the ego during infancy. Psychoanalyt. Quart. *11*:33–58, 1942.
15. Silverberg, William V.: Childhood Experience and Personal Destiny, New York, Springer, 1952.

16. Stern, Max: Anxiety, trauma, and shock. Psychoanalyt. Quart. *20*:179–203, 1951.

——: Pavor nocturnus. Internat. J. Psychoanalysis *32*:302–309, 1951.

——: Trauma, projective technique and analytic profile. Psychoanalyt. Quart. *22*:221–252, 1953.

17. Hughlings-Jackson, J.: On certain relations of the cerebrum and cerebellum (on rigidity of hemiplegia and on paralysis agitans). Brain *22*, 1899.

18. Sherrington, C. S.: The Integrative Action of the Nervous System, New York, Scribner's, 1906.

19. Magoun, H. W.: An ascending articular activating system in the brain stem. Arch. Neurol. & Psychiat. *67*:145–154, 1952.

20. Linn, L.: Psychological implications of the activating system. Am. J. Psychiat. *110*:61–65, 1953.

21. Bühler, Charlotte: The First Year of Life, New York, The John Day Co., 1930.

22. Gesell, Arnold L.: An Atlas of Infant Behavior, New Haven, Yale University Press, 1934.

——: Infant Development, New York, Harper, 1952.

23. Rangell, Leo: Some remarks on the psychic significance of the snout or peri-oral region. Paper read at the American Psychiatric Association, May, 1953.

24. Spitz, Rene A.: Hospitalism: an inquiry into the genesis of psychiatric conditions in early infancy, in: The Psychoanalytic Study of the Child, New York, International Universities Press, 1945, vol. 1.

—— and Wolf, K. M.: Anaclitic depression, in: The Psychoanalytic Study of the Child, New York, International Universities Press, 1946, vol. 2.

—— and ——: Autoerotism. Some empirical findings and hypotheses on three of its manifestations in the first year of life, in: The Psychoanalytic Study of the Child, New York, International Universities Press, 1949, vols. 3 and 4.

——: The psychogenic diseases in infancy, in: The Psychoanalytic Study of the Child, New York, International Universities Press, 1951, vol. 6.

25. Bernfeld, Siegfried: Vom dichterischen Schaffen der Jugend, Wien, Internat. Psychoanalyt. Verlag, 1924.

——: The Psychology of the Infant, New York, Brentano's, 1929.

26. Fenichel, Otto: The Psychoanalytic Theory of Neurosis, New York, W. W. Norton, 1945.

27. Klein, Melanie: The Psychoanalysis of Children, London, Hogarth Press, 1946.

28. Ferenczi, Sandor: Contributions to Psychoanalysis, Boston, Richard C. Badger, 1916.

——: Further Contributions to the Theory and Technique of Psychoanalysis, London, Institute of Psychoanalysis and Hogarth Press, 1926.

29. Szasz, Thomas: On the psychoanalytic theory of instincts. Psychoanalyt. Quart. *21*:25–48, 1952.

30. Abraham, Karl: Ejaculatio Praecox. Selected Papers on Psychoanalysis, London, Institute of Psychoanalysis and Hogarth Press, 1927.

31. Selye, Hans: The Physiology and Pathology of Exposure to Stress, Montreal, Acta, 1950.
———: Annual Report on Stress, Montreal, Acta, 1951.
———: Annual Report on Stress, Montreal, Acta, 1952.
32. Ribble, Margaret A.: Disorganizing factors of infant personality. Am. J. Psychiat. 98:459–463, 1941.
33. Lewin, Bertram D.: Phobic symptoms and dream interpretation. Psychoanalyt. Quart. 21:295–322, 1952.
———: Reconsideration of the dream screen. Psychoanalyt. Quart. 22:179–199, 1953.
34. Simmel, Ernst: Self-preservation and the death instinct, in: The Yearbook of Psychoanalysis, New York, International Universities Press, 1945, vol. 1.
35. Bell, John E.: Perceptual development and the drawings of children. Am. J. Orthopsychiat. 22:386–393, 1952.
36. Bartemeier, Leo H.: Eating and working. Am. J. Orthopsychiat. 20:634–640, 1950.
37. Bergler, Edmund: The Basic Neurosis, New York, Grune & Stratton, 1949.
38. Wilcox, D. and Solomon, Joseph C.: Conflicts regarding motility in rheumatoid arthritis. Unpublished manuscript.
39. Bonaparte, Marie: Time and the unconscious. Internat. J. Psychoanalysis 21: 427–468, 1940.
40. Korszybski, Alfred: Science and Sanity, New York, The International Non-Aristotelian Library Pub. Co., 1945.
41. Greenacre, Phyllis: Trauma, Growth, and Personality, New York, W. W. Norton, 1952.
42. Romm, May: The wish to be an only child. Paper read before the joint meeting of the West Coast Psychoanalytic Societies, Santa Barbara, 1951.
43. Solomon, Joseph C.: Psychiatric implications of deafness. Mental Hygiene 27:439–445, 1943.
44. Greenacre, Phyllis: Urination and weeping. Am. J. Orthopsychiat. 15:81–88, 1945.
45. Sperling, Samuel J.: On the psychodynamics of teasing. J. Am. Psychoanalyt. Assoc. 1:458–483, 1953.
46. Erikson, Erik: Sex differences in the play configuration of pre-adolescents. Am. J. Orthopsychiat. 21:667–692, 1951.
47. Finley, Malcolm H.: Personal communication.
48. Kinsey, Alfred C., Pomeroy, W. B., and Martin, Clyde E.: Sexual Behavior in the Human Male, Philadelphia, Saunders, 1948.
———, ———, ———, and Gebhard, P. H.: Sexual Behavior in the Human Female, Philadelphia, Saunders, 1953.
49. Meerloo, A. M.: Father time: An analysis of subjective conceptions of time. Psychiatric Quart. 22:587–608, 1948.
———: Father time. Part II. Psychiatric Quart. 24:657–671, 1950.
50. Allen, Frederick H.: Psychotherapy with Children, New York, W. W. Norton, 1942.

51. French, Thomas Morton: The Intergration of Behavior, Chicago, University of Chicago Press, 1952, vol. 1.
52. Fenichel, Otto: The pre-genital antecedents of the Oedipus complex. Internat. J. Psychoanalysis 12:141–166, 1931.
53. Lampl-de Groot, Jeanne: Re-evaluation of the role of the Oedipus complex. Internat. J. Psychoanalysis 33:335–350, 1952.
54. De Monchy, René: Oral component of the castration complex. Internat. J. Psychoanalysis 33:450–452, 1952.
55. Diamond, Bernard: Analysis of an oral incorporative fantasy. A case history read before the San Francisco Psychoanalytic Institute Seminar, Nov., 1951.
56. Kubie, Lawrence S.: Neurotic potential, neurotic process, and neurotic state. U. S. Army M. J. 2:1–12, 1951.
57. Berliner, Bernhard: Libido and reality in masochism. Psychoanalyt. Quart. 9:322–333, 1940.
—: The concept of masochism. Psychoanalyt. Rev. 29:386–400, 1942.
—: On some psychodynamics of masochism. Psychoanalyt. Quart. 16:459–471, 1947.
58. Thoreau, H. D.: Walden, Boston, Houghton Mifflin Co., 1937.
59. Wolff, Werner: The Dream, Mirror of Conscience, New York, Grune & Stratton, 1952.
60. Adler, Alfred: The Practice and Theory of Individual Psychology, New York, Harcourt, Brace, 1929.
61. Freud, Sigmund: Three contributions to the theory of sex, in: The Basic Writings of Sigmund Freud, New York, Modern Library, Random House, 1938.
62. Deutsch, Helene: The Psychology of Women, New York, Grune & Stratton, 1944, vol. 1.
63. Redl, Fritz: Pre-adolescents—what makes them tick. Child Study, 44, 1943–44.
64. Bornstein, Berta: On latency, in: The Psychoanalytic Study of the Child, New York, International Universities Press, 1951, vol. 6.
65. Bender, Lauretta: Mental hygiene and the child. Am. J. Orthopsychiat. 9:574–582, 1939.
66. Alpert, Augusta: The latency period. Am. J. Orthopsychiat. 11:126–132, 1941.
67. Levy, John and Monroe, Ruth: The Happy Family, New York, A. A. Knopf, 1940.
68. Trotter, William: Instincts of the Herd in Peace and War, London, T. F. Unwin, 1922.
69. Freud, Sigmund: Group Psychology and the Analysis of the Ego, London, International Psychoanalytic Press, 1922.
70. Finley, Malcolm H.: The classroom as a social group. Am. J. Orthopsychiat. 11:21–32, 1941.
71. Solomon, Joseph C. and Axelrod, P. L.: Group psychotherapy for withdrawn adolescent girls. Am. J. Dis. Child. 68:86–101, 1944.
72. Redmond, Louis: What I know about boys. Coronet Magazine, 1953.

73. Knight, Robert P.: Borderline states, in Loewenstein, Rudolph (ed.): Drives, Affects and Behavior, New York, International Universities Press, 1953.
74. Overstreet, H. A.: The Mature Mind, New York, Norton, 1949.
75. Shaskan, Donald A.: Evolution and trends in group psychotherapy. Am. J. Orthopsychiat. *18*:447–454, 1948.
76. Tannenbaum, Frank: Crime and the Community, Boston, Ginn & Co., 1938.
77. Solomon, Joseph C.: Adult character and behavior disorders. J. Clin. Psychopathol. *9*:1–55, 1948.
78. Freud, Anna: The Ego and Mechanisms of Defense, New York, International Universities Press, 1946.
79. Buxbaum, Edith: Transference and group formation in children and adolescents, in: The Psychoanalytic Study of the Child, New York, International Universities Press, 1945, vol. 1.
80. Freud, Sigmund: Totem and taboo, in: The Basic Writings of Sigmund Freud, New York, Modern Library, Random House, 1938.
81. Reich, Annie: Early identifications as archaic elements in the super-ego. Paper read before the American Psychoanalytic Association, mid-winter meeting, 1952.
82. Jacobson, Edith: Metapsychological differences between manic-depressive and schizophrenic process of identification. Paper read before the American Psychoanalytic Association, mid-winter meeting, 1952.
83. Holmer, P.: Identification. Discussion at meeting of San Francisco Psychoanalytic Society, 1953.
84. Sullivan, Harry Stack: Conceptions of Modern Psychiatry, Washington, D. C., The William Alanson White Psychiatric Foundation.
85. Spiegel, Leo A.: A review of contributions to a psychoanalytic theory of adolescence: Individual aspects, in: The Psychoanalytic Study of the Child, New York, International Universities Press, 1951, vol. 6.
86. Alexander, Franz and French, Thomas M.: Psychoanalytic Therapy, New York, Ronald Publishing Co., 1946.
87. Bühler, Charlotte and Hetzer, Hildegard: Testing Children's Development from Birth to School Age, London, Allen, 1935.
88. Schilder, Paul: Brain and Personality, New York, International Universities Press, 1951.
89. Josselyn, Irene M.: The ego in adolescence. Paper read before the 109th Annual Meeting of the American Psychiatric Association, Los Angeles, 1953.
90. Ginsburg, Sol. W.: The meaning and nature of work: A contribution to ego psychology. Paper read before the 109th Annual Meeting of the American Psychiatric Association, Los Angeles, 1953.
91. Arlow, Jacob A.: A psychoanalytic study of a religious initiation rite—bar mitzvah, in: The Psychoanalytic Study of the Child, New York, International Universities Press, 1951, vol. 6.
92. Ashby, W. R.: Design for a Brain, New York, John Wiley & Sons, 1952.
93. Jung, Carl G.: Two Essays on Analytical Psychology, New York, Bollingen Series XX, Pantheon Books, 1953.

94. Jones, Ernst: Papers on Psychoanalysis, Baltimore, Williams & Wilkins, 1949.

95. Wittels, F.: The ego of the adolescent, in, Eissler, K. P. (ed.) : Searchlights on Delinquency, New York, International Universities Press, 1949.

96. Fromm-Reichmann, Frieda: Principles of Intensive Psychotherapy, Chicago, University of Chicago Press, 1950.

97. Horney, Karen: New Ways in Psychoanalysis, New York, Norton, 1937.

98. Freud, Sigmund: Future of an Illusion, London, Hogarth Press, 1928.

99. Szurek, S. A.: Learning to love. Beacon, 1947.

100. Blitzsten, N. Lionel: Personal communication.

101. Colby, Kenneth: Paper read before Mt. Zion Psychiatric Clinic, San Francisco, 1950.

102. Burgess, E. and Wallin, P.: Engagement and Marriage, New York, Lippincott, 1953.

103. Shaw, George Bernard: Man and superman, in: Selected Plays, New York, Dodd, Mead, 1948.

104. Duvall, Evelyn Mills and Hill, Renton: When You Marry, Boston, D. C. Heath & Co., 1953.

105. La Piere, Richard Tracy: Sociology, New York, McGraw-Hill, 1946.

106. Fromm, Erich: Contributions of the social sciences to mental hygiene. Paper read at World Mental Health Congress, Mexico City, December, 1951.

107. Gary, Edelbert: News item, circa 1925.

108. Menaker, Esther: Masochism—a defense reaction of the ego. Psychoanalyt. Quart. 22:205–220, 1953.

109. Lantos, Barbara: Metapsychological considerations of the complex of work. Internat. J. Psychoanalysis, 33:439–443, 1952.

110. Polatin, Phillip and Philtine, Ellen C.: The Well-Adjusted Personality, Philaadelphia, Lippincott, 1952.

111. Burrow, Trigent: The Neurosis of Man, New York, Harcourt, Brace, 1949.

112. Lentin, M. E. and Courtney, D.: The human life cycle and its interruptions: a pathologic hypothesis. Studies in gerontologic human relations. Am. J. Psychiat. 110:906–915, 1953.

113. Benedek, Therese: Psychosexual Functions in Women, New York, Ronald Press, 1952.

114. Pitkin, Walter: Life Begins at Forty, New York, McGraw-Hill, 1932.

115. Fessler, L.: The psychopathology of climacteric depression. Psychoanalyt. Quart. 19:28–42, 1950.

116. Kroger, W. and Freed, C.: Psychosomatic Gynecology, New York, Saunders, 1951.

117. Kountz, W. D.: in, Cowdry, E. V.: Problems of Aging, Baltimore, Williams & Wilkins, 1952.

118. Ziffron, Sidney E.: Reduction in operative motility in the very aged. J.A.M.A. 152: July 11, 1953.

119. Dunbar, F. and Dunbar, F.: A study of centenarians. Paper read before the International Gerontological Congress, St. Louis, 1952.

120. Simon, Alexander: Psychological aspects of aging. California Med., *75*:73–80, 1951.

121. Lawton, George (ed.): New Goals for Old Age, New York, Columbia University Press, 1943.

——: Aging Successfully, New York, Columbia University Press, 1946.

122. Bowman, Karl: Personality changes in aged persons. Paper read before the meeting of the American Gerontological Association, San Francisco, 1953.

123. Freud, Sigmund: Wit and its relation to the unconscious, in: The Basic Writings of Sigmund Freud, New York, Modern Library, Random House, 1938.

124. Kubie, Susan H. and Landau, Gertrude: Group Work with the Aged, New York, International Universities Press, 1953.

INDEX